S0-AEC-385

New Media Theory

Series Editor, Byron Hawk

New Media Theory

Series Editor, Byron Hawk

The New Media Theory series investigates both media and new media as a complex ecological and rhetorical context. The merger of media and new media creates a global social sphere that is changing the ways we work, play, write, teach, think, and connect. Because this new context operates through evolving arrangements, theories of new media have yet to establish a rhetorical and theoretical paradigm that fully articulates this emerging digital life.

The series includes books that combine social, cultural, political, textual, rhetorical, aesthetic, and material theories in order to understand moments in the lives that operate in these emerging contexts. Such works typically bring rhetorical and critical theories to bear on media and new media in a way that elaborates a burgeoning post-disciplinary "medial turn" as one further development of the rhetorical and visual turns that have already influenced scholarly work.

The Two Virtuals

New Media and Composition

Alexander Reid

Parlor Press
West Lafayette, Indiana
www.parlorpress.com

Parlor Press LLC, West Lafayette, Indiana 47906

© 2007 by Parlor Press
Cover Illustration: "Absorbed" © 2005 by Eva Serrabassa. Used by
    permission.
All rights reserved.
Printed in the United States of America

S A N: 2 5 4 - 8 8 7 9

Library of Congress Cataloging-in-Publication Data
Reid, Alexander, 1969-

The two virtuals : new media and composition / Alexander Reid.

p. cm. -- (New media theory)

Includes bibliographical references and index.

ISBN 978-1-60235-022-9 (pbk. : alk. paper) -- ISBN 978-1-
    60235-023-6 (hardcover : alk. paper) -- ISBN 978-1-60235-
    024-3 (adobe ebook)

1. Mass media--Technological innovations. 2. Rhetoric. I. Title.

P96.T42R445 2007

302.23--dc22

2007026553

Cover design by David Blakesley.
Printed on acid-free paper.

Parlor Press, LLC is an independent publisher of scholarly and
trade titles in print and multimedia formats. This book is available
in paper, cloth and Adobe eBook formats from Parlor Press on the
World Wide Web at http://www.parlorpress.com or through online
and brick-and-mortar bookstores. For submission information or
to find out about Parlor Press publications, write to Parlor Press,
816 Robinson St., West Lafayette, Indiana, 47906, or e-mail
editor@parlorpress.com.

For Rhonda, Mirabel, and Jameson

Contents

Acknowledgments

I must begin by thanking my fine colleagues at Parlor Press: Byron Hawk and David Blakesley for their excellent feedback as I wrote this book and Marc Santos for his close reading.

Certainly I could not have accomplished this work without the support of my friends at SUNY-Cortland. David Franke and Vicki Boynton have built a Professional Writing program with me, and I could not have written this book without their encouragement. Teaching and building that program has served as a necessary touchstone for what I have written here. Thanks also to those faculty who played an important role in our writing program and have been willing to hear me out: Mary Lynch Kennedy, Karen Stearns, Ross Borden, Bernie Earley, Tim Emerson, Mario Hernandez, Homer Mitchell, and Jane Richards. I also thank the students who have been open-minded and willing to take on the challenges of technology with me.

Of course new media is about more than writing. Paul van der Veur and Charles Heasley have helped me understand in practical and local ways what it means to say that new media breaks down the boundaries between disciplines. Lorraine Berry's work with our *NeoVox* project has increased my appreciation of the international dimensions of networked education. And there are many others across our campus, folks who support our technology. If there is one thing I have learned about teaching with technology, it is that I cannot do it alone. In that respect, it is much like writing this book.

I must also acknowledge the great value of the community of bloggers with whom I have been fortunate to associate over the last few years. Collin Brooke, Jeff Rice, and many others have offered me a genuine appreciation of the broad and lively nature of our field. My thanks to those people and those who have read and commented on my own blog. The energy of this blogosphere has kept me going.

Finally I thank my family, my parents and my sister, as well as my in-laws, who didn't have to believe in me, but did. And, of course, my kids, Mirabel and Jameson, and my wife, Rhonda, for their love and patience. Thank you all.

The Two Virtuals

1 Introduction: The Two Virtuals

There are two virtual "realities," neither of which is reality in the way we have traditionally understood it. Nevertheless, both have a dramatic effect upon our professional lives and the future of higher education. The first virtual is quite familiar; it is the virtual reality produced by modern computing—the broad range of technologies from cell phones to mainframes that have transformed culture in the U.S. as well as around the globe. While the adoption of these technologies has been widespread, there is also some apprehension about the cultural and personal impact they will have. This is certainly the case in higher education, which is divided between enthusiasm for the integration of technology into education and concerns about the effects this technological emphasis will have on traditional, especially humanistic, educational values. The second virtual is likely less familiar; it is the virtual of a minor philosophical tradition that one can trace back to pre-Socratic philosophers, to the medieval philosopher Duns Scotus, to Spinoza and Leibniz, to Bergson and Simondon, and many others, including Deleuze and Guattari. It lies in the periphery of more familiar postmodern theories and concepts, such as deconstruction, the rhizome, simulation, and so on. This virtual does not specifically refer to computers or even technology in general; instead, it is no less than an alternate theory of cosmos, of matter, time, and space. As I argue in this text, the second, philosophical virtual provides us with a theory of materiality and thought, a theory of *composition* (of the way in which thoughts compose as media and media composes as thought), that allows us to approach the first, the technological virtual, in critical and productive ways.

Speaking on the issue of technological virtuality, Derrida (2002) poses the following question:

> This new technical 'stage' of virtualization (computerization, digitalization, virtually Immediate world-

wide-ization of readability, telework, and so forth)
destabilizes, as we have all experienced, the university
habitat. . . . Where is to be found the communitary
place and the social bond of a 'campus' in the cyberspatial age of the computer, of the World Wide Web?
Where does the exercise of democracy, albeit a university democracy, have its *place* in what Mark Poster
calls 'CyberDemocracy'? (p. 210)

As Derrida observes, the university has been a significant site of transformation. Not only must one think of new computer majors and
courses, computer classrooms, computerized class presentations, online course materials and discussions, and entirely online courses, but
also all the other aspects of university life: online advisement and reg-
istration, online grading, online libraries, campus networking, wireless campuses, networked computers for every student in every dorm
room. Nearly all of these are phenomena of the last twenty-five years,
many of the last ten years. Indeed, there are entirely online universities. What does it mean to say they offer a "virtual education" and
hand out "virtual degrees"? How "real" is an education that takes place
largely or totally online? These are legitimate questions asked by skep-
tical academics, for clearly a virtual education is different from one
that takes place in a physical classroom.

It is necessary for us to engage with the "second" virtual. Where
the virtual-technological deals with producing simulacra of reality,
this philosophical virtual, which I call the *virtual-actual* (following
Deleuze and Guattari), addresses the production of materiality itself.
Briefly put, where traditional Western philosophy describes a world of
discrete objects organized by inherent characteristics and fixed, measurable distances, the virtual-actual maps a continuous materiality
from which objects unfold in a perpetual flow of mutation. In this
sense it is quite different from the virtual-technological, which deals
with discrete, binary symbols, and, yet, the virtual-actual provides us
with a theory of materiality, of time and space, that allows us to understand better the role information technologies play in knowledge
production both on a cultural level and on the level of individual subjects. Such concepts may seem abstract and distant from the particular
challenges of our discipline or the practical future of the academy.
However, the distance is not as great as it might first appear. Information technologies have directly affected the ways we produce, organize,

and communicate information about our world and ourselves. Our conventional way of understanding the relationship between a writer (or thinker) and technology establishes a conflict or at least tension where the broader the role technologies play, the more likely they are to be perceived as a threat to "independent" thought. In some respects, the apparent threat of technology is not unlike the implications of ideology in its questioning of free will and agency. However, the virtual-actual provides a means to investigate the material processes of thought that incorporates the material, technological, and ideological, as well as our lived experience of what we call "free will." In doing so, the virtual-actual addresses the ways in which information technologies intersect with embodied cognitive processes in the composition of knowledge.

In short, this is immediately a question of *composition*. That is, if we ascribe to the belief that writing is not simply the recording of pre-existing ideas, but instead participates in the composition of knowledge, then we are committing ourselves to exploring these intersections between technology and the embodied mind. And I stress the status of "embodiment" here to emphasize that thought itself is material, even though we often think of the concepts that we manipulate in our minds as being abstract. Indeed in this text, thought or cognition is not only material but also distributed through a network of processes that are both inside and outside the body. This "cyborgian" dimension to thought is not a new phenomenon, though perhaps the computational power of modern information technologies and their rapid expansion over the past few decades have made the role of technology in cognition more palpable, creating increased apprehension. That point aside, rather than imagining technology as threatening to invade the sanctity of our consciousness, this text views consciousness as a *product* of the body's intersection with technology. Investigating the virtual-technological within the context of the virtual-actual allows one to understand the composition of thought (and media) as a material process that involves technologies as much as it involves ideology and culture. Postmodern theory, cultural studies, and post-process composition have built a critical understanding of discourse and representation in terms of ideology and culture. The virtual-actual, which in many respects underlies much of this philosophy, articulates a theory of materiality and the composition of thought that describes the role ideology and culture play in the material unfolding of consciousness. This description includes understanding how and why ideology fails to capture human thought in totality; it also explains the potential cybernetic (or managerial) function technologies play in the composition of thought. Given this philosophical perspective of the two virtuals, it is then possible to conceive of experimental, material compositional practices designed to play on the structural limits of ideological control. While such experiments may not create "freedom" in the traditional, humanistic sense, they offer new embodied experiences and potentials for thought.

In short, drawing on the concepts of the two virtuals, this book investigates potentials for using new media in rhetoric and composition to move in directions other than the all-too-likely outcomes that give us cause for concern. Specifically, I am looking to avoid a situation in which new media and information networks become yet another, increasingly sophisticated and effective means for regulating and pacifying thought. My argument in this text is founded partly on the premise that one effective strategy for engaging in these complex disciplinary, institutional, and cultural changes is through a critical understanding of the technologies that are playing such a significant (though I would not say *deterministic*) role in our "information society." That said, this is not a text aimed only at those rhetoricians who view new media as their "specialization"; it is more broadly a text for rhetoricians and compositionists as we collectively engage the challenges the virtual presents us. This inquiry pursues new possibilities for pedagogic and disciplinary practice with an eye toward imagining a rhetoric of new media that would provide us with the opportunity of engaging in the future formation of the university, to say nothing of the broader culture. The intersection between the two virtuals, the folding of the virtual-technological into the abstract materiality of the virtual-actual, suggests new approaches to the embodied, cognitive processes of media literacy that form the basis of our discipline. This in turn points to new understandings of compositional processes and pedagogy. These understandings, at least in this text, are not prescriptive. This book does not suggest "how-to" teach composition in the context of new media. Instead, it offers an alternate perspective from which new practices might unfold.

The question before us now is not *if* new media educational products and practices will be developed, as they already exist in many contexts. Instead, it is a matter of imagining *how* such experiences will unfold. Nowadays, most college classes get together for three hours a week. However, a robust multimedia environment could handle much of that activity asynchronously and on-demand. There would be no need for students and faculty to meet for a lecture or presentation. Even much of the class discussion could arguably be handled better this way, where students would have more time to be thoughtful. Though online learning will likely continue to become an increasingly popular option for non-traditional students and commuters, it is likely that many traditionally-aged students (and their parents) will still desire the conventional, on-campus college experience. For such students, not meeting face-to-face seems as impractical as meeting solely for the purpose of having students sit in a lecture hall and take notes. Instead, we will see the continuing development of hybrid courses (partly face-to-face and partly online), where the imperative for meeting would be different from our conventional practices: to satisfy our need to put a human face on learning and to ground our virtual experiences in the certainty of physical interaction.

Though undoubtedly there are many possible directions a hybrid, new media education might take, I see two primary trajectories that reflect two different ways of understanding the role of technology. The first, more traditional, perspective views technology as ancillary to human thought. Here the computer is a repository for information and a handler of mundane, repetitive computational tasks. Aside from giving us access to information and performing these calculations, computers do not, from this perspective, play a core role in human thought or creativity. However, because of their computational power, computers and networks do present dangers regarding information piracy and security, as well their academic counterpart, academic dishonesty, particularly plagiarism. Under such a model, computer networks become a way of distributing proprietary information (like textbooks) to students. Unless a student happened to be in a major that focused on computing, he or she would likely not use computer networks to produce media or information. Concerns of the proprietary nature of information and the potential for cheating would severely limit the use of such networks for student creativity. However, proprietary products would flourish. Instead of sitting through lectures with PowerPoint slides, students would sit in front of their computer clicking through on-demand video and interactive "learning objects." Physical classroom time would be reserved for labs, extended office hours, study groups, and, of course, secure testing. Composition programs could employ networks to provide uniform, canned instruction across sections on subjects from grammar and MLA-style to developing a thesis statement and revising one's writing. Networks would continue to be used as a watchdog, guarding against plagiarism by matching student texts with extensive databases of writing. In short, information technologies would be used to regulate and pacify human thought and creativity.

Alternately, drawing on the theory of the virtual-actual presented in this text, one might conceive of technology as integrated into processes of thought and creation and thus develop pedagogies that view new media as not simply a high-tech textbook. From this perspective, one would not eliminate the concept of proprietary media but would recognize that the protection of copyright must be balanced against other cultural interests. More importantly, one would not mistake the legal fiction of authorship, necessary for copyright and the media marketplace, with the material processes of composition, which indicate that thought and creativity are processes distributed across culture and technologies. As such, computer networks would serve as an opportunity for students to produce their own media through their integration of vast databases of information with their own compositional efforts. Courses would de-emphasize the largely uni-directional downloading of pre-formatted proprietary lessons and stress the multi-directional exchange of media among members of the learning community. In a writing class, much like composition today, the course would focus on becoming rhetorically effective and critical users of media, but instead of writing print texts, one would practice composing new media. Ultimately the students would construct their own learning objects, archaeologies of their own learning experiences. A large part of the process would be editing and mixing existing media objects and blending them with some new video, audio, and text. As I detail in Chapter 8, this composition process reflects the contemporary practices of ripping, mixing, and burning digital music. On some level, "beneath" all this content, is text, but the rhetorical effectiveness of the text lies in its ability to serve as a mechanism for a database. In this context, organization and arrangement become an issue of interface, of human-computer interaction (HCI), in relation to this database. Argument becomes secondary to what we call "experience design" today: the rhetorical effect of interacting with this learning object. Audience awareness is perhaps the one thing that remains constant, even if both the nature of the audience and certainly the way one addresses the reader-cum-user has changed.

Many academics will find neither option desirable. For those who have grounded their teaching on the time-honored practice of lecturing, the coming changes may be especially difficult. However, even for those with more experience in a distributed classroom environment, the notion of students composing new media learning objects may seem daunting, not only in terms of the technical challenges of learning to do such things for oneself but also in pedagogic terms of understanding how such practices might constitute learning. Certainly, in much of our regular ways of thinking about the teaching of writing, the focus lies on formal correctness, whether those forms reflect grammar conventions, MLA-style, or the organizational expectations of various generic forms of academic discourse. Beneath our everyday presentation of genre and convention lies a theory of rhetoric and composition, a predication of the compositional process and of the ways we think and learn. Undoubtedly, formal expectations will emerge for new media learning objects (if we pursue them as a mode of teaching), just as they have developed for websites. However, my argument here is that new media composition must be built upon a different theory of the embodied, cognitive processes of composition. Without such a theory, higher education is likely to move toward a more proprietary, corporate concept of information, which will increasingly restrict teaching and learning experiences. Such a theory begins in the virtual-actual, at the foundations of our understanding of materiality and thought.

COGNITION, CONSCIOUSNESS, AND SUBJECTIVITY

As this text details, the intersection between the virtual-technological and the virtual-actual deals heavily with the composition of thought. Clearly, the questions of how thought happens, of how the brain works, of how consciousness and subjectivity are produced, and what relationships may exist between these processes are fundamental to many disciplines from philosophy and psychology to cognitive science and robotics. They are questions of religious, scientific, ideological, and artistic concern, and certainly they are issues in English Studies, though perhaps more indirectly than in some other disciplines. The virtual-actual, as a theory of materiality, does not separate the question of thought processes from other material processes: that is, it does not separate thought from other material processes that provide its context. Though in English Studies we most often employ the term "subjectivity," and in rhetoric and composition we most often conceive of texts addressing audiences on a conscious level, English Studies also recognizes the role of the unconscious (as in psychoanalytic theory). This text investigates the interface between the subject and networked, symbolic, information systems. However, the text also studies the intersection of technology and the body's cognitive processes in the composition of thought at an unconscious level, and the emergence of thought into consciousness as it verges toward integration in subjectivity. In doing so, I make use of three terms: cognition, consciousness, and subjectivity.

Cognition describes the embodied processes that result in a thought of which the conscious becomes aware. I discuss extensively the concept of "distributed cognition," which emerges from the fields of robotics and artificial intelligence. The traditional model of cognition, from Plato onward, is a centralized, top-down model. That is, cognitive function is centrally located in the brain/mind and extends outward and downward to the rest of the body and into interactions with the external world. In the distributed model of cognition, thought processes not only occur throughout the body but also in the external, "smart" environment in which we are situated. For example, the eyes do not simply sense and transmit all visual information equally, calling upon a central processing brain to distinguish important from unimportant visual data. The eyes have their own filtering, information-processing function. Just as I rely upon various segments of my body to process information, I also depend upon my environment to record and process information for me. Obviously my computer performs any number of cognitive functions for me, sorting information on the Internet, filtering my e-mail, and storing data. However, I have any number of smart technologies, from things as basic as eyeglasses, clocks, books, and thermostats to my fax machine, the caller ID function on my phone, and various medications I might take. All of these technologies expand my cognitive functions, or more accurately they expand and *shape* my cognitive function. This combination of organic, embodied cognition with technological information processes creates the now familiar "cyborg" subject, the cybernetic organism produced by the distribution of cognition. However, as I argue here, the cyborg is not science fiction; it is not even a product of the postmodern condition. Following on Katherine Hayles and others, I argue that we humans, as language users, have always already been cyborgs. The emergence of what one might term "symbolic behavior," the use of both gestural and vocal communication and eventually written communication, externalized cognitive functions. As a result of symbolic behavior, knowledge no longer had to be stored within individual brains; it could be shared among a community and eventually stored in material form in rituals, in drawings, and in writing. This was the inception of the smart environment. It is also, arguably, the inception of consciousness as we know it.

Consciousness is the second term I employ here. As I discuss, the distribution of cognitive function to an external, smart environment calls for the development of consciousness to serve as an interface for symbolic behaviors. I'm not arguing this is the beginning of consciousness per se; I'm not interested in origins. Instead, I am suggesting that the distribution and externalization of cognition results in the mutation of consciousness into a form recognizable to us. I am interested in consciousness as we experience it. As such, I describe consciousness as the product of both external and embodied functions. This description fits well with the trope of the cyborg, but it is in opposition to the traditional notion of consciousness as internal, separate even from the functions of the body. However, by placing consciousness in the intersection of technology (including language) and the body, consciousness becomes an object of material, cultural, and historical development. This does not mean that "our" thoughts are not our own but rather that "we" are products of our bodies situated in a smart environment of distributed cognition with material, cultural, and historical dimensions and contexts. As I discuss in Chapters 2 through 5, media technologies present us with the fragmentation of our traditional concept of consciousness as internal and cohesive, a fragmentation that Derrida's grammatological investigation uncovers in writing (1976). This fragmentation is further intensified in mechanical media (e.g., typewriters, cameras, etc.) and in cybernetics. Where the traditional concept of cognition views the cyborg as a fragmentation of the mind, in the virtual-actual, the recognition that thought processes occur across a field of materiality constitutes an integration of cognition into materiality, as opposed to the traditional notion, which seeks to fragment and separate the human from his/her material context.

As such, where traditional consciousness is a relatively stable entity (e.g., "my consciousness"), this text discusses consciousness as virtual. That is, as cognitive processes enter into conscious awareness, they almost simultaneously enter into language. Of course, many thoughts (perhaps all thoughts) cannot be fully articulated in language. The moment when consciousness claims itself, names its thought, it is apprehended from the process of becoming and pinned onto a plane of reference where the conscious thought is represented and organized on the grid of thoughts that articulate subjectivity. As such, consciousness sits on the hinge between the material processes of cognition and the ideological, referential processes of subjectivity.

In this sense, subjectivity develops as an (ideological) address for consciousness. Our subjectivity establishes protocols that allow us to interact with other consciousnesses in a social, cultural context. As such, my body participates in a distributed network of cognitive functions and produces my consciousness as a means of interaction. Part of that interaction is necessarily establishing my relationship with other nodes on the network; this is my subjectivity. Thus as a professor or father or heterosexual white man, I am authorized for certain functions in certain contexts, much like a computer user logging onto a network. This is very much the Althusserian-cum-Foucauldian notion of the subject as a node in a circuit of power. However, as I will detail, I depart from that concept in a significant way. Put briefly, rather than imagining the imposition of the subject upon consciousness, the model of distributed cognition suggests that the articulation of subjectivity occurs through this network and is constitutive of the production of consciousness. This is closer to Deleuze's theory of a "control society." Nevertheless, subjectivity remains the ideological, cultural naming of consciousness. As such, I use both the term consciousness and subjectivity to differentiate between consciousness, as an emergent function of the body within a distributed network of cognition, and subjectivity, as the valuation of consciousness within a specific ideological framework.

Taken together, my use of cognition, consciousness, and subjectivity serve to provide an alternative approach to thought than that offered by the traditional notion of the disembodied mind. The latter notion occludes the material, historical, technological and cultural processes of cognition and thus naturalizes a particular ideological view of the subject. More importantly, my approach opens the possibility that consciousness and subjectivity can be mutated through material, technological experimentation with the network of distributed cognition. This creates the potential for discovering new realms of thought and new possibilities for social interaction and community. As it turns out, the "information revolution," including new media, represents a powerful historical opportunity for such experimentation by creating a wide range of new opportunities for symbolic behavior across the network of distributed cognition. Simultaneously, these same technologies represent significant potential dangers not only to human life but the entire planet through their promise to reframe the world in the reductive, commodifying logic of capitalism and a technologically-realized and managed, virtual reality. As Hayles (1999b) writes,

> The best possible time to contest for what the post-human means is now, before the trains of thought it embodies have been laid down so firmly that it would take dynamite to change them. Although some current versions of the posthuman point toward the anti-human and the apocalyptic, we can craft others that will be conducive to the long-range survival of humans and of other life-forms, biological and artificial, with whom we share the planet and ourselves. (p. 291)

As I argue here, long-range survival may rely upon the understanding of the virtual-technological as a material process intersecting other material processes of thought, culture, and ideology within a larger theory of the virtual-actual.

Learning to Live with New Media

I do not pretend to have an answer to this situation. However, this text does contend that rhetoric and composition's continued role in higher education will rely upon its ability to address new media in both a critical and productive fashion. In doing so, the discipline must address the "two virtuals." That is, we must develop an understanding of how media technologies shape the material practices of composition, as well as the recursive relationship between the materiality of composing and the discursive communities and practices attached to those media technologies (i.e. media technologies shape and are shaped by the discourse communities that employ them). However, such an understanding is not sufficient in itself. We must also address the "other" virtual, the virtual-actual. Only through our engagement with this minor discourse can we open a space for moving beyond the limits of the print-oriented philosophy and rhetoric that structure our current practices. As I explore, this latter approach further emphasizes that our practice need not focus on "fixing" our discipline or the university, on securing it to any particular set of ideological outcomes or critical methods or subject positions. Instead, the virtual suggests our focus might switch to the singular, material unfolding of cognition and media, as whatever it may be becoming. This emphasis on the singular, explored by Giorgio Agamben (1993), Jean-Luc Nancy (1991), and others, suggests an alternate politics for a "coming community" (to use Agamben's phrase).

This text is largely structured around this project. Chapters 2 through 5 focus primarily on the development of technologies that lead to the virtual-technological experience. Though an investigation into the development of new media might begin with an examination of print technologies or the development of various mechanical media, Chapter 2 goes back considerably further, while simultaneously looking at the contemporary moment. Cognitive scientists termed the 1990s the "Decade of the Brain" for the startling advancements made throughout their discipline. In particular, in an interdisciplinary field known as evolutionary psychology, recent investigations have been made to pinpoint the emergence of human consciousness as we understand and experience it. As I discuss in Chapter 2, this research provides significant evidence that the development of symbolic behavior—something that would go beyond the embodied gestures and grunts we see in other animals—is closely connected to this dawn of consciousness. Symbolic behavior is not simply speech; it is also gesture and codified gestures, such as the making of jewelry or cave drawings. I explore the implications of these understandings of consciousness as they relate to our classical notion of thought as "phonocentric," as a speaking in the mind that is later transcribed into writing. The chapter also jumps forward to discuss the invention of formal writing technologies and the treatment of writing by Plato (and the subsequent treatment of Plato by Derrida and others). In analyzing these two moments—the emergence of symbolic behavior and the development of writing—I lay out one of the fundamental arguments of this book: that writing, media, and cognition are intertwined material processes working through a shared network of symbolic information. Of course, our experience of consciousness and subjectivity as fairly cohesive obscures the fragmented and distributed processes that produce thought. While consciousness and subjectivity obviously have their uses in organizing individual and communal behavior, our ongoing insistence that they are the beginning and end of thought has prevented us from developing a better understanding of the composition of thought and ideas and the role media and other technologies play in it.

This network of distributed cognition becomes more apparent in Chapter 3, where I move my investigation several millennia to the invention of mechanical media, the typewriter and film camera in particular. Recent years have seen a number of excellent texts that investigate the history of media and cybernetics. Katherine Hayles's *How We Became Posthuman* (1999b), Lev Manovich's *Language of New Media* (2001), and Lisa Gitelman's *Scripts, Grooves, and Writing Machines* (1999), as well as collections such as *New Media 1740–1915* (2003), *Memory Bytes: History, Technology and Digital Culture* (2004), *Rethinking Media Change* (2004), and *Prefiguring Cyberculture* (2004), all deal with various precursors to the technologies and theories that drive new media. My objective here, in drawing on these and other texts, is to trace the symbiotic relationship between theories of the mind, media/information technologies, and our understanding of compositional processes. This relationship articulates a virtual-technological space that becomes more evident with the development of computers. With the emergence of mechanical media, one encounters a plethora of rethinking about compositional modes and the role of technology, from philosophers such as Nietzsche and Heidegger, to artistic manifestos such as those of the Futurists and Imagists, to more political and cultural investigations like Walter Benjamin's or Sergei Eisenstein's discussion of film and montage as revolutionary modes. For example, in my discussion of the typewriter, I focus on the multiple strategies involved to keep mechanical media separate from the (male) author. In the business world, the typewriter creates the invention of a new career, the female secretary. Academia, undergoing rapid changes to meet the educational needs of the American industrial revolution, invents, among other things, literary studies as the new focus of English. I discuss how the Arnoldian disciplinary viewpoint constructed literature and literary studies as insulation against mechanical media's "dehumanizing" dismantling of traditional authority.

The shifting concept of the subject in the Modernist era was not only an issue for literature and film. As I discuss in Chapter 4, the early cyberneticists were sorely aware of the potential implications their theories might have for how we view human cognition. Through the development of cybernetic theories, we have come to see that meaning is not so much transmitted as it is produced in the event of reception. That is, while a message-sender may have a particular meaning he or she wishes to communicate, that meaning is not sent. Instead, what is sent are symbols from which the receiver produces meaning (hopefully a meaning that approximates the one the sender meant to send). However, information processing is often not a conscious process; only when a meaning is especially ambiguous (like in literature) does the conscious mind actively participate. In this sense we can say that cognition is distributed throughout the body. Our sensory organs do not send our conscious mind sensory data indiscriminately. Similarly, our conscious mind does not receive garbled sounds or squiggly lines that must be consciously transformed into words. When we watch television we do not have to consciously transform light projections on a flat screen into images with depth. All of these and many other cognitive activities occur at an unconscious level. In addition, many cognitive activities are performed by technologies outside our body. As Chapter 4 investigates, this model of distributed cognition addresses the role technologies and embodied, but unconscious, cognitive functions play in constructing our conscious experience of the world. In doing so cybernetics offers a way of understanding the intersection of the virtual-technological with material space.

Chapter 5 brings together cybernetic theory with media technologies in its exploration of new media. New media intensifies the perceived fragmentation of the subject. If the film camera presented us with a fractured, mechanical body and mind, then the digital camera presents us a virtualized, informational body and mind. This is the new media state of virtuality, which Katherine Hayles (1999a) defines as "the cultural perception that material objects are interpenetrated by information patterns" (p. 69). In short, the development of new media establishes virtual-technological space as we now experience it. In this chapter, I investigate how the concept of the interface demonstrates the theory of simulation, where the surface representations of a computer application or a digital film present a simulacrum of an underlying informational and material system that does not exist as such. Subjectivity operates similarly, as the surface of a consciousness that does not exist as such. Instead, both subjects and computer interfaces are means for accessing and exchanging information. This does not mean that subjectivity does not exist, as in the familiar postmodern proclamation of the "death of the subject." Much like the computer interface exists, the subject also exists. As the voice or video recording presents us with an uncanny representation of ourselves by showing us our mechanical nature, the computer interface is an uncanny presentation of our consciousness as a surface product, floating on a sea of material, cognitive processes.

Chapter 6 marks a turning point in the text. Having analyzed the development of technological virtuality, I examine virtuality in more abstract terms as I look to the virtual-actual as a way of investigating the material unfolding of consciousness and the composition of thought in a network of distributed cognition. This chapter deals generally with concepts of space and time as they relate to cognition. Drawing on Manuel DeLanda and Brian Massumi (who in turn draw on Deleuze and Guattari and others), I discuss a topological approach that describes space as continuous rather than discrete and as mutational rather than fixed. I discuss these differences in time and space as they relate to the concepts of digital and analog. All information, even speech, enters our bodies in analog form, as light waves or sound waves as in the case of eyes and ears or chemical reactions (smell and taste) or physical pressure (touching). When we read a book or on a screen, embodied cognitive processes recognize the patterns of ink or light as letters, which form words and so forth. If we dispense with the belief that technology—whether it is speech, writing, or video—communicates an abstract packet of information, then instead we might recognize our networked, information environment as sending us analog material through a topological space of mutational vectors and intensities. New media does not transmit information but rather produces a topological space in which symbolic matter can be accessed and manipulated. While conscious interactions and decision-making seem to dominate in symbolic manipulations more than they do in other environments, our interactions with this information network are necessarily embodied and proprioceptive.

Chapter 7 takes up this general understanding of distributed cognition to develop a different mapping of the intersection between body and technology in the compositional process. It begins by articulating composition pedagogy in terms of cybernetics and Cartesian space, as a navigational strategy for steering students toward a goal. However, I then recontextualize writing in terms of the philosophy of the virtual-actual explored in previous chapters. In doing so I draw on the practice of ripping, mixing, and burning music as a more general process of new media composition. While "rip, mix, burn" is a familiar process for composing media in virtual-technological terms, here I employ these terms to describe composition in a broader sense as a mechanism of the virtual-actual unfolding of materiality. As I detail in the chapter, *ripping* describes the practice of pulling on informational resources whether they are sensed, remembered, or from some pre-existing media; *mixing* then describes the process by which this ripped data connects in a rhizomatic network where each new connection holds the potential for unexpected mutation; finally, by *burning* the composition, the mixture of data becomes translated and compressed into a material form that can be communicated across a network. In this way, the process can begin anew. Of course these compositional practices are not a result of new media. In fact, the chapter views these compositional processes as not being specific to any technology but rather as a description of the material unfolding of composition in the virtual-actual. The chapter closes by investigating how rip/mix/burn composition is already at work in writing classrooms. In particular, I look at Gregory Ulmer's textbook, *Internet Invention* (2003), as an example of this.

Following upon this discussion of rip/mix/burn and Ulmer, Chapter 8 investigates the pedagogic implications of undertaking a virtual-actual approach to new media composition. As I describe there, though pedagogy as a concept may inescapably belong to a cybernetic order, I suggest that it is possible to articulate a "pedagogic event" that operates through the virtual unfolding of time. Such an approach moves beyond the traditional constative knowledge of the university and its predictable, performative pedagogies to a pedagogy of surprise and mutation. I explore how such a pedagogy might extend from the practices of contemporary critical pedagogies, adapting those practices for the shifting technological and ideological contexts of an increasingly corporate academy. As I argue there, our future with ubiquitous computing in a globalizing economy and culture points to the necessity of a post-process mode of new media composition that demands what we might now call an interdisciplinary (though what might be better termed "post-disciplinary") ability to read, analyze critically, and integrate knowledge from texts native to disciplines across academia. Working in such an environment will require a broad knowledge base and a facility with critical-interpretive methodologies. Additionally, such environments call for strong rhetorical-compositional abilities and demand repeated practice at creative-conceptual thinking. As if such a challenge were not enough, all this must take place in the context of an ongoing process of collaboration, negotiation, and struggle with the increasing role of corporate capitalism on campus. It is not unnecessarily pessimistic to imagine this task to be impossible.

This impossibility becomes the subject of the book's ninth and final chapter, where I bring together the text's exploration of the virtual-technological and the virtual-actual to consider Derrida's questions, raised at the beginning of this introduction: "Where is to be found the communitary *place* and the social bond of a 'campus' in the cyberspatial age of the computer, of the World Wide Web? Where does the exercise of democracy, albeit a university democracy, have its *place* in what Mark Poster calls 'CyberDemocracy'?" (2002, p. 210) The chapter provides some history of the development of the current "corporate university" as documented by Bill Readings and others, as well as the significant role information technology has played in that development. As we consider how to "save English" or to "fix English," as we wonder whether rhetoric and composition should be a part of English Studies or a separate discipline, we see these issues in the context of technological innovation and the expansion of this corporate university. Multiple solutions abound for consideration. However, in the context of the topological unfolding of virtuality, the question is not how to get control of the disciplinary, or university, steering wheel: neither is it a question of where to steer once one has control. Instead, this context calls for an acceptance of "whatever discipline," a recognition of the singularity of writing and learning and thought rather than a conflict over defining the "essential" qualities of discipline or humanities or higher education. As I discuss, this is not a call for apathy or accepting someone else's rule; it is a shift in political action to insisting on the singularity of the unfolding of thought, a concept Giorgio Agamben details in *The Coming Community* (1993).

Such issues are intimately connected with the study of rhetoric, which, of course, concerns itself with the ways in which communities organize and maintain themselves through discursive practices. Through the development of the new media compositional practices and related pedagogies I explore here, a rhetorical space for the communal practices I am describing might be produced. This text ultimately is only an opening gesture toward thinking about how rhetoric will function in the coming virtual community. Fundamentally, the argument I am making is that we cannot simply expect to make minor adjustments and that our field will continue happily along its path of disciplinary inertia. New media is quite more than simply slapping a picture into an already existing essay and posting the whole thing on the Internet. It is instead part of a broader intellectual shift in the way we understand cognition, consciousness, and subjectivity, our relationship with information, our practices of composition, and the means by which we will develop productive relationships with one another. Now is the time for our discipline to engage these issues in earnest.

2 The Evolution of Writing

The emergence of new media has raised interest in the role media and information technologies play in the production of knowledge and the shaping of thought. For the most part, in the humanities this interest has focused on the ideological level, following on such works as Adorno and Horkheimer's investigation of the "culture industry." However, in the sciences, particularly in cybernetics, robotics, and cognitive science, greater interest has focused on understanding the information processes of the brain itself. Indeed, in the interdisciplinary field of evolutionary psychology, academics such as Steven Pinker investigate the evolution of language and consciousness using a discourse of mediation and information processing. Pinker (1997) writes,

> All reconstructions of our evolutionary history are controversial, and the conventional wisdom changes monthly. But I predict that the closing date of our biological evolution will creep later, and the opening date of our archeological revolution will creep earlier, until they coincide. Our minds and our way of life evolved together. (p. 205)

That is, Pinker contends that consciousness evolves in connection with technology, shaping one another. If this is indeed the case, then historically some of the most obvious technological candidates for having a powerful shaping influence on consciousness are writing technologies. Similarly, in the contemporary period, one would want to consider media and information technologies as technologies that play a significant role in the production of consciousness.

However, this avenue of investigation has been largely unexplored in our discipline. It has been more than twenty years since cognitive science had its heyday in rhetoric and composition. With the exception of history of rhetoric courses teaching *Phaedrus,* the historical invention of writing, to say nothing of the evolutionary development of language itself, has never been of much import to English Studies. At the core, the objection in the eighties to cognitive approaches to composition pedagogy was its essentialism, its inability or unwillingness to recognize the importance of social differences in the teaching of writing. This was part of a larger, postmodern turn toward discursiveness, toward understanding meaning-making as a social rather than an individual process. As such, cognitive science, particularly the kind of evolutionary psychology I address in this chapter, seems quite distant from an investigation of new media rhetoric, especially one as replete with postmodern theory as I have described this text to be. I should point out that where some scientists may be looking for the "origin" of consciousness, I am not interested in that here. What I see in their work, and in its connection with cultural theory, is an understanding of how thought mutates through its connection to the development of symbolic behavior (the use of sign systems either spoken or gestural). As I detail in this chapter, archeological records map the emergence of symbolic behavior in the production of jewelry, cave paintings, and related technologies. By tracking the trade of materials in wider and wider social circles, they also provide evidence for seeing dramatic changes in patterns of human organization and interaction. In short, archeologists theorize that a "creative explosion" occurs, roughly simultaneous to the development of symbolic behavior, which transforms human life and culture. Humans move into a society that is able to deal with a larger data set (more information) and to undertake more abstract and complicated tasks. The argument is that this expansion in cognitive ability is tied to the development of symbolic behavior. It may not be the "origin" of consciousness, but it is perhaps a prime example of how information technologies can affect human thought. I take this argument one step further and suggest that this evidence indicates that it is an error to imagine human thought as purely internal to an individual self; that in fact what makes human thought so dynamic and powerful is that it is largely external (or more precisely that the internal/external binary is misleading).

All this may seem quite distant from the virtual. Obviously, tens of thousands of years separate this creative explosion from virtual reality. However the other virtual, the virtual-actual, operates just as relevantly among cave paintings and shell necklaces as it does digital media. In terms of writing and composition, the fundamental philosophical difference between the virtual-actual and our conventional understanding of the writing process lies in how one understands the role of the "outside," of material culture, in the shaping of thought and text. A contemporary, post-process approach to composition accounts for the outside in the abstract, in terms of ideological discourses. We primarily focus on the concept of the subject, and, though shaped by cultural and ideological forces, the subject remains internal. The subject, affected by ideology, thinks internal thoughts. The virtual-actual deconstructs the internal-external boundary to map a continuous materiality. The creative explosion I discuss here was also an information revolution. Much like the modern experience of information overload (though perhaps significantly more intensive), this creative explosion demanded a new set of cognitive abilities and tools: or more accurately, the explosion, abilities, and tools emerge in concert with one another. As I elaborate later, prior to this explosion, it is theorized that humans thought in specific, limited, concrete terms and communicated only with a small group that shared very specific contexts. The explosion demanded an ability to abstract information, to divide knowledge into exchangeable processes, to store information in the world, and to be able to communicate with a wider social group, including people one saw only rarely. As I argue, this shift can be characterized as moving from a limited, internalized form of consciousness to a consciousness that functions liminally between internal and external cognitive processes and intelligent networks. In short, though cave paintings are distant from digital media, I seek to demonstrate that while the artificial intelligence and information networks of new media create a powerful network of distributed cognition, in doing so they do not change the fundamental relationship between embodied cognition, consciousness, and technology. As the philosophy of the virtual-actual indicates, we have always thought this way.

For what it's worth, a cognitive scientist reading this would be as equally perplexed by my argument as a rhetorician might. Steven Pinker, for one, is a prime example of those scientists who find postmodern theory and cultural studies particularly objectionable. As the "science wars" of the nineties demonstrated, many scientists wish to claim the knowledge they produce is an objective, verifiable representation of reality; postmodernism and cultural studies contends that all representations are cultural and ideological and cannot be objective. Science may wish to see the humanities conform to the rational structures and claims of scientific inquiry; in turn the humanities may largely ignore science or use scientific concepts in only the most metaphorical ways. In this chapter and throughout this text, I am looking to connect scientific and technological concepts to rhetorical-philosophical ones in a fashion that allows each to maintain its specific traits while also transforming the other. As Brian Massumi (2002) observes,

> When you poach a scientific concept, it carries with it scientific affects . . . A kind of conceptual struggle ensues, producing a creative tension that may play itself out in any number of ways (depending in part on how much the importer of the concept actually understands of the system left behind—or cares). However it plays out, it is certain that the humanities project into which the concept has been imported will be changed by the encounter. (p. 20)

As such, the argument in this book relies heavily on this first, surprising step, this "poaching." In order to build a writing and teaching practice upon an understanding of the material connections between new media and thought, it will be necessary to reconcile a critical understanding of ideology and discourse with an investigation into materiality.

In part, this argument begins with recognizing the partial gesture that rhetoric and composition has made toward postmodern theory. Specifically, while incorporating the critique of foundational knowledge and coming to view knowledge as social, discursive, and ideological, our field has struggled with postmodernity's implications for the writing process itself. The writing process, as it is generally taught, remains an internal, autonomous process, even if it is one that is learned socially and must ultimately account for the expectations of a discourse community. Our discipline has never been able to account for the radical exteriorization of the subject or the rhizomatic distribution of the compositional process. Yet it is precisely these traits that are intensified by the emergence of new media composition. In new media studies, the blurring of author/reader/user is commonplace, as is the disappearance of authority and intent in the iterative revision of new media texts such as wikis or blogs. In addition, though it is difficult to speak uniformly of a discourse as discontinuous as postmodernism, in general, the critique of foundational or essentialist knowledge about cognition does not suggest that materially speaking the brain does not exist or that it does not have functions. Instead, the point is to recognize the dis/continuity between sign systems (discursive knowledge) and materiality. Mark Hansen's *Embodying Technesis* (2000) provides a very thorough critique of postmodernism's turn toward textuality (though I would characterize this turn more as a matter of the way the work of Derrida, Deleuze and Guattari, and others have been interpreted and employed, especially in English Studies in the U.S. than as a necessary feature of their philosophies). Rhetoric and composition's focus on the social and ideological features of discourse, while retaining its traditional notion of the individual writer and autonomous writing process, specifically produces a blindspot in understanding the role of technology and the body (including the brain) in the composition and communication of knowledge. One way of understanding this book is to see it as an attempt to introduce a theory of the materiality of writing/media and cognition that is consonant with our theories about ideology and discourse.

What was objectionable about cognitive approaches to composition were their insistence that the challenges of composition pedagogy lay strictly with understanding the universal cognitive operations of individuals writing in a way that downplayed or even occluded the social dimension of writing. However, as I will discuss, evolutionary psychology, anthropology, and archeology provide different theories of the development of cognition and symbolic behavior. Taken together, these theories indicate that the adaptation of symbolic behavior was largely about being able to gain a social, competitive advantage—both individually and socially (for one's kin group). In short, symbolic behavior has always been discursive and rhetorical. More importantly from my perspective, the theory that modern consciousness and symbolic behavior emerged together forms a scientific foundation for arguing that consciousness is indeed a product of the exteriorization of embodied mental processes. That is, it is our ability to store and process information in spaces outside our body that allows us to engage in the complex thoughts on which consciousness is founded.

As this chapter details, this articulation of the intersection of cognition with sign systems, and the resulting exteriorization of thought, imply a radical rethinking of the compositional process that moves it beyond the private, interior domain of the individual and into a material-historical-cultural space. This move is crucial in understanding how technologies participate in the composition process as elements in a distributed network of cognition.

SPEECH AND GESTURE

Some 20,000 years ago in southern France, humans ventured into the caves of Lascaux to produce elaborate drawings and symbols. It was not the beginning of art but rather the apogee of Upper Paleolithic civilization in Western Europe. There can be no precise date for the origin of art any more than there can be a precise definition of what art is, though archeology suggests that artistic expression can be traced back tens of thousands of years before this, at least as far back as 75,000 years ago. However, even this date in Lascaux precedes the invention of "formal writing systems" by more than 15,000 years. Nevertheless, as archeologists contend, significant social changes were taking place as these peoples banded together in larger groups and developed more complicated and extensive socio-economic networks. One theorized effect of these changes was an explosion in cultural information, which, in the absence of writing systems, had to be stored in human memory. In this situation, some external mechanism or practice had to be developed to ensure the successful imprinting of information on human memories and to allow for effective communication between individuals who were not intimately associated with one another. As such, the Upper Paleolithic period is identified as the era in which symbolic behavior emerged.

As I mentioned above, the current trend in fields like evolutionary psychology is to suggest that the historical moment when our species emerged as "us" coincides with what has been termed a "creative explosion," the rapid development of a range of tools *and* various forms of expression from jewelry to carvings to cave paintings. According to evolutionary psychology, humans (and our direct ancestors) are the only species to enter this "cognitive niche," as it is termed. It represents our evolutionary gamble to bet our continued survival on our ability to reason abstractly and develop novel approaches and solutions to problems such as killing prey larger and/or faster than us and negotiating the often vicious and competitive politics of our social group. Foundational to the success of this strategy is our ability to articulate our knowledge in language and share it with others. This is a fundamentally rhetorical skill, as is the ability to negotiate the politics of communication to figure out how and when to share our information. As this argument proceeds, a kind of symbiotic relationship exists between our mind's ability to construct ever more complex, abstract strategies and the development of symbolic means in which those strategies could be understood and communicated.

How does this relationship develop? As archaeologist Clive Gamble (1999) explains, the "transition, anatomically from Neanderthals to Cro-Magnon peoples, behaviorally from an ancient to a modern pattern, and culturally from the Middle to the Upper Paleolithic, represents, in evolutionary terms, the Other becoming Us" (p. 268). Specifically, Gamble sees that transition as

> socially, technically, and culturally the separation of the gesture from the body. Objects now took on a social life. . . . [Language] is a further aspect of this separation of the act from the body, the creation, if you like, of a society as a severed limb rather than an integral social and technical gesture. (1999, pp. 269–272)

In other words, however we might typify the communication of earlier periods, during this time our ancestors developed a new cognitive power of abstraction that allowed them to separate speech, gesture, and action from the immediate contexts of their bodies. The big difference, Gamble explains, between modern humans and Neanderthals "is that we move from social occasion to social occasion while Neanderthals moved at most from gathering to gathering" (1999, p. 356). Neanderthals did not stock locales with supplies or materials; instead, they carried their tools with them. "What they carried was a sequence of embodied gestures (artifacts) which were an extension of their hands. In the same way the form and shape of the clothes which they most certainly wore were conditioned by the bodies they concealed" (1999, p. 356). Neanderthals relied upon the immediate presence of their bodies to provide their tools with meaning. Tools and supplies had immediate value for an individual and those with whom the individual shared close, emotional bonds. Meaning hinged on physical proximity; artifacts were not seen as having independent value. By tracing the dispersal of raw materials from a particular source, archeologists can see that Neanderthals did not transport goods farther than 20km, nor were such goods passed from hand to hand farther than this distance. Gamble concludes that Neanderthals lived in simple social networks not extending beyond immediately present individuals. Where gatherings of Neanderthals did occur, communication was based upon embodied gestures and artifacts whose meanings did not persist beyond the gathering's immediate moment.

Modern humans, on the other hand, did stock locations with materials and supplies. They were able to abstract artifacts from the immediate context of their bodies. Among other things, this results in the production of new technologies:

> the saw (and blades in general) as well as the needle belong to a class of truly synthetic tools in the sense that they have no close analogue in any part of the human body. They present new tricks to the neural system that coordinates manual dexterity—tricks for which our brain is not hardwired. (Ofek, 2001, p. 170)

This capacity for abstraction is the fundamental cognitive activity upon which symbolic behavior emerges. Furthermore, unlike the early Neanderthals, evidence from the Upper Paleolithic period indicates a marked increase in the transfer of materials beyond 20km. This can be correlated with a transformation in the social networks inhabited by these peoples. As individuals in more insulated networks "criss-crossed through nodes and along the paths of a wheel or star-burst network, their effective and intimate networks were frequently affirmed. People were available for negotiation without assigning a special temporality to such action" (Gamble, 1999, p. 361).

Haim Ofek (2001) argues that it is during the trade exchanges made at these occasions that symbolic behavior begins. Trade over long distances indicates exchanges being made between individuals whose relationship is not predicated upon regular co-presence (i.e., they do not see each other on a regular basis). Instead, the exchange is made possible by the cognitive ability to abstract the value of objects and establish a *symbolic* value (what Ofek terms "monetarization"). As he argues, "by its very nature, money is a fiction . . . and dealing with it is the ultimate ritual" (p. 180). For Ofek, this argument is made even more compelling by the appearance of "wall paintings, portable art, personal ornamentation, elaborate burials—that is, the sudden increase in symbolic behavior" (p. 180). It is important to note that the creation of trade networks does not necessarily mean the development of a marketplace logic of *exchange value*. While some economy is in place, it is difficult to know what and how symbolic value was attributed to objects. What is important here is the realization that the existence of trade necessitated the ability to engage in symbolic behavior.

For Gamble, this extension into broader networks marks a shift from "complex" to "complicated" societies. In complex societies, information is embodied and each activity is discretely stored in the memory. Members of complicated societies, however, chunk information into sequences of simpler tasks. As Gamble notes,

> to become information these chunks require signs and symbols to provide a code for action. . . . The categories created by chunking allow us to explore the possibilities of an infinitely rich world of information based on movement and interaction. Instead of dealing with each information source on a one-by-one basis, the individual now groups and categorizes such sources into a variety of patterns. (1999, pp. 363–4)

Setting aside the question of the origin of symbolic behavior, what is clear in both Gamble and Ofek's assessment is that the creative explosion of modern human cognition is grounded in non-phonic activity. That is, artistic expression, whether in the form of naturalistic representations or abstract symbols, would appear to have its foundation in the cognitive demands of complex technological activities and economic demands. Obviously, there can be no direct physical evidence of speech, but the point here is that there is no historical basis for asserting that symbolic communication begins with the attempt to abstract speech, as would appear to be the case in our traditional view of non-phonic symbolic communication (e.g., writing) which sees such activity as an attempt to represent ideas first articulated in speech.

Instead, in the examination of the Paleolithic emergence of symbolic behavior, spoken and gestural symbols develop contemporaneously, specifically to produce knowledge, including consciousness. That is, we learn to speak not so that we can articulate a knowledge of the world already pre-existing within our own minds: knowledge does not exist internally to then be represented externally; knowledge is produced through the process of externalization, through its articulation in symbols. Gamble notes that with the development of the complicated society

> artifacts were no longer adjuncts to persons, mean-
> ingful only when attached in acquisition, manufac-
> ture, or use and linked in action by rhythms. Arti-
> facts now become personified since they represented
> either that person or the existence of an extended
> network *in absentia*. When associated with social oc-
> casions and the transformation of locale into place,
> they formed a substitute for co-presence that can be
> understood because they belonged to a complicated,
> sequenced set of routines. (1999, p. 365)

Given its place within a social network, an artifact retains its meaning
even when the person who gave it to you is no longer there. This is the
general sense of symbolic or representational meaning, that objects
in the world have meanings outside of their immediate local context
and use. This externalization of information into the social landscape
becomes a necessary step in human development.

Of course, externalized, symbolic information cannot exist in an
independent fashion; symbolic information relies upon its connection
to a social network that can interpret the symbols and access the data.
In short, through their attachment to a symbolic, social landscape,
these Paleolithic peoples attached themselves to a cybernetic network,
a system of distributed cognition, a smart environment. I term this
network "cybernetic," not simply because it was a network of symbolic
information, but because it also served to secure information and ensure that information could be communicated to other tribe members.
As has been suggested by archeologists, this would be the moment
when modern human consciousness as we understand it comes into
existence. Before this, prehistoric humans could not think beyond the
context of the body and their immediate kinship group. Now humans
entered a social landscape, with the power of abstraction and symbolic thinking. Human consciousness, if we are to understand this
as corollary to symbolic behavior, is not then a product of self-presence. Neanderthals had self-presence of some sort and non-symbol-
ic, embodied, spoken and gestural communication for hundreds of
thousands of years before this. Consciousness and symbolic behavior
emerge only when presence is exteriorized—exteriorized so that technological processes, social practices, and systems of exchange could
be effectively organized and communicated. Consciousness then becomes not so much the pinnacle of our internal self but the hinge, the

point of interface, between internal processes and external networks of data, information processing, and technological activities; in order to become conscious, one must articulate oneself through a network of distributed cognition.

THE EVOLUTION OF WRITING

Understanding the fundamental moment of the emergence of symbolic behavior and consciousness significantly impacts how we understand later technological developments in media. In this current informational crisis, our inundation in media makes the study of writing's evolution important not only as a scholarly, philosophical enterprise but also as a subject of undergraduate curriculum as well. If our contemporary challenge as writers and rhetoricians is responding to new media, then our students will require a historical context for this technological development. In addressing this challenge, programs in rhetoric and professional writing might explicitly incorporate questions of technological development into courses on new media writing. However, as I have suggested, this issue goes beyond the specific context of writing in electronic environments; it becomes a fundamental question of how we understand writing itself. Though the *Phaedrus* is a long-standing and common text in "Rhetorical Traditions" or "History of Rhetoric" courses, the dialogue's definition of rhetoric and its analysis of the problems with writing take on different implications in the context of new media. In this way, the rhetorical implications of new media become present in writing courses across the curriculum even though they may not be acknowledged.

More than 10,000 years passed between the caves of Lascaux and the emergence of farming. Another 5,000 years passed before the development of a formal writing system. Entry into an agricultural economy requires increasing specialization of a community's members. As Ofek notes, the switch was not an easy one, as "expressed in skeletons dating to the time of the first human acquaintance with agriculture. Small overall size, knobbly joints, thinning in the outer layer of bones, abscesses and dental cavities—all bear testimony to diets badly out of balance" (2001, p. 213). This meant that an increasingly elaborate trade network was required to provide farmers the variety of diet and other goods they needed in exchange for their excess harvest. In addition, agricultural technologies did not develop in isolation; such developments relied upon trade and information networks as well. Formal writing systems may have developed from these exigencies. Certainly some of the earliest forms of writing were on clay tokens likely used for counting and recordkeeping in the emerging towns and cities where these trades took place. Such trade engendered the development of towns and thus the possibility of specialized trade labor, like writing. However, prior to the development of fertilizer and irrigation, farmers were forced to live an itinerant existence, picking up and moving when they exhausted the soil of its nutrients. This itinerancy shifted trading sites and patterns and thus limited the development of an urban culture.

The eventual creation of these agricultural technologies resulted in the building of more permanent cities. These trade centers allowed for the pursuit of even further specialization in crafts and personal services, including schools:

> Around 3200 BC . . . fertile regions undergo massive terraforming along rectilinear plots. Rivers are diverted into rectangular irrigation systems. Cities emerge, themselves rectilinear. Zoom in with me now into the squarish walls of the cities, and into the very squarish rooms of the city, and we will find the intimate source of this sudden change. There, a row of hard stone benches arranged regularly. It is a schoolroom for scribes. Hundreds of boys, mostly the sons of privileged nobility, sit for hours hunched over clay tablets, learning to scrawl in regular lines. Indeed, if we superimpose the scratching of these lines they look like the lines of irrigation written on the face of the earth itself, as seen from an orbiting satellite. The harsh discipline of the schoolchildren being tutored in a script "canalizes" their thought processes, re-enforcing certain pathways. It's hard not to imagine that what's written on the brain gets projected onto the world, which is literally "canalized," too. (Porush, 1998, pp. 48–9)

David Porush's observations regarding the emergence of civilization make clear connections between the shape of farms, the design of cities, the architecture of buildings, and the appearance of writing. From this description it is not possible to identify the origin of the rectilinear shape or the canalizing brain (i.e. which caused which), but one can see a symbiotic relationship where the brain shapes, and is shaped by, technology. Porush specifically identifies writing as a technology that leaves a significant mark upon the shape of the brain, by imposing an abstract grid upon the brain's physical-mental space.

Porush's description reflects Jay Bolter's observation that in a culture's attempt to understand the impact of writing technologies, "the behavior of writing space becomes a metaphor for the human mind as well as for human social interaction" (2001, p. 13). This issue is already present in the *Phaedrus*, where Plato addresses the impact of writing technology upon memory. The *Phaedrus* serves as a link between the early history and pre-history of writing and our own understanding. Oddly, since Socrates and Plato represent the "beginning" of rhetoric and philosophy, in historical terms they stand at about the mid-point between the invention of formal writing systems and the contemporary moment. However, despite the 25 centuries or more of writing that precedes classical Greece, Plato is dealing with writing as a new challenge in this dialogue. So what occurs when the dialogue is put into this technological and theoretical context? The *Phaedrus* has traditionally been considered a poorly formed dialogue, either written by a young and inexperienced Plato or an old and doddering one. The section addressing writing in particular has been viewed as an unnecessary addendum. However, in Derrida's reading (1981a), writing becomes a key concept for the dialogue tied through its association with the term "pharmakon," the Greek word meaning both remedy and poison. Where the immediate reading of the dialogue might result in one believing that Plato is condemning writing, a closer analysis reveals a subtler approach that establishes some of the key philosophical issues surrounding writing technology even now as we approach new media.

One of the key issues of Derrida's "Plato's Pharmacy" is the articulation of the *pharmakon* as a dangerous supplement that troubles the boundaries between inside and outside, living and nonliving:

> What Plato is attacking in sophistics, therefore, is not simply recourse to memory but, within such recourse, the substitution of the mnemonic device for live memory, of the prosthesis for the organ, the perversion that consists of replacing a limb by a thing, here, substituting the passive, mechanical "by-heart"

for the active reanimation of knowledge, for its reproduction in the present. The boundary (between
inside and outside, living and nonliving) separates
not only speech from writing, but also memory as an
unveiling (re-) producing a presence from re-memoration as the mere repetition of a monument; truth
as distinct from its sign, being as distinct from types.
The "outside" does not begin at the point where what
we now call the psychic and the physical meet, but at
the point were the *mneme,* instead of being present to
itself in its life as a movement of truth, is supplanted
by the archive, evicted by a sign of re-memoration or
of com-memoration. The space of writing, space *as*
writing, is opened up in the violent movement of this
surrogation, in the difference between *mneme* and *hy-
pomnesis.* The outside is already *within* the work of
memory. (1981, pp. 108–9)

By turning to the text, one receives support for *hypomnemsis,* which is a
support for a spoken language that, in turn, supports a *living* memory
of thought. As Plato recounts in his formulation of a myth of writing's
invention: writing dulls the living memory and cures only its symp-
toms. That is, the text allows us to recall the words, but it does not re-
create presence. Of course, if it simply remained exterior and served to
support spoken language, then writing would have its uses. However,
it does not remain on the outside. Instead, writing takes place at the
moment where the *mneme* is supplanted by the "archive," an activity
that occurs in the cognitive act of writing. Writing in 2001, Bolter
echoes these same concerns raised by Plato: where does thought end
and writing begin? However, Bolter is clear to make the distinction of
referring to the "materiality of writing" as opposed to writing as a cognitive activity. Nevertheless, this remains a gesture to define writing
as exterior to the self. The trope of the *pharmakon* questions whether
this can be enough. Can one draw a boundary between the self and
the text somewhere between the fingertips and keyboard, the eye and
the screen?

Derrida's argument casts doubt on this possibility. If indeed the addition of the notion of materiality were somehow to succeed in insulat-
ing the conscious mind from writing, then it would only be able to do
so insofar as we viewed cognition as an immaterial process. That is, if

thought were abstract and writing material, then a clear point of interface and translation could be mapped. But this is clearly not the case.
Thought is a material process in that some*body* has to do the thinking;
writing as a symbolic behavior is likewise abstract. The problem, however, lies not in trying to sort out these complex interactions, but rather
in recognizing that consciousness is a specific consequence of exter-
nalizing human information processing and storage demands. This is
not to suggest that our conscious thoughts do not emerge within our
minds, but rather that their production relies on a series of processes
that are both "internal" and "external" in the way we conventionally
think of these things. Nor should the notion of consciousness as external immediately invoke the loss of agency. Many internal, unconscious
processes are out of our control; alternately, we can regulate many of
the external sources of information, though obviously they are not entirely within our control either.

Despite his reservations, Plato relies heavily upon writing, seemingly choosing writing where Socrates does not. Gregory Ulmer (2003)
argues that only with the arrival of text can the close analysis of language make possible the production of philosophic concepts. For example, developing the concept of justice requires a careful study of the
use of the term:

> it would be an easy matter to recollect what Agamem-
> non or Achilles did or what happened to them, [but]
> the names of "dike" and "hubris" and related terms
> were buried deep in the oral matrix. To rely on oral
> memory not only to recollect but to collect what hap-
> pened to them would be beyond existing capacity.
> But place the language of the study visibly before the
> eye, so that the flow is arrestible and the words be-
> come fixed shapes, and the process of selection and
> collection can begin. (Havelock cited in Ulmer, 2003,
> pp. 30–31)

In other words, the existence of the written text allows Hesiod, and
then Plato, to study the use of the term "dike" (justice) in a way not
possible before. However, in developing these philosophical concepts
(indeed the concept of concepts itself), Plato needs to prevent the slip-
page of concepts from one category to another, from outside to inside.

Writing thus becomes the means by which philosophic concepts are produced and secured but remains in excess of those concepts.

Writing's operation outside of the conceptual is demonstrated in the *Phaedrus,* where Plato must describe writing in mythic rather than conceptual terms. At the outset of the dialogue, Socrates warns against putting too much credence in myths. Curiously, in the context of this warning, Plato invents two myths in the dialogue's examination of writing. Though created by Plato, these myths reflect already existing mythic structures, particularly, as Derrida presents, the Egyptian god Thoth. The truth of writing, Derrida (1981) explains,

> is not the object of a science, only of a history that is recited, a fable that is repeated. . . . One should note most especially that what writing will later be accused of—repeating without knowing—here defines the very approach that leads to the statement and determination of its status. One thus begins by repeating without knowing—through a myth—the definition of writing, which is to repeat without knowing. (pp. 74–5)

In other words, what one discovers, here at Western philosophy's beginning, is that despite the binaries it establishes, rational scientific knowledge cannot separate itself from irrational, mythic knowledge, for it is within that mythic space that writing, the founding tool of philosophy and science, emerges. What this suggests, in typical Derridean fashion, is that binaries such as rational, scientific knowledge versus irrational, mythic knowledge cover a more fundamental condition of knowledge that is neither rational, irrational, or some synthesis or joining of the two. Instead, we require an understanding of the process of knowledge production that does not rely upon this type of systemic logic.

Neither our scientific nor our mythic narratives can account for the development of writing or symbolic behavior in general. What is certain however is that questioning the evolution of writing raises further questions regarding the construction or evolution of consciousness. With symbolic behavior at the root of the anthropological definition of modern humans and formal writing systems as the foundation of human civilization and history, this should come as no surprise. The binaries Derrida seeks to deconstruct, such as those between speech and writing, science and nonscience, inside and outside, and philosophy and rhetoric, are important for understanding how rhetoric and composition might move forward in relation to new media. Here further binaries appear, such as technology versus humanism, professionalizing education versus liberal art education, and writing pedagogy as the delivery of skills versus writing pedagogy as a critical-cultural activity. These tensions between humanistic education and professional writing education reflect that of the philosopher and the sophist, the lover and the non-lover in the *Phaedrus*. And as Derrida explores, these binaries each rest upon the myth of writing.

The development of symbolic behavior and the invention of formal writing systems create a pattern of exteriorizing cognitive processes that continues with further technological change. The developmental process archeologists and evolutionary psychologists theorize resonates strikingly with Derrida's critique—all the more striking given the general antipathy among scientists for contemporary philosophy. However, if modern, human consciousness, symbolic behavior, and technology all develop in concert, then this reflects Derrida's deconstruction of the traditional relationship between thought as internal and primary and writing as external and secondary. Furthermore, we necessarily must turn to some alternate understanding of thought and composition that manages to forego such binary stipulations. The virtual-actual provides this by articulating the abstract and the material as part of a continuous plane. I discuss this in detail in Chapter 6. However, before reaching that point, I want to explore in greater detail the historical relationships between cognition and media technologies. While socio-technological revolutions such as Gutenberg's invention may not result in as dramatic a shift as the development of symbolic behavior, they clearly have extensive cultural effects. Furthermore, they serve to exemplify the continuation of both the founding logocentric concept of writing as secondary to speech and the instability of that concept. This instability intensifies in the nineteenth century when new inventions such as the gramophone and the camera serve to further exteriorize apparently internal mental processes. André Leroi-Gourhan (1993) observes,

> tools detached themselves from the human hand, eventually to bring forth the machine: in this latest stage speech and sight are undergoing the same process, thanks to the development of technics. Lan-

guage, which had separated itself from the human through art and writing, is consummating the final divorce by entrusting the intimate functions of pho-nation and sight to wax, film, and magnetic tape. (p. 216)

Of course, he was writing before the arrival of digital media, but his point is no less valid: it is these technologies, the new media of the *nineteenth century,* that signal the mechanization of the composition process. As I examine in the next chapter, the typewriter, gramophone, and camera initiate a new level of cognitive exteriorization that lays the foundation for the challenges of the contemporary moment.

3 Nineteenth-Century New Media

In 1874, as weapons manufacturing declined following the Civil War, Remington began serial production of typewriters and

> the typewriter became a discursive machine-gun. A technology whose basic action not coincidentally consists of strikes and triggers proceeds in automated and discrete steps, as does ammunitions transport in a revolver and a machine-gun, or celluloid transport in a film projector. (Kittler, 1999, p. 191)

The typewriter mechanized the writing process and in doing so participated in the transformation of cultural ideas about writing and the relationship between author and reader. This transformation was broad, ranging from changes in business practices to the development of new literary and philosophical ideas about writing. If, as I suggest in Chapter 2, consciousness emerges through a network of symbolic behavior shaped by the technologies of speech and gesture, such as writing, then the development of mechanical means of information production will have a significant effect upon that production and the way we understand cognition. The impact that these and other related composition and communication technologies (e.g., the telegraph, the telephone, the gramophone) had on our concepts of writing and thought are not coincidental. As Lisa Gitelman (1999) argues, "inventing new ways to write or new kinds of writing presupposes a model of what writing and reading are and can be . . . In this way, shorthand alphabets, phonographs, typewriters, and other nineteenth-century innovations in the area of inscriptive practice are so many theories of language and textuality" (p. 4). Gitelman thus suggests that these technologies do not determine our conception of thought or writing; instead, they meet, to some degree, existing expectations, understand-

ings, and practices of writing, while clearly at the same time promising
to transform them.

In the traditional scheme, the "author," keyed as male, maintains
his presence in the text and speaks his unified voice through history.
He views writing technologies as transparent. This transparency hinges upon a broader philosophy that sees the body as secondary to the
mind. The author's intellect and his ideas exist in an abstract, symbolic space and thus may pass unaffected from the materiality of his
body to the materiality of the text. However, as I will discuss, the
typewriter ushers in more than a new mode of composition; it signals
a change in the way we understand the functioning of the mind. The
mind becomes a less abstract, more biological entity whose operation
more closely resembles the industrial mechanisms of the nineteenth
century, like the typewriter, with a electrical network whose communications echo Morse code. The virtual-abstract I have been describing lies beneath these metaphors. On that continuous, material plane,
the typewriter, camera, and other media technologies intersect our informational network and our embodied cognitive processes; through
this intersection, technologies and practices of distributed cognition
unfold. In short, these technologies participate in the composition of
both thought and media. However, recognizing the integral role technology plays in these compositions was as unacceptable in the nineteenth century as it was for Plato: writing and media technologies were
a danger the author must avoid. In response, the male author attempts
to insulate himself from these implications by the installation of a new
partner in the compositional process: the female typist. In addition,
literary study emerges as a discipline to secure that threatened traditional concept of the author, which serves as a lynchpin in protecting
culture from the dehumanizing effects of industrialization. However,
in terms of literary production, the typewriter contributes to the development of Modernist aesthetics and the shift to a more fragmented
presentation of both the mind and the world.

Of course, the movie camera contributed at least as much as the
typewriter, if not more, to this emerging aesthetic. As I will discuss,
the camera combines the fragmentation of the mobile world (into 24
frames per second) with an illusory re-integration of that world into a
new cohesive reality enabled by collusion between the screen and the
human eye. The new reality presented by the camera is hailed for its
revolutionary scientific and political potential. In this chapter, I ex-

plore how filming and editing techniques provide a new understanding of human physiology and psychology through the documenting of patient behaviors. These same editing techniques are employed to support politics from Soviet montage to fascist propaganda. However, despite film culture's insistence on the "reality" of its images, film technique has always included a variety of editing processes, optical illusions, and other camera tricks. As I investigate, filmic representation, even "unedited," is never "real." Film's simulation of the real includes consciousness itself. This simulation presents viewers with a disturbing reflection of the mechanical production of human consciousness. Taken together, the typewriter and camera confront the Modern world with the multidimensional quality of media composition and suggest significant implications for consciousness that would be further developed through cybernetics. The history of these technologies also reveals the multiple techniques deployed to insulate the traditional, masculine, free-willed, rational consciousness from those implications.

The Discourse Machine Gun

While the original typewriter was designed to enable visually impaired people to write, it quickly became adopted by the industrializing business world of the late nineteenth century. As the number of typists employed by business rapidly increased, the position was quickly identified as a job for women. According to U.S. Census Bureau data, in 1870 there were 154 stenographers and typists in the United States. Only seven (4.5%) were women. By 1890 there were 33,400, and 21,300 (63.8%) were women. By 1930, over 95% of stenographers and typists would be women (Kittler, 1999, p. 184). In addition to creating new economic conditions for women, this new role altered the rhetorical relationship between the male author and the women who were both his readers and the subjects of his narrative. Women could no longer be perceived as being innocently outside the realm of textual production (even if, in historical fact, they had not been so for some time). Kittler suggests that this shift in gender was tied to a shifting perception of writing itself as the typewriter replaced handwriting as the mode of textual production:

> The fact that the minimal unevenness between stroke
> and paper can store neither a voice nor an image of

> a body presupposes in its exclusion the invention of
> phonography and cinema. Before their invention,
> however, handwriting alone could guarantee the per-
> fect securing of traces. . . . And what applied to writ-
> ing also applied to reading. Even if the alphabetized
> individual known as the "author" finally had to fall
> from the private exteriority of handwriting into the
> anonymous exteriority of print in order to secure "all
> that's left of him, as well as his self-propagation"—al-
> phabetized individuals known as "readers" were able
> to reverse this exteriorization. (1999, p. 9)

Kittler's argument here is that prior to the typewriter, the handwritten
nature of writing established a high level of intimacy between author
and reader. This intimacy was partly a result of a technological reality: the hand was the only means by which memory could be stored
outside the body. There were no sound recordings, only sheet music.
There was no cinema, only written narratives. There were no cameras,
only portraits. The hand was *the* means of media composition and
communication. And this means of communication was dominated
by men. For women of this time, hands were meant for other kinds
of work, sewing in particular. However, industrialization mechanized
the production of both text and textile. Writing became word processing, a technical skill separated from the intimacy of handwriting. In
making this transition, writing became an increasingly embodied skill
requiring speed and precision; along with this embodiment, the role of
the word processor, if not the "author," became feminized.

These technical and aesthetic developments were supported by the
emergence of human sciences during this period. As Foucault has argued, the human sciences served an important role in creating discourses about human nature and behavior. These discourses were crucial for the careful management of humans that became necessary in
an industrial culture. That is, in order to create optimal conditions for
the interactions between humans and machines, it was necessary to develop discourses about humans and machines that articulated them in
common terms. For example, Kittler explains that scientists studying
aphasia (an inability to communicate or understand language) "had
figured out the number of milliseconds it takes for a letter to travel
from the eye to the hand muscles via the brain's reading and writing
centers," and that from their study "the equation of cerebral circuits

with telegraphic dispatches had become a physiological standard" (1999, pp. 189–90). In other words, the passage of information from the eye to the brain to the hand was understood as a kind of internal telegraph system. If one thinks of reading and writing as a process in which a series of discrete signals is telegraphed through the body, then the typewriter, as an encoder of discrete letters, makes more sense as a writing machine than the pen with its continuous script. In such studies it is clear that the pen had lost its special quality and become instead an ineffective extension of the human nervous system. This is a significant shift: from the connection of the continuous handwritten line communicating an intimate knowledge of the author's mind and soul to the discrete signs of the typewriter translating electric signals, with the typist's body at the center of the network.

As much as the typist was at the center of this compositional process, her body was also subject to a process of invisibility. That is, the entire mechanical process of typing was obscured. Gitelman (1999) discusses the shift from "invisible" typewriters (typewriters whose "upstrike" printing technology prevented the typist from seeing what "she" typed) to "visible" typewriters. As she observes,

> Skilled typists do not look at the keys or at the body of the machine; rather, they experience what William James undeniably would have called a "cultivated motor automatism" or a "mild case of possession," when they cease to exert intention before every action of hitting the keys. And admittedly, if the "visible" typewriter become gradually less visible, unnoticed, then the same fate befell the typist during the early twentieth century. (1999, p. 210)

In maintaining the authority of the author, who, in a twisting of Nietzsche's comment about Socrates, is "he who does not type," the role of the typewriter must be occluded, and during this early period the term typewriter referred to the machine, the person, *and* the activity ("to typewriter" a letter). The entire process becomes part of the background.

This perception of the typist's body as a conduit for information underlies later plans for developing more computerized forms of word processing. In his landmark 1945 essay, "As We May Think," Vannevar Bush outlined plans for a machine he called the "Memex," a

form of hypermedia that relied on 1940s technologies such as micro-
film. However, his essay also anticipates a future where the electrical
impulses of the human nervous system might be directly translated
into electrical impulses in machines without being translated first into
mechanical operations (e.g., typing on a keyboard or speaking into a
microphone). He explains,

> The impulses which flow in the arm nerves of a typ-
> ist convey to her fingers the translated information
> which reaches her eye or ear, in order that the fingers
> may be caused to strike the proper keys. Might not
> these currents be intercepted either in the original
> form in which information is conveyed to the brain,
> or in the marvelously metamorphosed form in which
> they then proceed to the hand? (2001, pp. 152–3)

It is no accident that Bush refers to the typist as female. By this time
this was almost uniformly the case in the business world. These two
attributes must be considered in concert: the feminizing of the writing
process and the articulation of writing in electro-mechanical terms.
Bush's formulation begs the question, why have a typist at all? Why
not create this interface directly with the author? The answer reveals
powerful ideological commitments to a particular concept of authorship. Maintaining the female typist preserves the sanctity of the male
authorial intellect. The male author dictates his thoughts to the female
typist, and it is her body that then becomes the electro-mechanical
interface with the typewriter. It is her mind that produces the "mar-
velous metamorphosis" of language into electrical impulses. As I will
discuss later in the Cybernetics segment, preserving the masculine,
rational, free-willed consciousness from the possible implications of
information technology was a primary concern of cyberneticists during this early period of their discipline.

Of course, cybernetics was hardly the first discipline to concern
itself with maintaining the sanctity of the author. In 1900, as the typewriter was becoming a regular feature of offices and writers' desks, the
study of English literature was an emerging phenomenon at universities across the United States. Literary study develops in the university
at a time when the curriculum in general is gaining a more professional, business orientation. From 1870 to 1910, the number of professional jobs widened from 230,000 to 1,150,000; likewise, there was an

increase in trade, finance, and real estate from 800,000 to 2,800,000. Most of these jobs required certification from an educational institution. Specifically in terms of colleges: in 1870 5,553 faculty taught at 563 institutions; by 1900 23,868 faculty held positions at 977 institutions (Berlin, 2003, pp. 22–23). Not surprisingly, these numbers parallel the increase in demand for typographers and stenographers that Kittler discusses. Together they represented a new industrial professional and managerial office culture. The increasing demand for an educated workforce did not simply require an enlargement of the existing educational system but a significant reworking of its curriculum as well.

For English departments, one of the most substantial curricular reforms of this period was the introduction of the *literary* study of English literature. While literary works had been studied earlier in the nineteenth century, their "literary" qualities were subordinated to a view of "literature as an extension of public forms of speech and argument" (Berlin, 2003, p. 19). One of the reasons for this subordination was the belief that literature was "self-interpreting," a belief grounded in the idea that reading literature was a cultural practice already shared by the students and faculty. Literary study, then, emerges when the increase in student population introduces doubt in that belief; it responds to a perceived concern that incoming students do not have sufficient cultural knowledge to balance their increasingly business-oriented education. Therefore, from its inception, the study of literature was seen as tangential, if not oppositional, to capitalistic interests (and is still largely viewed that way, at least in the mainstream culture). In fact, as industrialization proceeded, literature was viewed as a valuable salve against the dehumanizing effects of an increasingly mechanical culture. As Matthew Arnold argued at the time, culture

> is a study of perfection, and of harmonious perfection, general perfection, and perfection which consists in becoming something rather than in having something, in an inward condition of the mind and spirit, not in an outward set of circumstances . . . above all in our own country has culture a weighty part to perform, because here that mechanical character, which civilization tends to take everywhere, is shown in the most eminent degree. (1993, pp. 22–3)

For Arnold that cultural perfection was best exemplified in poetry. In making this argument, Arnold countered a vision of culture hinged on scientific curiosity and the practical development of society: that is, a belief that the improvement of culture would occur through scientific and technological progress. Culture, in Arnold's sense, is "sweetness and light," the contemplative pursuit of a human perfection divorced from the material concerns of daily life.

Arnold's articulation of culture, particularly high art, as an insulation against the dehumanizing effects of modern life becomes a central value of English departments that largely remains with us today, though Arnold's bourgeois ideological commitments might be objectionable. We still often read literature to connect to an experience of humanness (whether we brand that experience "universal" or historically and culturally specific) that identifies us as being more than the mechanical cogs (or today, informational networks) our technoculture asks us to be. As such it is not uncommon to encounter significant resistance to technology in English departments. However, as George Landow (1997) argues, this neo-Luddism is contradictory within the discipline:

> Scholars and theorists today can hardly be Luddites, though they can be suspicious of the latest form of information technology, one whose advent threatens, or which they believe threatens, their power and position. In fact, the self-presentation of knowledge workers as machine-breakers defending their chance to survive in conditions of soul-destroying labor in bare, subsistence conditions tells us a lot about the resistance. Such mystification simultaneously romanticizes the humanists' resistance while presenting their anxieties in a grotesquely inappropriate way. In other words, the self-presentation of the modern literary scholar or critical theorists as Luddite romanticizes an unwillingness to perceive actual conditions of their own production. (pp. 272–3)

Those actual conditions include the mechanization of both the composition and publication of books. The disciplinary study of literature is a product of industrial culture, just as much as the books purchased and read in literature courses are. The Romantic-cum-Arnoldian view of literature as critical of industrialization obscures literary study's dependency on that industrialization. Landow suggests that if English Studies fails to recognize the extent to which it is a product of industrial culture and technology, then the discipline will fail to recognize the role post-industrial culture and technology (e.g., new media) will play in shaping its future.

On the other hand, by examining the impact of industrial technology on literary production, one might come to realize that the technological challenge to authorship does not begin with the Internet. Kittler's analysis demonstrates that these disciplinary values were already being challenged at the moment of their inception: "In standardized texts, paper and body, writing and soul fall apart. Typewriters do not store individuals; their letters do not communicate a beyond that perfectly alphabetized readers can subsequently hallucinate as meaning" (1999, p.14). The typewriter does not determine the mode of authorship to come, but it does indicate that authorship cannot travel unchanged through differing writing technologies. After the typewriter, writing is different. It is done in different places, by different people, for different purposes.

> T. S. Eliot, who will be "composing" *The Waste Land* "on the typewriter," "finds" . . . "that I am sloughing off all my long sentences which I used to dote upon. Short staccato, like modern, French prose." Instead of "subtlety," "the typewriter makes for lucidity," which is, however, nothing but the effect of its technology upon style. (Kittler, 1999, p. 229)

The typewriter transforms literary style through its mechanization of the writing process. The neurological relationship between the hand and the brain, which functioned in a particular way with handwriting, is transformed when the hand is attached to the typewriter. Rather than the continuous smooth relationship, the typewriter (and the computer keyboard to follow) is "staccato." Where sight is integral to handwriting, for insuring the formation of letters, it is unnecessary for typing, where the letters are preformed. Nietzsche, who turns to the typewriter when he begins to lose his vision (and a whole new aphoristic philosophy emerges), observes, "our writing tools are also working on our thoughts" (cited in Kittler, 1999, p. 200).

It is this Nietzschean observation that literary studies occludes. But
of course, this occlusion is neither an invention of nineteenth-century
English Studies nor of Arnoldian or Romantic anti-industrial sentiments (though such sentiments surely shaped the particular attitudes
of the discipline toward technology). Nietzsche puts the entirety of
Western philosophy to question here by doubting the ancillary role
not only of writing technology but also of writing itself. For to make
such a statement one must first recognize that thoughts are produced
through writing. However, another possibility is also emerging. As
Vannevar Bush's piece indicates, it becomes possible to begin imagining a new relationship between humans and machines, one in which
"pure thought" is communicated directly into the "pure" electronic
memory of the machine, bypassing any physical or mechanical process. If Plato introduced us to the notion of a realm of pure thought
from which all material things are (imperfectly) derived, then here we
see the development of a parallel, technologically-produced immaterial realm of electronic thought. As I will explore, the development
of such cybernetic technologies raises important concerns regarding
the value of embodiment, specifically the psychological and political
implications of asserting the capacity of technology to capture, represent, and finally simulate reality. Ironically, the insistence on *both* the
abstract nature of thought *and* the abstract transparency of communication will create a crisis with the invention of modern computing
and cybernetics in which technological information processing threatens to supplant human thought. This technological invasion of the
mind is precisely what the masculine tradition sought to avoid. On the
other hand, by acknowledging the occluded virtual-abstract space, it
becomes possible to understand thought as the intersection of technology and embodied cognition and realize that information technologies
are not necessarily or entirely about "thought control" (even though
they are clearly powerful ideological tools that must be approached
with critical care). While these concerns will become clear with the
advent of new media, they were already being raised with the development of the camera.

24 Frames Per Second

Perhaps even more significant than the typewriter for our changing
ideas of media composition was the development of the movie camera. In his 1936 essay, "The Work of Art in the Age of Mechanical

Reproduction," Walter Benjamin saw film as a means for a revolution in which art is stripped of its ritualistic, cultic aura: "the instant the criterion of authenticity ceases to be applicable to artistic production, the total function of art is reversed. Instead of being based on ritual, it begins to be based on another practice—politics" (1968, p. 224). In short, Benjamin believed film had the capacity to alter the relationship between art and the masses. Where the Arnoldian view of culture valorized the cultic value of art as protection against mechanization, Benjamin saw film's mechanization of artistic reproduction as an opportunity to confront the class biases that informed traditional art forms. Specifically, the camera created the possibility for the masses to be reproduced themselves:

> some of the players whom we meet in Russian films are not actors in our sense but people who portray *themselves*—and primarily in their own work process. In Western Europe the capitalist exploitation of the film denies consideration to modern man's legitimate claim to being reproduced. (Benjamin, 1968, p. 232)

From a contemporary perspective, where television, particularly cable, programming is filled with "reality-based" shows, it is difficult to appreciate Benjamin's belief in the revolutionary potential of "man's" claim for reproduction. Nevertheless in the Modernist period, the camera represented entry into a new reality, an opportunity to remake the world through a new mode of perception. As Benjamin noted,

> a different nature opens itself to the camera than opens to the naked eye—if only because an unconsciously penetrated space is substituted for a space consciously explored by man . . . the camera intervenes with the resources of its lowerings and liftings, its interruptions and isolations, its extensions and accelerations, its enlargements and reductions. The camera introduces us to unconscious optics as does psychoanalysis to unconscious impulses. (1968, pp. 236–7)

This new, unconscious-optical space suggested the camera's revolutionary potential: "our taverns and our metropolitan streets, our offices and furnished rooms, our railroad stations and our factories appeared to have us locked up hopelessly. Then came the film and burst this prison-world asunder by the dynamite of the tenth of a second" (1968, p. 236). In other words, from Benjamin's Marxist perspective the camera's technical capacities provided a lens for seeing the intersection between capitalist ideological interests and the mechanization of daily life. It is as if the camera's ability to produce a mechanical view of the world inaccessible to the organic human eye revealed a mechanization of culture that would be otherwise invisible.

Benjamin was not alone in his assessment. For filmmakers like Sergei Eisenstein, montage was the cinematic version of the Marxist dialectic: the combination of disparate spliced images led to a realization of material conditions and a lifting of false consciousness. The camera's ability to break apart reality allows it to penetrate into otherwise unseen spaces. The filmmakers' editorial ability to reintegrate these fragments and create wholeness, either in a material dialectic as with Soviet montage or a more "realistic" Hollywood-style film, then demonstrates the ability of film to produce a new reality from these fragments, one that participates with the viewer in the production of reality. However, this technological capacity also produces new opportunities for social control and manipulation of subjectivity. The shift from revolutionary montage to social control is well exemplified by the mutation of the revolutionary worker's claim for reproduction, which Benjamin hails, into contemporary reality TV. In Benjamin's description, the camera allows revolutionary filmmakers to peer beneath the veil of ideology to represent lived experience, and as such to give a true voice to the people. Reality TV offers its participants an opportunity to express themselves but constrains the context and conducts heavy edits, over which the participants have no say (witness the almost cliché complaints afterwards about being misrepresented). Reality TV rarely provides any insight into the actual material conditions of the individuals' lives. In fact, the programs are specifically filmed in a foreign context and depictions of home only appear to the extent that they might be molded into sympathetic family narratives. Rather than using editing techniques to present a revolutionary reality, reality TV programs edit their "real life" footage to represent the imaginary realm of the viewers (and the participants, even though some may not like what they see).

While the power of film exists in its ability to create cuts and edits, it also relies upon the camera's proclaimed technical ability to capture a cohesive reality. As media theorist Lev Manovich (2001) contends, "Cinema emerged out of the same impulse that engendered naturalism, court stenography, and wax museums. Cinema is the art of the index; it is an attempt to make art out of a footprint" (pp. 294–5). In other words, the purpose of cinema was to capture the reality of motion. Part of this impulse was a product of the technological lineage from which the movie camera emerged. The Phenakistiscope, the Thaumatrope, the Zootrope, the Praxitnoscope, the Choreutoscope, and other proto-cinematic technologies all relied upon hand-drawn and animated cells (Manovich, 2001, p. 296). Relying upon drawings necessarily meant a certain lack of verisimilitude; in addition, since a hand-operated crank animated the cells, the speed of the film was inconsistent. The film camera combined the reality of photography with a motorized, and hence regularized, system of animation. Despite the many elaborate techniques and artifices used to produce cinema, "cinema's public image stressed the aura of reality 'captured' on film, thus implying that cinema was about photographing what existed before the camera rather than creating the 'never-was' of special effects" (Manovich, 2001, p. 299). In other words, even in the case of Hollywood movies where narratives are clearly fictional, the cinematic composition relied on the perception that the events recorded reflected reality.

The paradox between the cut-up technical quality of film and the viewer's experience of a cohesive whole is foundational to cinema. Since, to this day, technology does not exist for real-time optical signal processing, cameras can only sample optical information, recording the information in chemical exposure (film) or digital code. Clearly, however, the cuts between these samples occur too quickly for the human eye to register. As a result, film appears as a seamless, cohesive representation of reality:

> every cinematic aesthetic has developed from the 24-frame-per-second shot, which was later standardized. Stop trick and montage, slow motion and time lapse only translate technology into the desires of the audience. As phantasms of our deluded eyes, cuts reproduce the continuities and regularities of motion. (Kittler, 1999, p. 119)

In this collusion between the eye and the screen, Kittler contends that viewers desire to misidentify film as real, to participate in the illusion of reality that it presents. Film becomes a manifestation of the audience's imaginary realm, on which Hollywood has so thoroughly capitalized. However, the inverse problem also presents itself. If the illusory cohesiveness of film is misidentified as the flowing world of the imaginary, then the fragmentary composition of film unmasks the mechanical underpinnings of the imaginary realm. This results in a potential psychological difficulty in which the more realistic a film seems (i.e. the more seamlessly it matches with the viewer's imaginary realm), the more likely that the discontinuous, mechanical attributes of filmic production might be transferred in the viewer's mind to their own imaginary realm (where, as I explain below, it might lead to a traumatic revelation of one's own mechanistic unconscious). In short, the filming process neatly demonstrates the foundation of any composition: a continuous materiality persists "out there," which can only be partially apprehended (by technology or human sense) and partially articulated (in discourses of writing, film, and so on), but this fragmentation is occluded in our assertion and experience of continuity (in the apparent seamlessness of a 24 frame-per-second video or our faith in the cohesiveness of originary, authorial intellectual property communicated through the reading experience).

During the early years of film, this challenge not only confronted the film entertainment industry but the scientific community as well. It was particularly crucial in the emerging field of psychiatry, where the filming of hysterics became a key form of scientific evidence. Early psychiatrists remarked upon the difficulty of having their patients perform their psychoses at appropriate times, during their lectures for example. Film technology solved this problem, as Hans Hennes, a psychiatrist of the period, explains, "The person doing the filming is in a position to wait calmly for the *best possible moment* to make the recording. Once the filming is done, the pictures are available for reproduction at any moment. Film is always 'in the mood.' There are no failures" (cited in Kittler, 1999, p. 145). As Kittler continues,

> The only thing [psychiatrists] have to do is shoot silent films, which as such (through their isolation of movements from the context of all speech) already envelop their stars in an aura of madness. To say nothing of the many possible film tricks that could

> chop up and reassemble these body movements, until
> the simulacrum of madness was perfect. (p. 146)

The insistence on the camera's reliable reproduction of reality was necessary for maintaining the veracity of this science. This insistence was not an attempt to cover up their "doctoring" of the film evidence. The psychiatrists were not deliberately misrepresenting their patients; in fact, the doctors asserted that this filming process revealed their patients as they really were and thus represented the patients more accurately than actually bringing them physically to the lecture hall.

However, it is likewise clear that the madness these psychiatrists studied was as much a product of a mechanical, technological process as a psychological one. In this simulacrum of madness it is impossible to tell who is mad and who is only faking. Neither reality nor unreality exists; simulation replaces both with a world produced through technological means. Interestingly, as Kittler notes, if the traditional history of film marks its movement from the entertainment of tent spaces toward experimental film, here we see a movement from psychiatric experimentation to the entertaining Hollywood film where the actor mimics the madness of the patient (p. 146). In other words, the camera's insertion between the patient and the doctor is reflected in the filmic interface between actor and audience. Our insistence upon the reality of one becomes our expectation of the reality of the other. Both the patient's and the actor's movements are recognized as "performances," but both are also identified as representing a deeper reality about the human condition.

However, alongside this recognition of the camera as producer of a new reality is a paranoid fear of the technology as threatening the purity of the human body and mind with its interfaces.

> Films anatomize the imaginary picture of the body
> that endows humans (in contrast to animals) with a
> borrowed I and, for that reason, remains their great
> love . . . On celluloid all gesticulations appear more
> ridiculous, on tapes, which bypass the skeletal sound
> transmission from larynx to ear, voices have no tim-
> bre . . . And all that not because media are lying but
> because their trace detection undermines the mirror
> stage. That is to say: the soul itself, whose technologi-

cal rechristening is nothing but Lacan's mirror stage.
(Kittler, 1999, p. 150)

Kittler here refers to the common experience of hearing one's voice on
tape (perhaps an answering machine) or watching one's self on a screen
(perhaps a security monitor). In confronting our doppelganger, we experience a disconnection from our own imaginary picture of ourselves.
In short, film, like the typewriter, presents us with a crisis in subjectivity. If Lacan's mirror stage represents a moment when we obscure
our fractured mechanistic production within the illusion of linguistic
wholeness, then the film and typewriter continually return us to that
moment of crisis by shattering that presumed wholeness with their
fragmentary composition. It becomes necessary for us once again to
assert an illusion of the whole. For film, this wholeness relies upon
a separation from cinema's past as a form of animation and a value
on erasing "any traces of its own production process, including any
indication that the images that we see could have been constructed
rather than simply recorded" (Manovich, 2001, p. 298). However, just
as the typewriter broke the continuous, intimate script of handwriting into discrete, impersonal elements, the camera transformed the
organic personal vision of an individual perspective into a mechanized
series of images. And just as the typewriter forever changes our ideas
about the writer and the audience, the camera has altered the way
we see the world. As Kittler contends, the invention of the gramophone, film, and the typewriter divided the recording of history and
memory into separate media, which only now are being reintegrated
in digital form. However, this reintegration in no way marks a return
to the continuous, intimate reality of handwriting. In fact, if anything,
the digitization of media exponentially magnifies its cut-up condition
(from thousands of frames or typewritten letters to millions of bytes).
It is important to note that this fragmentation is not *caused* by these
technologies. Human cognition *is* a fragmentary process composed
from multiple data flows into and within the body. Our consciousness
might give us a sense of cohesion, but even that is often disrupted by
strong emotions or unconscious habits or even a sudden noise.

An analysis of media technologies reveals ways in which the compositional process (whether as a composition of texts or other media)
might be understood as the partial apprehension of a continuous materiality (the virtual-abstract) and the integration of those partial elements into thoughts and symbolic structures (the virtual-technologi-

cal) that represent or simulate that material space. As I have discussed, from Plato onward, this understanding has been the foundation of a condemnation of writing, media, and technology, a basis for warning us against the dangers these represent. However, such warnings have always been founded on the belief that the mind was the cohesive and originary site of conscious thought. In Chapters 2 and 3, I have presented writing and media as necessary participants in the production of thought and suggested that thought, media technologies, and information are partial apprehensions of the material world. This should not be viewed negatively (as a failure to capture reality as it "truly" is) but rather as a demonstration of the necessary survival skills of conscious, rational thought: to filter through information, to abstract and make connections, and to communicate key pieces of data when they are needed. In reactionary responses to postmodernism, one often finds "theory" articulated as claiming consciousness and rationality do not exist. Here, and at least in my understanding, this is a significant misreading. Instead, what is asserted in postmodernism is a different understanding of the cognitive experiences we generally term consciousness and rationality—how they emerge and what relation they bear to materiality on one hand and culture/ideology on the other. In stepping into this argument, postmodern theory does not so much create a new debate but finds itself integrated into this ongoing concern over the role of writing and media in thought and communication. As I investigate in the next chapter, this anxiety over the writing and media intensifies with the development of the field of cybernetics or information science, which of course ushers in the development of computer technology.

4 Cybernetics

Though fears over media's externalization of thought go back at least to Plato, they have been particularly intensified by the development of modern computing. It is with modern computing, of course, that we begin to realize the virtual-technological reality with which we are familiar today: that is, a reality that is not simply a realistic representation of the real, but a real-time, fully interactive virtual space that maps onto material reality. Through this virtuality, users make changes in real time to both informational, digital spaces and physical spaces as well. Equally important, our connection to computers provides us with a powerful external means of data processing, organizing, communicating, and storing. Thus they serve as a significant element of our distributed cognition. That said, as the past two chapters have indicated, the virtual-technological has been with us since the emergence of symbolic behavior; since that time we have relied upon a virtual, informational space. And as I have been arguing, our consciousness serves as a hinge, an interface between that digital-symbolic information and the analog processes of embodied cognition. Those analog, embodied processes participate in the other virtual: the material unfolding of space. However, both Western philosophy and theology have insisted on the separation of consciousness from the body, occluding or downplaying the mind's embodiment. In Chapter 3, the invention of the typewriter, camera, and other technologies begin to unravel this separation by presenting us with a view of the fragmentary, material processes of thought. As I explore in this chapter, the familiar mind-body dualism becomes a source of anxiety as the development of computers presents us with machines that simulate the disembodied intelligence we have traditionally ascribed to ourselves. In a sense, given the obvious material differences between human and computer information processing, this anxiety seems odd, and yet it is such a common feature of our culture, we pay little attention to these differences. While the history of cybernetics can be read as a series of attempts to insulate human cognition from the implications of information theory, I describe here how a contemporary cybernetic theory of distributed cognition offers us a powerful way of understanding the role new media plays in the composition of thought and text.

As with many other twentieth-century technologies and technological theories, cybernetics grew from military applications: cryptology and targeting systems. Though military applications continue to be an important aspect of cybernetics, the field cannot be reduced neatly into the masculine fantasy of increasingly destructive toys. At its core, cybernetics focuses on the task of developing intelligent systems, a task that continues in the form of Artificial Intelligence (AI) and Artificial Life (AL). As a result of this focus, cybernetics has opened a scientific field of inquiry only to discover fundamental questions about humanness and unlikely modes of social critique. From the start, early cyberneticists such as Norbert Wiener were concerned about how their theories might be applied to human consciousness, particularly how cybernetics might come to suggest ways that human consciousness could be shaped or even controlled by machines. Their concerns led them to create a "homeostatic" version of intelligent systems that emphasized the capacity of a system to maintain its independence from its environment. As I will discuss, Wiener's and others' attempts to insulate cybernetics from social or psychological theory actually led directly to social and psychological crises. The objectification of information contributes to the removal of the subject from the communication process that was initiated by earlier media technologies, and the separation of humans from machines creates a relationship of paranoia between the two where the cyborg appears as a frightful double. The insistence of maintaining this separation, however, was predicated on the belief that human intelligence is an abstract control mechanism. That is, while the mind obviously is connected to the body and relies upon the senses for input, it is separable from those inputs and functions independently of them. The mind takes in information, creates a representation of the world, and then directs the body's actions in that world. With such a model of the mind, the image of thinking machines performing the functions of human minds, interfacing with those minds, and even replacing some human mental functions induces paranoia. Of course, as I have been suggesting, an alternate understanding of cognition as a material, networked process that includes brain, body, and machines offers an opportunity to move beyond the problems created by the binaries of inside/outside and human/machine. Such an understanding is also offered by contemporary cybernetics in the concept of distributed cognition. However, as I will explore, this concept still leaves open many questions about the fate of traditional humanistic values such as free will and creativity.

Cybernetics undergoes several developments en route to distributed cognition. Along with homeostasis, from the earliest stages of cybernetics, an alternate theory of information, communication, and intelligence was articulated. This "reflexive" model viewed information as a subjective product, produced in a symbiotic relationship between sender, receiver, and environment. In this model, consciousness is far less separable from environment, though even on this side of the field there was a concern for preserving the rational, free-willed subject. From this perspective, the "autopoietic" theory of intelligent systems developed. In my discussion of autopoiesis I focus on its important social and political implications as articulated by Humberto Maturana and Francisco Varela. Maturana and Varela contend autopoiesis suggests a biological ethos of utopian anarchy, and their theories end up having an influence upon Deleuze and Guattari and the broader field of post-Marxist and cyborg theory. However, autopoiesis still seeks to maintain a fundamental independence of intelligent systems from their environments, while contemporary philosophy moves away from such positions.

In contemporary cybernetics, autopoiesis has been replaced by theories of artificial intelligence (AI) and artificial life (AL). Despite the advancements of the field, the fundamental issue of how to model intelligent systems remains at stake. Some roboticists, such as Hans Moravec, continue to ascribe to an abstract theory of consciousness that suggests building AI by installing massive processing power to produce internal, abstract representations of the world. This might be termed a "top-down" approach. Others, like Rodney Brooks, prefer a "bottom-up" approach and model consciousness as an emergent phenomenon that results from the intersection of multiple systems. Rather than building representations of the world, Brooks contends, "it turns out to be better to use the world as its own model" (1991). Brooks's model of "subsumption architecture" draws upon a variety of disciplines including cognitive science, linguistics, and philosophy, and in turn his work suggests important implications for those fields.

As with the previous chapter, my purpose here is not to provide a full accounting of the history of this field as Katherine Hayles's (1999b) does. Instead, I continue to investigate the development of two inter-related phenomena, the erasure of distance between subject and object and the fragmentation of subjectivity. While mechanical media had a dramatic effect upon our sense of self and our secure sense of separateness from the outside world, cybernetics greatly intensifies those effects through its investigation of how communication and information processing function. By moving through this analysis, it becomes possible to move beyond seeing the "two virtuals" as dialectic opponents or dualistic poles and instead as two integrated elements. The virtual-technological becomes a means for apprehending the virtual-actual, for composing and sharing thoughts, that cannot be separated from the materiality of the virtual-actual any more than computer or human intelligence can be separated from a material computer or human brain.

HOMEOSTASIS

If cybernetics' nascent elements emerged during WWII, then its articulation as a disciplinary field took shape through the Macy Conferences on Cybernetics, which began in 1943 and continued until 1954. During this time, the foundational concepts of cybernetics would be developed. As Katherine Hayles (1999b) explains, the Macy Conferences were only one of several such conferences taking place during this period. However, they were unique in their interdisciplinary nature and in the fact that the presentations were not finished papers but rather brief sketches designed to initiate discussion. In this way they were an attempt to bring together scholarly work being done with information in a variety of fields, from literature and philosophy to psychology and anthropology to electrical engineering and neurophysiology (Hayles, 1999b, pp. 50–51). However, despite this interdisciplinary flavor, the conferences were certainly dominated by a hard scientific perspective as seen in the work of Norbert Wiener and Claude Shannon, whose theories founded cybernetics as we understand it today.

The basic purpose of the conferences, and information theory, was to develop an understanding of how intelligent systems communicate information. To accomplish this, the attendees had to develop working definitions of information and intelligent systems. Only then could the communication of information between these systems be considered. The participants shied away from the consideration of humans as intelligent systems. In general they preferred to think about the design of information-processing machines. The question of how humans processed communications clearly introduced issues of psychology (and rhetoric), which they wished to avoid. However, their focus on information-processing machines inevitably led to a technological concept of intelligence. If machines could be said to have intelligence, then that was because intelligence itself was the product of technological processes whether that intelligence rested in a piece of technology or a human body. While this would not mean that human intelligence was a technology, it certainly suggested that it had technological attributes. This blurring of machine and human was furthered by their definition of information. In Claude Shannon's equations, information was abstracted, decontextualized, from its material form and the medium in which it was transmitted. This decontextualization was necessary to avoid the slippery slope into psychology (to claim information required a context would necessarily include the context of the human mind). Decontextualized information could be examined in terms of noise and structure, without any consideration given to how one individual might interpret the transmission.

The decontextualization of information identified information as an *object*. The sender produces information, and then that information is sent to the receiver. Providing that errors and noise are kept to a minimum, the receiver gets the exact information the sender produced. The receiver then processes and makes use of that information according to its own purposes. In this way information systems were defined as "homeostatic": homeostatic systems use information for the purpose of maintaining both internal stability and a stable relationship with their environment (Hayles 1999b). The alternative was to conceive of information as a *process* and information systems as *reflexive*. When information is a process, it is produced through the relationship between sender and receiver. It does not exist as a pre-formed object. Information systems thus become reflexive because the information they use depends upon relations with external systems and not simply upon internal organization. As Hayles notes, "Homeostasis won in the first wave largely because it was more manageable quantitatively. Reflexivity lost because specifying and delimiting context quickly ballooned into an unmanageable project" (1999b, pp. 56–7). As we shall see, reflexivity will eventually supplant homeostasis as the dominant information theory of the sixties and seventies. However, reflexivity will build upon, rather than abandon, the decision to imagine information as abstract and disembodied. Furthermore, reflexivity and the theories of virtual reality that follow upon it, do not arise because of a new willingness to accept ambiguity or unmanageability, but rather from the technological ability to model increasingly complex systems.

The decontextualizing of information perpetuates the Western philosophic tradition of viewing signs as divisible into sensible (signifier) and intelligible (signified) elements, but problems emerge in extending this tradition into cybernetics. Within such sign systems, "the written signifier is always technical and representative. It has no constitutive meaning" (Derrida, 1976, p. 11). The signifier is in itself meaningless, an empty marker for the signified. As such, the intelligible signified can be seamlessly translated across signifiers, as between languages, or, as in the case of cybernetics, between different media or intelligent systems. However, in the Platonic tradition, this translatability is grounded on the effacement of any difference between the world we sense and our initial sense of that world, which occurs through voice. "In every case, the voice is closest to the signified, whether it is determined strictly as sense (thought or lived) or more loosely as thing" (Derrida, 1976, p. 11). In this phonocentric logic, written signs are then derived from speech, particularly with the phonetic alphabet. This raises a problem for cybernetics, which, despite its intention to remain within this scheme, had already abandoned this logocentric formula by moving beyond the phonocentric universe. As an extension of symbolic mathematics, information theory relies upon a non-phonetic language. The encoding of all information and communication into this mathematical symbology goes far beyond the exteriorization of writing in general. As Derrida notes,

> the *practical methods* of information retrieval extends the possibilities of the "message" vastly, to the point where it is no longer the "written" translation of a language, the transporting of a signified which could remain spoken in its integrity . . . phonetic writing, the medium of the great metaphysical, scientific, technical, and economic adventure of the West, is limited in space and time. (1976, p. 10)

In other words, cybernetics hails the end of Western philosophic tradition by shattering the relationship between voice and signified even as it seeks to retain it through decontextualizing information.

One of the more significant implications of this deconstruction deals with notions of presence or being. Derrida argues that the traditional concept of presence is phonocentric; it denotes the speaking subject's presence to authenticate the meaning of his words. A being must be able to speak his own being, to be present to himself. Presence is paired with its opposite, absence, and Derrida articulates writing as a metaphysical problem in terms of presence and absence: writing is addressed to an absent audience, who then receives the text in the absence of the author. The metaphysical problem comes in mediating presence across this gap, a problem that has been addressed by imagining the author's voice as carried in the text (for example, in the personal strokes of handwriting). However, in the non-phonetic encoding of cybernetic communication, the question of presence and absence is seemingly moot, at least from Derrida's perspective. The dialectic of presence and absence is replaced by one of pattern and randomness, which Shannon's equations incorporate as necessary elements in information. Conventionally, one would think of information as pattern and randomness as interference, as the absence of information. In such a case, pattern and randomness would match up with presence and absence. However, Shannon's equations indicate that information cannot be so simply defined: information requires randomness. That is, in order for a message to contain information, it must include unexpected elements. For example, if you are watching TV and a test pattern appears for five minutes, there is a pattern but no information. On the other hand, if you are watching your favorite program, there are still patterns, but there is also randomness as the colors on the screen change through time. These changes contain information within the context of the pattern.

This complex relationship between pattern and randomness leads the pair to be viewed as symbiotic partners in the production of structures, rather than as opposites. Instead of meaning being secured by a presence that can give a voice to the message, the message is transmitted in non-phonetic symbols that transmit both constant and variable data. Hayles explains, "the dialectic between absence and presence came clearly into focus with the advent of deconstruction because it was already being displaced as a cultural presupposition by randomness and pattern" (1999b, p. 43–4). This is not solely a result of Shannon's theories. The typewriter and camera are already enacting this replacement by transforming presence into traces inscribed either on the page or on film. Homeostasis completely elides the sender and receiver from the equation of communication. All that matters is the code itself. In seeking to insulate humans from cybernetics, the theory effectively writes them out of the process of communication. However, in doing so, the phonocentric metaphysics of presence is replaced by a cybernetics of decontextualized information, and as a result, the interior self is fully exteriorized. That is, Western metaphysics links its solution to the problem of communication with its protection of the sanctity of the self: thoughts can be communicated because the mind can produce an accurate, independent, internal representation/signification of the world and transmit that representation through its voice. The phonocentric signification of sense and thought simultaneously creates a seamless match between internal and external worlds and secures the border between the internal and external. Writing, however, exteriorizes that internal representation and as a result exteriorizes the mind as well. In the non-phonetic, cybernetic, informational universe, the process of signification deliberately elides the role of the self and voice in producing information. Information production is external to the self and speech. In fact, cybernetic signs are unpronounceable.

The unforeseen and ironic result of the decision to objectify information is that the human subject that cyberneticists sought to protect is radically exteriorized. That is, if information can be produced, communicated, and processed within a non-phonetic sign system, then the processes of the conscious mind are not necessarily internal to itself. Machines can do our thinking and perhaps, as the paranoiac claims, already do. Given its focus on signs and information, Derrida sees cybernetics as within the scope of writing and his project of deconstructing Western metaphysics:

> Whether it has essential limits or not, the entire field covered by the cybernetic *program* will be the field of writing. If the theory of cybernetics is by itself to oust all metaphysical concepts—including the concepts of soul, of life, of value, of choice, of memory— which until recently served to separate the machine from man, it must conserve the notion of writing, trace, grammé [written mark], or grapheme, until its

own historico-metaphysical character is also exposed.
(1976, p. 9)

That is, if cybernetics does indicate a closure to Western metaphysics, it will occur through its connection to writing as a means of exteriorizing the self, of breaking down the binaries upon which metaphysics is founded.

However, Shannon, Wiener and the others certainly had no intention of pursuing this or any other philosophical project. They struggled to confine themselves to engineering problems. That said, they did register some concerns about the potential social and political implications of their theories and hoped to prevent them from being employed in social contexts. If questions regarding individual and social contexts that might have been addressed by psychologists or anthropologists participating in the conferences were elided, then a space for human freedom outside cybernetics would continue to exist, and cybernetics would not be applied to the controlling of human populations. This left cyberneticists a narrow line to walk, particularly Wiener, who saw cybernetics as integral to the future. As he argues in *The Human Use of Human Beings,*

> society can only be understood through a study of the messages and the communication facilities which belong to it; and that in the future development of these messages and communication facilities, messages between man and machines, between machines and man, and between machine and machine are destined to play an ever-increasing part. (1988, p. 16)

In such a future, such as the one in which we now live, Wiener's argument would lead us to view machines as constitutive of human society. Paranoia might be a reasonable response if one viewed machines as an external threat to an interior self.

Wiener ascribed to this belief and often reflected on the importance of humans not allowing machines to control their lives. In her analysis of Wiener's work, Katherine Hayles remarks upon his ambivalent shifting between an advocacy of machines and a concern for their impact on humans:

> When I think of him, I imagine him laboring mightily to construct the mirror of the cyborg. He stands

proudly before this product of his reflection, urging us to look into it so that we can see ourselves as control-communication devices, differing in no substantial regard from our mechanical siblings. Then he happens to glance over his shoulder, sees himself as a cyborg, and makes a horrified withdrawal. (1999b, p. 87)

Hayles's imagined scene alludes to Victor Frankenstein's confrontation with his creation in Mary Shelley's novel. Much like Victor, Wiener confronts his double in the image of the cyborg, and much like Kittler's account of the crisis of seeing oneself on film, Wiener revisits his own mirror stage when confronted with the mechanistic, cyborgian production of his own consciousness. His desire to identify himself as a control-communication device reflects that next Lacanian step into identifying with the Law of the Father. That is, it is the control-communication aspect of cybernetics that places the machine under the regulation of language, and, at least in homeostatic theory, provides the machine a cohesive consciousness. In this regard, control-communication is much like the child's acceptance of "phallologocentric" language as a means of articulating his own "I." However, as Hayles suggests, the machinic creation is too much to witness. It is fragmented and horrifying. Only by accepting lines of communication and control can the creature become unified and identified, though this traumatic moment is apparently always there for Wiener. This psychological crisis has a sociological dimension as well. Unable to accept the monstrous, cyborgian other as himself, Wiener identifies the creature as an external, social threat—that is, as the danger of what could happen to his cohesive identity if machines took over (much like being "assimilated" by the "Borg" in *Star Trek: The Next Generation*). On the one hand, cybernetics is a psychological threat in its promise to reveal our own mechanistic functioning, to expose us as always already cyborgs. On the other hand, cybernetics poses a socio-political threat: what transformations will these technologies enact upon us? The cyborg, then, represents the Other hinted by the cinematic doppelganger. That is, if our on-screen double confronts us with a mechanical representation of our selves, the cyborg demonstrates our mechanical production as both a psychological trauma and a social threat.

Homeostasis and the inception of cybernetics thus present a difficult situation. Having defined information as an abstract and thus encoded object, cybernetics has written presence out of the communication system. Information is code and senders and receivers are thus encoders and decoders, who perform their functions primarily to maintain their own internal organization (homeostasis). Extending on the subjective effects of the typewriter and camera, cybernetics further fragments media composition by articulating communication in algorithmic terms. The replacement of presence and absence by pattern and randomness obviates the need for subjects and objects, articulating both in a common space. Humans and machines are defined in common terms even while cyberneticists seek to insulate consciousness from cybernetics. As a result, paranoia seeps out. There is the fear of one's own mechanistic nature and the fear that machines will take over. The insistence on making machine intelligence human intelligence's "other" establishes these conflicts. Of course, the conflicts already existed in *Frankenstein,* in Luddite revolts, in Matthew Arnold's concerns, and so on, but here they take shape within the realm of information.

Autopoiesis

Following the period of homeostasis, cybernetics begins to swing in the direction of reflexivity. This swing reinstates the interior space of the subject, but in doing so, it also opens the human mind to cybernetic investigation. As I mentioned, reflexivity was considered in the early days of cybernetics but rejected for primarily two reasons: it was not easily quantifiable, and it represented a threat to the individual. Reflexivity suggested that the internal processes of the message's recipient needed to be considered in understanding communication. The concept clearly extended to the observer of an information system as well (i.e., the scientist). This was a problem not only for cybernetics but also for experimental science in general. Since the beginning of experimental science, the veracity of the knowledge discovered was hinged upon the scientist being a "modest witness": that is, a disinterested, objective observer (see Haraway 1996). However, in the early 1960s, Humberto Maturana and several participants from the Macy Conferences brought the issue to the foreground in a seemingly innocuous way. They had conducted experiments with the visual cortex of frogs and made the following discovery: small objects, moving in a fast, erratic pattern, registered a large response from the frog's eye, where large, slow-moving objects elicited little or no response (Hayles,

1999b, p. 135). This suggested that the frog's eyes (and presumably human eyes) *construct* reality rather than objectively representing it to the brain. From this modest beginning Maturana, with his colleague Francisco Varela, continued experiments with other animals, particularly with their perceptions of color. Hayles summarizes their early conclusions: "certainly there is something 'out there,' which for lack of a better term we can call 'reality.' But it comes into existence for us, and for all living creatures, *only through interactive processes determined solely by the organism's own organization*" (emphasis in original, 1999b, p. 136). In other words, the world we call "reality," which is obviously a function of sensory data, is not the world as it "really" is but rather a representation of the world to our brain that matches up with the human organism's own interests in maintaining its self-organization. Maturana and Varela termed this state *autopoiesis,* which they defined as the circularity of "organization that makes a living system a unit of interactions . . . and it is this circularity that it must maintain in order to remain a living system and to retain its identity through different interactions" (cited in Hayles, 1999b, p. 136). Thus autopoiesis constituted an extension of homeostasis that integrated reflexivity. As with homeostasis, autopoietic systems strive to maintain self-organization, however now an epistemological element was integrated into the system: the knowledge we receive as organisms is a function of systematic self-interest.

Autopoiesis had the benefit of maintaining an independent consciousness. However, unlike homeostasis, that consciousness now entered into a close relationship with the outside world. Rather than receiving "objective" information about the world upon which to act, as a homeostatic system would, autopoietic systems gain autonomy *through* their connections to other systems. As a result of this interdependence, autopoietic systems develop ethical obligations to one another. That is, the observed and the observer exist in a structural coupling with one another; the information that is produced comes from this coupling and alters both the observer and the observed. This had very clear social implications, and Maturana and Varela pursued those implications extensively by constructing a second category, allopoiesis, to describe systems that have goals other than maintaining self-organization (Hayles uses the example of a car, whose organization is subordinated to her desire to go somewhere). Political danger arises when autopoietic systems (humans) are forced to become allopoietic and subordinate their interests to those of larger systems. Maturana uses this distinction to talk about social systems, where the ideal is a kind of utopian anarchy. In this way, autopoietic theory strives to maintain a sense of the liberal human identity. The ethical foundation focuses on the freedom of individual systems to pursue self-organization. However, it also requires individuals to consider their ethical obligations to others with whom they are "structurally coupled."

In part, Maturana and Varela protect human autonomy by restricting their discussion of autopoiesis to biological entities. However, Félix Guattari contends,

> Autopoiesis deserves to be rethought in terms of evolutionary, collective entities, which maintain diverse types of relations of alterity, rather than being implacably closed in on themselves. In such a case, institutions and technical machines appear to be allopoietic, but when one considers them in the context of the machinic assemblages they constitute with human beings, they become ipso facto autopoietic. (1995, pp. 39–40)

Guattari indicates two, interlocking issues with autopoiesis. The first is its difficulty integrating theories of evolution and the second is that this problem might be addressed by viewing autopoiesis on the larger scale that Guattari terms the "mecanosphere." Hayles also notes the problem with evolution. Essentially, autopoiesis contends that systems function to maintain their own internal organization, but evolutionary change would suggest this is not necessarily the case. As Hayles explains,

> Either an amoeba and a human have the same organization, which would make them members of the same class, in which case evolutionary lineages disappear because all living systems have the same organization; or else an amoeba and a human have different organizations, in which case organization—and hence autopoiesis—must not have been conserved somewhere (or in many places) along the line. (1999b, p. 152)

Guattari's proposed response to this problem broadens the concept of autopoiesis by viewing "machinic autopoiesis" as a consciousness-producing process in which structures break down and become something other through their intersection with other assemblages. Guattari's approach points to the way in which autopoiesis suggests a mode of cognition and individuation that moves away from the humanistic model of subjectivity. That is, Guattari is suggesting understanding all materiality (the mecanosphere) as an autopoietic system, and humans as entities within that system. Again, as with homeostasis, the implications of a reflexive, autopoietic cybernetic system appear to point toward the erasure of the autonomous, internal, self-controlled and controlling subject.

Donna Haraway sees a similar, extensive autopoiesis in James Lovelock's "Gaia hypothesis" that our planet is a "complex entity involving the Earth's biosphere, atmosphere, oceans, and soil; the totality constituting a feedback or cybernetic system which seeks an optimal physical and chemical environment for life on this planet" (1995, p. xii). If the entire planet has an autopoietic function, then all the organisms living on the planet are mechanisms in its ongoing function. This perception is fundamental to the contemporary environmental movement that recognizes our planetary interdependence. However, from the perspective of cybernetics, it means that the "earth—itself a cyborg, a complex auto-poietic system that terminally blurred the boundaries among the geological, the organic, and the technological—was the natural habitat, and the launching pad, of other cyborgs" (Haraway, 1995, p. xiii). Both Haraway and Guattari draw the ethical imperatives of autopoiesis from Maturana and Varela's original hypotheses. However, they demonstrate a willingness to leave behind the necessity for human autonomy and instead articulate interdependent systems where consciousness and subjectivity emerge from the interactions between living and non-living systems.

AI-AL

Over the past twenty-five years, the field of cybernetics has moved beyond autopoiesis to investigate theories of artificial intelligence (AI) and artificial life (AL). In doing so, cyberneticists have explored issues such as evolution that autopoiesis had found particularly difficult to address. In addition, though the field remains focused on practical, engineering problems, its theories reflect the general shift toward post-humanism that marks the last quarter of the twentieth century. In fact, the cybernetics theory of distributed cognition becomes a particularly useful way of understanding what happens to subjectivity in postmodern theory. Rodney Brooks, head of the Artificial Intelligence Lab at MIT, explains the general shift that occurs with AI and AL:

> Recent trends in artificial intelligence, cognitive science, neuroscience, psychology, linguistics, and sociology are converging on an anti-objectivist, body-based approach to abstract cognition. Where traditional approaches in these fields advocate an objectively specifiable reality—brain-in-a-box, independent of bodily constraints—these newer approaches insist that intelligence cannot be separated from the subjective experience of a body. (Brooks and Stein, 1994, p. 1)

Brooks's description of the field lays out the current conflict in cybernetics between those who continue in the traditional approach and seek to create a disembodied "brain-in-a-box" and those like himself who pursue a "bottom-up," embodied approach to consciousness. Brooks explains his approach in comparison to the biological evolution of consciousness. Single-cell life forms emerged around 3.5 billion years ago. A billion years later, photosynthetic plants evolve, and not until 550 million years ago were there any fish or vertebrates. Dinosaurs appeared 330 and mammals 250 million years ago. The first primates evolved 120 million years ago, but human-like beings have existed for only 2.5 million years. The agricultural revolution began 10,000 years ago; writing was invented 5,000 years ago, and as Brooks puts it, "'expert' knowledge only over the last few hundred years" (1991, p. 3). From this Brooks deduces that

> problem solving behavior, language, expert knowledge and application, and reason are all pretty simple once the essence of being and reacting are available. The essence is the ability to move around in a dynamic environment, sensing the surroundings to a degree sufficient to achieve the necessary maintenance of life and reproduction. (1991, p. 2)

This leads Brooks to focus on creating robots capable of dynamic movement and sensory reception, with the idea that higher-level consciousness will emerge from such developments. Based on this approach, Brooks and his associates have created successful robots. Essentially, they have decided that rather than attempting to simulate human intelligence in some abstract way, they would simulate the embodied processes by which they theorize this intelligence emerges.

Drawing on research in cognitive science and neuroscience, Brooks explains what he sees as the three primary errors made about human intelligence: that humans produce "monolithic internal models" of the world; that they have "monolithic control" over brain and body functioning; and that the brain is "a general purpose machine, acting with equal skill on any type of operation that it performs by invoking a set of powerful rules" (Brooks et al, 1999, p. 4). Rather than producing total internal models, humans continually interact with their environment. For example, when asked to make a copy of a complex display of blocks, participants in an experiment fail to notice any but the most drastic changes made in the display. They do not create complete mental pictures of the display but rely on continually referring back to the existing model. However, cybernetics has relied upon the concept of a "monolithic internal model" since the homeostatic period, largely because this concept fits with our cultural ideas about consciousness as an independent entity.

Similarly, we have imagined the conscious mind as a unified system of control regulating the brain and body. In this traditional model, once sensory data has been centralized to produce an internal model of the world, mental and physical activity precedes from that central location. Only in this way can we articulate a unified consciousness as being fully aware of the world and fully in control of its body's actions. Such a conclusion leads logically to the third error, that humans are general-purpose machines. That is, a centralized consciousness is assumed to function by abstracting general principles from an environment and applying a set of general rules to guide action in that environment. However, studies of split-brain patients suggest, "there are multiple independent control systems rather than a monolithic one" (Brooks et al, 1999, p. 4). Various parts of the brain act on their own, without connection to other parts, based on the information to which they have access. Furthermore, rather than functioning through general abstractions, humans tend to rely upon specific contexts for achieving cognitive tasks. For example,

> subjects were unable to apply the negative rule of if-then inference when four cards were labeled with single letters and digits. However, with additional context—labeling the cards such that they were understandable as name and ages—subjects could easily solve exactly the same problem. (1999, p. 4)

In other words, studies in cognitive science indicate that human intelligence is fragmented and relies upon its intersection with an embodied, material world.

For Brooks this leads to engineering robots that have their processing power distributed through multiple systems. In terms of human cognition, however, there are substantial implications for our traditional model of consciousness. Put succinctly, human consciousness, as the rational, free-willed seat of human behavior, does not exist. Instead, consciousness would appear to be an "epiphenomenon," an emergent psychological effect of the intersection of multiple cognitive routines functioning throughout the body and into the external environment. Katherine Hayles describes these routines as "discrete and semiautonomous agents."

> Each agent runs a modular program designed to accomplish a specific activity, operating relatively independent of others. Only when conflicts occur between agents does an adjudicating program kick in to resolve the problem. In this model, consciousness emerges as an epiphenomenon whose role it is to tell a coherent story about what is happening, even though this story may have little to do with what is happening processurally. (1999b, p. 157)

What does this mean? Perhaps it's easiest to think in terms of example. As I write this, it is late in the morning, and I haven't eaten yet. My hunger "agent" takes over, and I have to stop to get something to eat. Or a more complicated example: I drive my car to work. I am driving, listening to music, thinking about what I have to do in the office, letting my mind wander, etc. Who is doing the driving? Who is doing the listening? Who is thinking about work? My consciousness floats above these interactions. Even more complexly, writing: where do the ideas, the words, I am writing at this very moment come from? Certainly, after they are written, I can read them on the screen and create a "coherent story" about what I wrote and why I wrote it, but does that explanation capture the process that has occurred? Does it explain the neurolinguistic construction of language, the interactions between my brain and fingers, the intersection of memory and rhetorical considerations, my practically unconscious application of usage conventions, and so on?

This is where reflexivity takes us, to a space where consciousness becomes secondary to sensory inputs and "discrete and semiautonomous agents." And these agents need not be internal or unconscious processes. We might also think of technologies as fitting into these categories—as altering sensory input and as contributing their own discrete, semiautonomous agency to our consciousness. This is certainly what Kittler has suggested. And he is far from the first to raise this possibility. As I mentioned earlier, Nietzsche sees writing tools shaping our thoughts. Similarly, Heidegger states, "when writing was withdrawn from the origin of its essence, i.e., from the hand, and was transferred to the machine, a transformation occurred in the relation of Being to man" (cited in Kittler, 1999, p. 199). Nietzsche and Heidegger's statements, and Benjamin's similar ideas about the camera, imply that consciousness has always been shaped by technologies, just as conscious minds have shaped technologies; and when new technologies are developed, they can have a dramatic effect upon the mind. Cybernetics, as it develops, allows us to understand that conscious intelligence—in all beings—emerges from a series of mechanistic processes.

For Brooks, as with other cyberneticists, the task has never precisely been to define human intelligence. In fact, as the discipline's history indicates, extraordinary measures have been taken to insulate the human mind from their practical, engineering concerns. However, the human mind has been taken as a model of intelligence upon which to establish artificial intelligence. This has been the case ever since the famous Turing test. Brooks's AL approach simply shifts the focus to an evolutionary and embodied approach to the production of intelligence. This has resulted in us imagining human intelligence in technological terms. And as much as contemporary cybernetics is influenced by neuroscience, cognitive science, psychology, and sociology, these fields could not exist in their present form without the information processing and simulating power of computers. That is, these disciplines are themselves cybernetic to a large degree. This is a significant observation as it indicates an important divergence from Western metaphysics. That is, the long history of metaphysics has hinged upon the speaking subjecting knowing himself, speaking himself into being. Now, however, the human, as an object of science, is known through nonphonetic, cybernetic-mathematical symbology. Human identity is completely exteriorized from the self. If human scientific discourses of the nineteenth century articulated human bodies as machines so as to maximize their intersection with industrial technologies, then this cybernetic articulation of the human mind and body allows for the interface with cybernetic technologies, an interface that we now familiarly know as creating the cyborg.

Though many of these concerns have been made visible in contemporary cyborg studies, they were already in place in the originary moment of the cyborg. Manfred Clynes and Nathan Kline coined the term cyborg (cybernetic organism) in a 1960 article that addresses the challenges of manned space flight. Clynes and Kline identified numerous difficulties that might be faced in space in trying to maintain humans at an optimum level of performance.

> The purpose of the Cyborg, as well as his own homeostatic systems, is to provide an organization system in which such robot-like problems are taken care of automatically and unconsciously, leaving man free to explore, to create, to think, and to feel. (1995, p. 31)

The cyborg immediately applies the concept of homeostasis to humans, viewing them as cybernetic systems. The technologies Clynes and Kline imagine attaching to the astronaut, such as an osmotic pressure pump that could regularly provide doses of various pharmaceuticals, were designed, in their eyes, to address lower-level concerns of functioning in terms of the spacecraft, the spacecraft's environment, and the astronaut's physiology. This frees the cyborg to focus its intelligent systems (i.e. his/her mind) on higher-level functions. Of course, on those higher-level functions, a different set of cybernetic connections are being made as the cyborg interfaces with computers that take over a range of cognitive functions, such as lengthy calculations and the recording and retrieval of data.

In other words, the cyborg is constructed from multiple smart systems each designed to perform specific cognitive functions that are then attached to the human. (Arguably, that human is itself an assembly of smart systems as well, as the cognitive science Brooks cites suggests.) The result of this assembly is a model of intelligent systems that is described as "distributed cognition." Brooks's "subsumption architecture" is an example of distributed cognition in which his robots' cognitive functions are spread through the system, each performing its own task. For example, Genghis, an insect-like robot, has six separately programmed legs that are designed to stabilize themselves in relation to the other five. The robot has no central program for walking, but rather learns to walk after a few seconds each time it is activated. In other words, the balance of the entire system is produced as an emergent behavior resulting from the intersection of these intelligent systems (Hayles, 1999b, pp. 236–37). The insect robot exemplifies both the distribution and emergence of cognition in a relatively simple system. However, these concepts become even more powerful when we begin to consider them in the context of human cognition.

Drawing on Edward Hutchins, Hayles discusses James Searle's "Chinese Room" as a further example of distributed cognition. In Searle's example, he is stuck in a room, not knowing a word of Chinese. Messages in Chinese are slipped into the room. Making use of a basket filled with Chinese symbols and a rulebook for how the symbols might be arranged, Searle constructs responses and sends them back. Searle's contention is that this provides an illusion of his knowing Chinese when he doesn't and that this is evidence that machines can appear to have intelligence when they are simply responding to preformatted rules. Hutchins, however, points out that in this example it is not Searle but rather the entire room that knows Chinese. "The situation of modern humans is akin to that of Searle in the Chinese room," Hayles continues,

> for every day we participate in systems whose total cognitive capacity exceeds our individual knowledge . . . Modern humans are capable of more sophisticated cognition than cavemen not because moderns are smarter, Hutchins concludes, but because they have

constructed smarter environments in which to work.
(1999b, p. 289)

In other words, the essential problem with Searle's argument is that
it is based on what Brooks terms a faulty model of cognition, specifically his first error, that humans produce monolithic models. It's
not simply the case that Searle does not "know" Chinese; he doesn't
"know" English either, at least not in the way his argument would
suggest a machine would have to know it in order to prove its intelligence. Searle's knowledge, or my knowledge, of English, according to
distributed cognition, is an emergent phenomenon based on multiple
subroutines. This is similar to an analogy Brooks provides of an ant
walking along a beach. Looking at the insect's gait as it tries to move
across the sand, one might imagine that its motions are quite complex.
But the complexity is not built into the ant, it emerges in the intersection of the ant with the sand (Brooks and Stein,1991, p. 4). Likewise,
the complexity of language is not as much a reflection of internal complexity as an indication of the complexity of the environment with
which we interact as language-users.

Taken together, the past sixty years of cybernetics maps out an in-
exorable move toward understanding human cognition as a fragmentary process incorporating multiple mechanisms that are both internal
and external to the body and brain. Ironically, as a science reliant upon
notions of rationality and objectivity, the field has sought to develop
its theories of artificial intelligence in a way that would prevent them
from affecting our ideas of human intelligence. This insulation has
been largely unsuccessful as cybernetic concepts of humanity abound
from Hollywood movies to cognitive science. While pop cultural references to the cyborg have clearly emphasized a paranoid response to
technology, contemporary information theory offers us a fruitful way
to understand human intelligence as an embodied process. Unfortunately, for a variety of disciplinary reasons, the implications of cognitive science have been largely separated from the humanities. Those on
the scientific side have viewed traditional humanities as outdated and
postmodern theory and cultural studies as both absurd and threatening. In turn, traditional humanists have seen science and technology as
dehumanizing and theory and cultural studies as absurd and threatening. However, as I am presenting here, there are significant and useful
connections between distributed cognition, experimental media, and
postmodern theories of the virtual, which have been largely overlooked

(even though some, like Rodney Brooks and Katherine Hayles, have recognized them). In the next chapter, I will complete my "historical" investigation by examining the contemporary new media in relation to the fragmentation of traditional notions of the self and the collapsing of time and space in virtuality. Together with Chapters 2, 3, and 4, this investigation will provide a usable understanding of the virtual-technological. I will then move on to consider how a contemporary theory of the virtual-actual, in conjunction with this understanding of the virtual-technological, might open new practices and a new understanding of new media composition.

5 Into New Media

The intersection of mechanical media composition and computing create the foundation for the development of new media: a compositional space in which recordings of material events and strictly digital productions are combined in the common medium of digital information. New media suggests a number of related (though quite different) productions including software applications, the Internet, video games, DVDs, digital cinema, and various digital appliances such as MP3 players (e.g., iPods), cell phones and digital video cameras. This chapter seeks to examine phenomena common to all of these in their collective reliance upon real-time information processing and the production of a simulated environment. That said, I am going to focus on one in particular, digital cinema, as a means to provide some specificity and continuity in terms of examples of the phenomena I am describing. Furthermore, I will examine in some detail one especially salient example of digital filmmaking, *The Matrix* trilogy.

In conducting this analysis, I am continuing the task of the previous two chapters: to investigate the role media and cybernetics play in the simultaneous fragmenting of materiality and collapsing of spatial and temporal distances (the boundary between subject and object). If the typewriter opened cracks in the seeming continuity of consciousness and the film camera presented us with our uncanny doppelganger, then new media intensifies those experiences in the shift from thousands of frames to millions of bytes. This effect results from the collapse of distance between the subject and object and causes an affective crisis by shattering the illusory cohesion of interiorized self-presence. Digital production intensifies this collapse, as Paul Virilio (1997) explains, through its ability to produce real-time data interaction. As I explore, consciousness and materiality are thoroughly atomized in new media and produced as exteriorized simulation. In short, new media and simulation constitute the final and complete deconstruction of the abstract, cohesive, internalized subject of traditional humanism. That said, the material analysis of technology and information indicates that consciousness and subjectivity can never be simply abstract, neither as a humanistic individual nor as an empty simulation. Instead, one must understand information, media, cognition, consciousness, and subjectivity as embodied, material processes. This chapter concludes with a discussion of such theories and lays the foundation for the extended investigation of these issues that follows.

SIMULATION

Generally speaking, our cultural imagination of simulations focuses on realistic, full-sensory, virtual environments, such as the holodeck on *Star Trek: The Next Generation*. However, in the contemporary moment, the power of simulations has more to do with access to real-time information than with the verisimilitude of their presentations. The dominant form of interface between the body and the computer remains the screen, a technology which has developed as different technologies have been constructed for interfacing with it (e.g., the mouse, the joystick). These technologies of simulation represent the combination of cybernetics with technologies of mechanical reproduction to open a new digital space of media. The relationship between clicking on a screen (actually clicking a mouse button that simulates clicking on a region of the screen, which has in turn simulated the appearance of a button) and the response of the computer's memory and processors appears seamless. However, the process involves translation between different programs and programming and machine languages. As I will explore, the relationship between the simulated surface interface and the machine beneath reflects a similar relationship between human body and consciousness.

While simulation would appear to be a product of modern technologies, Lev Manovich contends that just as modern screens (in cinemas, televisions, and computer monitors) bear a relationship to framed paintings, simulations draw a conceptual heritage from frescos and mosaics. A screen, whether it is a Renaissance painting or computer monitor,

> is intended for frontal viewing—as opposed to a panorama for instance. It exists in our normal space, the space of our body, and acts as a window into another

> space. This other space, the space of representation,
> typically has a scale different from the scale of our
> normal space. (Manovich, 2001, p. 95)

However, frescos and mosaics are intended to create an illusion of a
physical space. They typically match the scale of the world around
them; they "are 'hardwired' to their architectural setting [which] allows the artist to create a continuity between virtual and physical
space" (2001, pp. 112–13). Manovich explains that framed paintings,
which are obviously mobile, demand *immobility* from their viewers:
there is only one perspective from which to view the screen. Frescos
and mosaics, on the other hand, allow the viewer to move through
the space. In a sense frescos sacrifice their own mobility to the viewer.
This is a significantly different tradition from cinematic screens where
the media demands that the viewer focus his or her attention in one
direction upon a preformatted, linear experience. The screen's insistence on immobility has historically applied both to the viewers and
objects of representations (e.g., those who would sit for a portrait or
a photograph). Manovich articulates this immobility as a form of in-
carceration, equating movie houses with prisons where "the prisoners
could neither talk to one another nor move from seat to seat" (2001,
p. 107).

However, the combination of cybernetics with the screen results in
a new kind of screen-based simulation and mobility based upon access
to real-time data. While the viewer remains linked to the screen as before, the screen itself becomes fluid, changing in real time. Real-time
data interaction means not only that one can *receive* information as it
happens anywhere around the world (thus compressing the dimensions
of space and time) but also that one can *respond* to that data, enacting
changes around the world (whether those changes are as mundane as
updating information in a database or playing an online video game or
as deadly as launching a satellite-targeted missile). Manovich identifies
the key difference here:

> in contrast to older action-enabling representational
> technologies, real-time image instruments literally
> allow us to touch objects over distance, thus making
> possible their easy destruction as well. The potential
> aggressiveness of looking turns out to be rather more

innocent than the actual aggression of electronically enabled touch. (2001, p. 175)

In other words, while there has been extensive criticism of the violence of the male gaze, the postcolonial gaze, even panoptic-disciplinary culture, this violence is symbolic or representational compared to the real-time violence made possible by global telecommunications.

As a result of this collapse, global telecommunications exponentially increase the exteriorization of the self initiated by the camera. Virilio notes the potential danger of our being able to "touch" at a distance, but the connection runs in both directions. The self finds itself connected on a global scale, the vast expansion of the nervous system McLuhan imagined. In this situation, the self cannot directly experience the world at a "distance" but instead always finds its experience preceded by an exteriorized, mediated engagement. Jean Baudrillard (1994) describes this precession:

> Simulation is no longer that of a territory, a referential being, or a substance. It is the generation by models of a real without origin or reality: a hyperreal. The territory no longer precedes the map, nor does it survive it. It is nevertheless the map that precedes the territory—the precession of simulacra—that engenders the territory. (p. 1)

Baudrillard's simulations no longer reference a territory, but rather *precede* that territory. As a result, simulation becomes a way of managing, if not producing, the "real" in the absence of reality. This disappearance of the real that Baudrillard theorizes occurs through the technological erasure of distance. In a digital environment the self, the object, and the distance between them are all simulated. And this is not simply an experience that happens "online," any more than the subjective effects of the typewriter occurred only while one was typing. Digital mediation precedes the subject everywhere. As Manovich notes,

> Benjamin's and Virilio's analyses make it possible for us to understand the historical effect of these technologies in terms of progressive diminishing and finally, the complete elimination of something that both writers see as a fundamental condition of human perception—spatial distance, the distance between

the subject who is seeing and the object being seen. (2001, p. 174)

The first such first modern simulations develop from the Allied decoding of the Nazi Enigma cryptography.

> Under the conditions of high technology, war coincides with a chart of its organizational structure. Reason enough for the Government Code and Cipher School to model, in miniature, its organization after the German army, that is, after the enemy. Turing's game of imitation became a reality. (Kittler, 1999, pp. 256–57)

Kittler's reference to Turing's imitation game is to the famous Turing Test for establishing artificial intelligence. In this game a man sits in a room and slips messages through two slots. In one adjoining room is another man who writes back messages pretending to be a woman. In the other room is a computer that also generates messages. If the first man cannot identify which respondent is the computer, then, Turing contends, this would be evidence of the computer's intelligence. The point? Simulation is the foundation of intelligence. That doesn't mean that we are all "faking it." It suggests instead that if cognition is in fact a fragmented and distributed process then the appearance and experience of a cohesive consciousness has always been a simulation, just as the computer "desktop" offers an experience of cohesion and organization that does not exist materially as such in the computer's hardware. The British used the strategy of simulation to break the Nazi codes. Eventually, however, this process of imitation is translated from the offices and personnel of the code-breakers into a computer. This takes the process of simulation one step further as the imitation game is translated into Boolean algebra. The COLOSSUS (the Allies' first computer) improves upon the typewriter decoding that preceded it by incorporating a series of IF/THEN conditional statements. IF/THEN statements create a feedback loop in which the computer evaluates data and makes decisions.

Kittler examines the subjectivity of such machines through an analogous comparison of bees to humans. While one bee can communicate specific instructions to another for finding pollen, the second bee cannot decode or retransmit this information. Human language, of course, works differently. It relies upon our ability to decode and retransmit. The form of one's language, the interaction between sender and receiver, Kittler contends, shapes subjectivity.

> In other words: bees are projectiles, and humans, cruise missiles. One is given objective data on angles and distances by a dance, the other, a command of free will. Computers operating on IF-THEN commands are therefore machine subjects. Electronics, a tube monster since Bletchley Park, replaces discourse, and programmability replaces free will. (1999, p. 259)

In this case, programming replaces language (the concept of a programming "language" being a crude approximation of the term since conventional languages are spoken and programming languages are not really pronounceable). Programming, as non-phonetic writing, has no referent within a phonocentric consciousness; instead, the subjectivity it produces is an exteriorization of the machine's processes. As a result, the computer does not present a simulation of an interiorized consciousness, but rather presents consciousness itself as a simulation, as an interface with smart systems.

DIGITAL CINEMA

The production of digital cinema is a powerful example of this with its computational power to manipulate time and space. The landmark special effects of *The Matrix* films, such as "bullet-time photography," demonstrate the potential directions in which new media might take us. While digitally produced films do not offer such interactions to moviegoers (and DVDs offer limited interactivity), the digital production of the film itself does involve this technical capacity. As such, in examining the subjective effects of digital cinema, the most fruitful sites for investigation are not in theaters but on movie sets, in special effects labs, and in post-production studios. In a manner similar to the advent of the camera, the development of digital cinema has opened access to a new mode of reality. Manovich argues that digital cinema now makes it reasonable to group the entirety of twentieth-century filmmaking under the "supergenre" of "fictional-live action film" (1999, p. 174). By this, he suggests that past filmmaking was characterized in part by the "unmodified photographic recordings of real events that took place in real physical space" that constitute the basic form of film footage (1999, p. 173). However, with digital technologies it becomes possible "to cut, bend, stretch, and stitch digitized film images into something that has perfect photographic credibility, although it was never actually filmed" (1999, p. 175). Despite the technical limitations or philosophical caveats one might observe about the camera's representation of reality, it is indeed an optical recording of a perspectival space. The pixelated reality of digital cinema, while having the ability to simulate a perspectival space, is not such a space. Within its narrative, *The Matrix* keeps the digital world of the Matrix and physical world of Zion as separate as possible. Much is done visually, even with the overall color tones of the film, to mark the difference between the worlds. However, in the filmmaking process, this separation is not so easily done. While there are some shots that are purely live action footage and some that are solely digital images, many scenes in the film are constructed from the combination of live action and digital production.

The trilogy's most famous effect, which the Wachowskis nicknamed "bullet-time photography," demonstrates how the distinction between live action and effects becomes blurred. Filmed at speeds approaching 12,000 frames per second, this process was seen as a transportation of Japanese anime into a live action context. The special effects team and the filmmakers

> blocked out the action that was going to be rendered and filmed the scene using conventional cameras. Then they scanned the images into a computer and, using a laser-guided tracking system, "mapped out" the movements of the camera that would capture the final scene. A series of sophisticated still cameras was placed along the mapped path, each of which would shoot a single still photo. Then the photos were scanned into the computer, which created a strip of still images, similar to animation cels. The computer generated "in-between" drawings of the images, much as animators draw frames to move their characters smoothly from one pose to another, and the completed series of images could be passed before the viewers' eyes as quickly or slowly as the filmmakers wanted without losing clarity. ("Bullet-Time Walkthrough," 2003, para. 3)

The Matrix's "bullet-time photography" technique has now been replicated in various contexts and is a recognizable feature of our visual culture. Such digital processes are precisely what Manovich anticipates when he defines digital cinema as "a particular case of animation that uses live-action footage as one of its many elements" (1999, p. 180). While digital film may lack the interactivity we associate with virtual environments, it would be a mistake to construe interactivity as the sole defining characteristic of virtual reality. Digital cinema's implosion of the realms of information and reality may in fact be a more fundamental element of VR and a key to understanding the dangers and opportunities it offers for human subjectivity, particularly in the context of the history of media production and cybernetics.

In fact, Manovich steers away from "interactivity" in his attempt to define new media, noting, "all classical, and even more so modern, art is 'interactive,'" which is, of course, what makes literary interpretation possible (2001, p. 56). Instead, as I discussed in the introduction, Manovich details five "principles" of new media: numerical representation, modularity, automation, variability, and transcoding (2001, pp. 27–48). Manovich's first two principles, numerical representation and modularity, form the foundation for the following three. Numerical representation marks the new media's translation of all information into binary code. As a result "a new media object can be described formally (mathematically). For instance, an image or shape can be described using a mathematical function" (2002, p. 27). Furthermore, such objects can be modified algorithmically, as when one applies an effect in an image-editing application (e.g., Adobe PhotoShop). This permits media to become programmable. Modularity refers to the fact that new media objects "are represented as collections of discrete samples (pixels, polygons, voxels, characters, scripts). These elements are assembled into larger-scale objects but continue to maintain their separate identities" (2002, p. 30). These two principles can be seen at work in bullet-time photography. The production of the scenes begins with taking a series of digital photographs of the scene's location. These images become the foundation for producing a three-dimensional digital model of the scene. The virtual camera viewpoint can be shifted around the model and an image with proper perspective can be produced. This requires the ability both to numerically represent an image and to program that image. Once the digital model is produced, the images of the actors, taken with the bullet-time photography technology, must be situated with the space. The ability to separate representations of the actors from the scene, as well as the discrete quality of each image in the series, creates the potential to swing the camera perspective and slow down motion in ways not possible with earlier technology. This modularity allows each piece to be defined and programmed independently.

This ability to program modular media elements creates the possibility of automation, Manovich's third principle. As Manovich notes, "In Hollywood films, flocks of birds, ant colonies, and crowds of people are automatically created by AL (artificial life) software" (2002, p. 32). Such software was employed in the creation of the immense battle scenes in Peter Jackson's film version of the *Lord of the Rings* trilogy. Automation occurs in new media whenever the computer performs programmed activities on media objects. In the bullet-time photography scene, the computer animates action between the series of photographs taken of the actors, creating a smooth motion. This allows the directors to move through the action in any manner they choose. This process, called tweening, originated in animation and is now a regular part of new media applications such as Macromedia Flash and Director. As Manovich's reference to AL suggests, automation requires the production of computers that are intelligent on some level; that is, they must be able to make decisions—an ability that means "human intentionality can be removed from the creative process, at least in part" (2002, p. 32). Another common example of automation is the appearance of artificial intelligence in the creation of video games. From IBM's notorious chess-playing machine, Big Blue, to the mundane monsters in a first-person shooter, AI/AL programming allows the computer to respond to the human player's actions.

The fourth principle, variability, indicates "a new media object is not something fixed once and for all, but something that can exist in different, potentially infinite versions" (2002, p. 36). Certainly *The Matrix* is a fixed object, but during the production of these scenes, different versions are possible. In conventional filmmaking, if a director is unhappy with a shot, the scene must be re-filmed. While the bullet-time photography scene was carefully designed and multiple takes of the actors were done, the digitization of the scene meant that the material recorded for the scene could be combined to produce different final products. Variability appears commonly in our user experiences in our ability to set preferences, the personalization of websites using cookies, and the scaling of information to conform to our computer (as when we download a movie file based on our connection speed). Variability also creates the experience of interactivity. Because new media objects, for example Web pages, are modular, they can be arranged in any fashion. Thus, in the most common example of interactivity, navigating the Web, the ability to choose from a set of hyperlinks allows for a certain, limited variability. In addition, the user can always enter any Internet address and thus shift from any one website to another. This expands the potential variability of Web-browsing to the entire expanse of the Web.

Manovich views his final principle, transcoding, as "the most substantial consequence of the computerization of media" (2002, p. 45). Transcoding is a particular form of translation that shifts information between a "cultural layer," where it is experienced by human users, and a "computer layer," where computers process it. This transcoding suggests a reflexive relationship between computers and culture.

> The ways in which the computer models the world, represents data, and allows us to operate on it; the key operations behind all computer programs (such as search, match, sort, and filter); the conventions of HCI—in short, what can be called the computer's ontology, epistemology, and pragmatics—influence the cultural layer of new media. (p. 46)

In turn, cultural expectations and values regarding computers, as well as other factors such as economics, affect the direction computer technology takes. Transcoding, then, is a broad principle of new media/ computer culture. A large part of *The Matrix*'s acclaim was due to its development of unique, digital, special effects. While the Wachowskis' idea for bullet-time photography may have been inspired by Japanese anime, the final result was clearly a product of digital technologies. Looking at a broader cultural picture, however, one might surmise that the final scene is also informed by pre-existing aesthetic principles, budgetary constraints on the film's production, audience expectations, and any number of other not immediately technological forces. All of these forces, however, had to be funneled through the technical capacities available to the Wachowskis.

How do these principles help one understand how new media shapes subject production? Where traditional film exteriorizes the self through its capture of the body's image, digital film goes further to translate the image into a discourse wholly inaccessible to the person being depicted. The resulting uncanny experience goes beyond the confrontation with a mechanical double to the confrontation with a digitized self whose construction and operation suggest that conscious subject has virtually no role in its own functioning. This process is more clearly exhibited in the signature scene of *The Matrix Reloaded,* the Burly Brawl. In the Burly Brawl, Neo fights dozens of Agent Smiths using his super-human abilities. As with the bullet-time photography scene (the technology of which was included in the brawl), the background set had to be recreated digitally. The entire fight scene was then choreographed and

> was then input into the computer using a motion capture setup. Since the scene involved dozens of people, it had to be broken down and captured a few people at a time, and then rebuilt afterwards. The mocap data was then mapped to the corresponding Neo and Smith models. ("Creating the Burly Brawl," 2003)

While it is commonplace to use a stunt double in filmmaking, here there is a virtual double whose motions are mapped onto a virtual character (a similar process was used in the animation of Gollum in *Lord of the Rings*). However, the ultimate production of the Neo and Smith models was not complete.

> Each actor's likeness, facial expressions, skin tone, and clothing all had to be recreated and simulated in the computer in photo-realistic quality. A process called Universal Capture (UCAP) was developed to capture and recreate each actor's head and facial characteristics. Five high-definition cameras and a small army of computers were set up to record the various facial expressions of each actor . . . . Combined with a cyberscan cast of each actor's head, the Universal Capture information allowed ESC to create an exact moving replica of each actor's head. (Neilson, 2003, para. 6)

Finally, the filmmakers simulated the actors' clothing and its interaction with light "using a Bidirectional Reflectometer, which captures the light reflectance (Bidirectional Reflectance Distribution Function or BRDF) values for all kinds of cloth," and by combining all these elements "a virtual human is created." (Neilson, 2003, para. 8). These "virtual humans" are computer codes, mixtures of different pieces of information patched together. These scenes, while planned and choreographed by humans, are automated by computers that process all this information; "before rendering out a given frame, each shot exists in the computer as lines of code, millions of assets compressed into one final shot" (Neilson, 2003, para. 9).

These digital replications intensify one of the earliest cinematographic special effects, the doppelganger. Technically speaking, the trick worked by covering half of the lens and shooting a scene with an actor. The film was then rewound, and the other half of the lens was covered. Then, without moving the camera's position, the scene was shot again with the same actor playing the part of his or her double. This "doppelganger trick," Kittler writes, "is nothing less than uncanny" (1999, p. 153). Indeed, the double is central to Freud's understanding of the uncanny. Uncanny experiences do not require literally meeting one's double, but rather seeing in someone or something else a repressed element of oneself. In his examination of E. T. A. Hoffman, Freud notes the role of dolls and automata in generating uncanny feelings. Though Freud reads literature in his investigation, Kittler notes,

> The psychoanalysis of the *uncanny* does not touch upon modern technologies of trace detection with as much as a single word. Freud and Rank, in their hunt for the remainders of an archaic reaction, return mobile mirrors to stationary ones once again, turn cinema and railroad into the romantic world of books. (1999, p. 152)

However, as I discussed earlier, Kittler views film as presenting us directly with the image of our double, producing this uncanny experience. If, as Freud suggests, part of the uncanny is the "impression of automatic, mechanical processes at work behind the ordinary appearance of mental activity," then the mechanically reproduced movements on the screen would literalize that impression (1999, p. 157).

With the appearance of digital filmmaking, however, one encounters yet another splitting and mutation. If traditional film and psychoanalysis presented us with a double and a mechanized unconscious, then digital film reveals a multiplicity of others and an unconscious penetrated by information and linked to assemblages of distributed cognition. Much like the filmic doppelganger represented the film experience on film, the replication of Agent Smith in *Matrix Reloaded* presents the digital film experience in digital film. Digital media reinforce Maturana and Varela's conclusions about autopoietic perception: the world we see is cybernetic, information processed by preprogrammed sensory organs. Where the narrative of *The Matrix* trilogy suggests that technology can precede the eye's function by inserting itself into the brain stem, digital cinema indicates how technology can intervene between the "real" and the eye, preceding the real in human perception as simulation. New media's capacities enable this possibility: the translation of images into symbolic, mathematical information; the fractal-modular structure of new media objects; the automation of media production by intelligent machines; the real-time variability of objects; and finally the transcoding of media from the machinic realm into cultural discourses. In seeing Agent Smith replicated we encounter the postmodern uncanny (or is it something else now?) experience of our own multiplicity and our own status as informational networks of distributed cognition: consciousness as one of many applications running on an immense cultural network.

From Digital to Analog Virtuality

The convincing and seductive simulation of digital cinema presents us with the all too familiar postmodern problem of the disappearance of the subject. However, it is important to remember that while the production of the film is digital, the *experience* of the film is not. Ultimately the film is expressed in analog media (of light and sound) and processed by a body whose informational mechanisms are chemical and electrical. Furthermore, while the software applications of new media operate digitally, they rest upon an analog system of electronic switches and voltage intensities within the material operation of the computer. In fact, Kittler (1996) argues, "there is no software," that, in a sense, the binary between hardware and software is a false one. Kittler's seemingly counter-intuitive claim rests on the highly technical problems surrounding the limitations placed on hardware by the insistence that systems be programmable. As Kittler explains, digital, programmable systems define information in relation to logical depth and the reduction of noise. Logical depth measures the difficulty in computing the algorithm beneath an output (in essence, the complexity of the system). However, this insistence on the programmability of hardware, Kittler continues, results in a limitation of computation power. The logocentric logic that governs programmable systems limits the possibilities of their connectivity. Basically, logic dictates the possibility of connections. These limitations, indeed the entire functionality of hardware, are hidden from users, just as the discontinuous quality of film is hidden from viewers.

Setting aside Kittler's technical language, the underlying gesture here is to deconstruct the apparent supremacy of software over hardware. Digital cinema may present us with the illusion of a cohesive, digitally-produced world, but the programmable sign system on which it rests is incapable of generating this level of complexity. Ultimately, the digital relies upon shifting into an analog technical system and the interfacing with the analog cognitive processes of human cognition in order to produce a seductive technological virtuality. In essence, as Kittler's central argument goes, software does not exist as such (as abstract sign systems); it exists as analog electronic intensities (in computer circuitry, emanating from the screen and speakers as image and sound): that is the materiality of the digital. The interface, or the projection of a digital film, is thus a simulacrum, a copy of some purported internal structure that does not in fact exist as such. In as much as such simulacra display traits of intelligence, they are exteriorizations of a consciousness that does not exist internally. No doubt, cognitive processes/information processes are taking place "within," and there are points of connection between the surface and these internal processes. But there is no internal twin of the surface, exteriorized consciousness/intelligence with which one interfaces.

The exteriorized intelligence of the computer simulation requires a compatible exteriorized consciousness of the user with which to interface in order to create a smart environment. This simulation of subjectivity, of intelligence, allows the computer to become a cognitive extension of the human. This interface is visible, for example, in the process of composing text on a computer. The graphical user interface's (GUI) ability to simulate prior media can easily lead us to conflate the compositional processes of writing on a computer with prior modes. This simulation creates the needed conditions of compatibility with user expectations. The ability to cut and paste text, an often-touted advantage of electronic composition, recalls prior compositional modes in which one might literally cut and paste pieces of written text together. It also reflects film-editing techniques, which have their own cutting and pasting. In more abstract terms, the movement of blocks of text (either within a document or from one document to another) harkens Aristotelian *topoi* and Ramus's advocacy of outlining following the Gutenberg Revolution. These simulations allow us to interface comfortably with the machine from within a traditional authorial identity. However, as one begins to consider the actual technical processes involved beneath the screen, the radical difference between new media and these earlier modes becomes evident. Hayles writes,

> As I write these words on my computer, I see the lights on the video screen, but for the computer, the relevant signifiers are electronic polarities on disks. Intervening between what I see and what the computer reads are the machine code that correlates alphanumeric symbols with binary digits, the compiler language that correlates these symbols with higher-level instructions determining how the symbols are to be manipulated, the processing program that mediates between these instructions and the commands I give the computer, and so forth . . . The longer the chain of codes, the more radical the transformations that can be effected. Acting as linguistic transducers, the coding chains impart astonishing power to even very small changes. Such amplification is possible because the constant reproduced through multiple coding layers is a pattern rather than a presence. (1999b, p. 31)

These multiple coding layers are not unlike the layers of discrete and semiautonomous agents of distributed cognition. Like human consciousness, the text on the screen is a non-linear, dynamic structure capable of (or susceptible to) dramatic transformations, precisely because what is present in the text is not consciousness (as Derrida has argued) but rather a trace, an epiphenomenon, of embodied processes. That is, what one witnesses with consciousness or in a text is a product of multiple interlocking cognitive and technological mechanisms. We might imagine ourselves to be fully-present authors, "speaking our minds," but that simulation of consciousness is simply a superficial interface, an exteriorized program, that allows us to communicate with the smart environments of discourse communities, intellectual marketplaces, and telecommunications technologies.

Rodney Brooks makes a related observation in his description of robot minds. He notes that while it may be useful for a designer to conceive of a robot's mind in digital terms, "combinational circuits are built out of raw voltages, not out of ones and zeroes . . . Similarly the symbolic abstraction is a crucial tool in the analysis and synthesis of our humanoids; but we do not necessarily expect these symbols to appear explicitly in the humanoid's head" (Brooks and Stein, 1994, p. 5). In other words, on their most material level, computer circuits function through an exchange in voltage intensity. These voltages form the simulacrum of the digital environment, which then through various intermediate steps becomes the simulated interface with which a human interacts. It is on this final level of simulation that consciousness appears. The same might be said of human consciousness. Like the simulated screen responding to an extensive circuit of real-time information, the human conscious provides an interface to the subterranean mechanisms of real-time processing. In other words, consciousness, as epiphenomenon, is also simulation, but that does not make it any less real. It is rather an indication that consciousness is a means for gathering, presenting, and processing information.

This new media model of consciousness as interface marks the erasure of distance between the traditional internalized subject and the external, objective world. Clearly this can suggest a threat to the conventional notion of human agency. As I discussed earlier and is a theme of *The Matrix* films, simulation appears to leave little room for human action. It suggests how easily humans can forget themselves and become fascinated with the disappearing images of a seductive simulation. And yet, the imminent reversibility of seduction applies to seduction itself. As Kittler's critique of software indicates, the simulation ultimately relies upon an analog materiality that always exists in excess of the simulation's cybernetic control. Because simulations are intertwined with materiality, they contain the possibility of their own reversal. This reversal lies in repulsion: the repulsion of the body, of the material, against its cynical disappearance in the mediascape. Arthur Kroker (2001) writes, "seduction is the annihilation of difference except as an indifferent rule of topological play; repulsion is a dark and missing otherness of embodied subjectivity . . . repulsion is the forgotten term for that implacable stubborn presence which we call a human being" (pp. 80–81). This stubborn presence is the physical embodiment of human consciousness, that material entity whose responses to an event can never be fully predicted or controlled. While the conscious mind finds itself seduced by the imaginary doppelganger and reality projected by simulation, the body reacts to the fragmentary composition of simulation itself.

Michael Heim (1998) describes this experience in less abstract terms in his discussion of Alternate World Syndrome (AWS), "the relativity sickness that comes from switching back-and-forth between the primary and virtual worlds" (p. 182). Heim explains that AWS is not unlike earlier technology sicknesses such as simulator sickness, motion sickness, and jet lag. It occurs when there is a substantial disconnection between various sensory inputs into the body: for example, our eyes register movement but our inner ears do not. Heim insists this is more than a technological glitch, that "AWS concerns not the system per se, but the system within the broader context of world entrance and exit" (1998, p. 185). In other words, AWS is the repulsion of the body against the seductive images of simulation. Heim moves forward optimistically, stating his faith in the human "power to transport ourselves elsewhere . . . Call it memory or expectation, teleportation lies at the basis of virtual reality. Teleportation is also a key for understanding our evolution and for mitigating its technostress" (1998, p. 193). Through our human ability to imagine ourselves elsewhere, Heim believes we will ultimately evolve beyond problems like AWS and establish a smoother interface between body and machine. This teleportation allows us to project our consciousness outside of our bodies, carried forth by technology, only to return later to the body, an experience Heim imagines as parallel with the spiritual voyage undertaken by aboriginal Pintupi tribespeople and symbolized by the boomerang: "the soul, they discovered, could transport itself through space and time, with at least as much magic as the boomerang" (1998, pp. 198–199). Heim pursues a similar trajectory for VR in his description of a spiral interface, which "moves us into virtual worlds that return us to ourselves, repeatedly deepening the awareness we enjoy as primary bodies" (1998, p. 75). Underlying this perception of VR is the hope that technology can open new subjective spaces which ultimately will enrich our experience of our bodies and renew our commitment to the physical world rather than becoming a disembodied, escapist fantasy (or nightmare).

Electronic devices, as virtual as the information they contain might be, are themselves material, as obviously are the bodies that hold our conscious minds. The argument for embodiment begins with this materiality. It is the repulsion of the body Baudrillard and Kroker describe; it is the cause of AWS that reminds us that we must always return to our bodies, the direct, physiological shocks that reconnect us to our bodies. The physiological shocks of technology are an insistent message that we incorporate the body into our understanding of technology and look upon the disappearance of materiality as a making-aesthetic of life (e.g., turning life into "lifestyle"), which Benjamin termed the foundation of fascistic politics. This cluster of values continues to present cultural challenges in the present moment, and though much postmodern theory has presented a pessimistic view of human agency, some more current theorists have sought ways to develop new possibilities for human action in concert with technology. As Katherine Hayles writes,

> although some current versions of the posthuman point toward the anti-human and apocalyptic, we can craft others that will be conducive to the long-range survival of humans and of the other life-forms, biological and artificial, with whom we share the planet and ourselves. (1999b, p. 291)

Hayles's critique hinges upon the contention that an *embodied* theory of consciousness that accounts for the role of both bodies and machines is crucial if we are to develop an ethical, ecologically and socially responsible technoculture. Any such theory will need to account for the seductive power of simulation; it will also have to respond to the concerns and cultural fallout generated by the critique an embodied, technologically-mediated consciousness poses to the disembodied, rational, free-willed mind.

6 Waking Up in the Machine

The last three chapters have focused on virtuality as a technological production, as a result of mechanical-cum-digital media composition and cybernetics. Now I will investigate virtuality as a philosophical concept. However, I will reiterate that these two virtuals are not opposed to one another but are intersecting concepts in which the virtual-technological operates within a materiality that unfolds through virtual-actual processes. The virtual-technological references the ways in which technologies capture, represent, simulate, produce, and participate in materiality; as I have been discussing, these technological operations also affect subjective experience and cognition. The virtual-actual enters this conversation on an even more fundamental level, in the production of materiality itself. The virtual-actual describes a morphogenetic process in which materiality unfolds. I am particularly interested here in the implications of the virtual-actual for understanding media composition in the intersection between technology and cognition. As such, the text shifts the investigation it has undertaken so far, which has operated under our regular conception of material space and time, to open a new way of thinking about the role of subjects in media composition. This chapter focuses on the work of Deleuze and Guattari and its extension in the contemporary work of Manuel DeLanda, Brian Massumi, and others. Fundamentally, the shift into Deleuzian philosophy marks a movement away from both the essentialist foundations of Western traditions *and* the discursive, ideological postmodern representation of subjectivity, and a movement toward a more dynamic universe where subjectivity and consciousness emerge as a product of non-linear, energetic interactions. Specifically, this chapter is interested in the virtual-actual as a process by which consciousness (and hence subjectivity) emerges from a continuous material space. At stake is the development of a mode of individuation and thought that replaces the traditional humanistic-Cartesian dualistic model, without becoming wholly captured within the logic of ideology or the will to technology.

The potential impact of computers and the virtual-technological upon rhetoric and composition is fairly apparent. We find ourselves surrounded by computers everyday and recognize that an increasing amount of writing takes place electronically, for electronic formats, and in conjunction with other media. However, I have been tracing a parallel discussion, which while long-standing, has not been a central element in our discipline's discourses on computers: the ways in which these technologies alter our understanding of cognition. Despite the relative absence of these issues from our discipline, it would seem clear that rhetoric and composition must be founded, implicitly if not explicitly, upon a theory of human thought. After all, writing is a fundamentally cognitive act, though significantly a cognitive act that is inextricably intertwined with technologies. And furthermore, as if any additional weight were required, writing in turn becomes a principle mechanism for the development of the foundations of Western philosophy. Now, writing technologies are undergoing a substantial technological transformation that is not unrelated to significant changes in the ways we understand human thought, beginning with Freudian psychoanalysis and developing into contemporary cognitive science and cybernetics. All of this threatens the basic principles of a humanistic, Enlightenment individual upon which the modern university and modern democracy and capitalism developed. As I have been discussing, however, there exists a third space (neither conventionally scientific nor traditionally humanistic) in which a constellation of heterogeneous theories of embodied cognition have been developing.

All of this has significant implication for rhetoric and composition, as significant as the direct effects of computers in the classroom that have been a site of study in our field for more than twenty years. The previous four chapters have laid the groundwork for exploring these implications by establishing the connections between symbolic behavior, cognition, and technology. Arguably, rhetoric and composition faces a radically different theory of composition based upon a post-humanistic conception of cognition. It is this conception that I begin to explore in this chapter through an articulation of the virtual-actual. To understand the implications of the virtual-actual for new media composition, one must begin more generally with the differences between virtual and conventional notions of space and materiality. Our conventional conception views the material world as being composed of discrete objects with essential differences distributed metrically through a relatively stable three-dimensional space. That is, for example, I sit in a room with a couch, a chair, a table, and four windows. These objects are separate from me and from one another, and one might measure their size and spatial relationship from one another. The windows have essential characteristics that define them as windows and as "not-chairs."

This notion of "essence" is eliminated in the virtual-actual. The philosophical problem with essence is that it requires the existence of some external set of qualities or reference points on which materiality must be organized. For an object to be a table, it must represent the essential qualities of "table-ness," qualities that insist upon an *a priori* tautological, ideal table. Assuming that one does not want to accept the literal existence of some Platonic realm of forms, our conventional notions of objects in space can only be understood as descriptive of our apprehension of them rather than as articulations of their material development. That is, we may distinguish a tree from a bush by certain characteristics, but the processes shaping the object we categorize as a tree have nothing to do with the essential characteristics of tree-ness. The virtual-actual describes these processes, termed "multiplicities," by which materiality unfolds. One might be tempted to view these processes as essences (and simply shift the notion of essence from the object to the process that produces the object). However, as I will describe in this chapter, multiplicities are material as opposed to the conceptual abstractions of essence. Furthermore, multiplicities bear no essential or determining relationship to the material objects that emerge from their processes. That is, multiplicities do not determine the characteristics of the objects; multiplicities establish conditions of possibility for the emergence of the processes or tendencies that produce objects. I realize this might seem to be a rather nuanced and esoteric distinction. The next section of this chapter provides greater detail about the operation of multiplicities and the role they play in the development of material conditions. As I explore there, and throughout this chapter, moving toward the virtual-actual, thinking about space and matter in these non-conventional ways, is integral to understanding the insight of the virtual into compositional processes.

My investigation of multiplicities is followed by a discussion of the relations between Cartesian and topological spaces. This continues my brief foray into articulating the difference between the virtual-actual and conventional notions of space. In the previous three chapters, my discussion of the collapse of distance has been predicated upon a conventional Cartesian understanding of objects and their spatial relationships. However, as I will describe, topological spaces do not have fixed dimensions but rather proceed through a process of unfolding. This is not simply a way of describing existing spaces but a way of describing the way in which spaces *become*. Clearly here the notions of space and time are already becoming mixed. This is unavoidable. In Cartesian space, where objects are described primarily as points in relation to an external grid, time does not have to be a factor. However, the topological spaces I am describing exist in flux, between points; to arrest the topological and define a particular point in its fluctuations is to apprehend it within a Cartesian mode. And this is certainly possible. The Cartesian represents one possible apprehension of topological spaces. However, topological spaces are not limited to Cartesian geometry. Such spaces are virtual in that they are undecided; they do not have a fixed, Cartesian identity. But they are also actual in that they have a physical, material existence. They simply cannot be fully described in Cartesian terms.

From this articulation of space, I move more specifically into an investigation of cognition. While we conventionally conceive of thought as abstraction, cognition is clearly a material event taking the form of energetic interactions within an embodied brain, in concert with a material-informational environment accessed through the senses. In short, if the virtual-actual establishes the conditions of possibility through which the processes of material production emerge, then this would include the material production of cognition. This articulation of the unfolding of thought is quite different from more familiar concepts of subjectivity grounded in the operation of ideological power and demands a significant rethinking of how consciousness and agency might function. This chapter investigates this rethinking through a second analysis of *The Matrix* trilogy. In the previous chapter, I focused on the new media technologies used in the production of the films. This time, I focus on the films' narrative, which takes us through a series of potential modes of individuation. At the outset, Neo's primary identity is as "the One": a messianic figure conceived to combat a paranoid fear by demonstrating his power to control machines and free the humans. However, the simple duality of humans versus machines is dispensed in the second film, and the redemptive story of the One is revealed as a simulation. Instead, we are presented with a conundrum about the apparent impossibility of free will and choice. In the conclusion, however, we move beyond that postmodern problem to encounter the aporia of consciousness. Neo does not save humanity or the machines from the fascism of Agent Smith by becoming the "one" but rather by becoming the "other," a mutative force that keeps the topological space unfolding. In Cartesian terms, the uncanny experience of digital cinema presents us with the fragmentation of the subject and our intersection with intelligent machines as the disappearance of identity: when machines invade the processes of thought, we lose our being. However, in this chapter and in *The Matrix* trilogy thought is not being. As I will explore, thought and being are only temporary captures of a topological process of unfolding in which we are always becoming other than our thoughts, paradoxically other than what (we think) we are. Specifically, the text pursues the trope of "waking up" as it unfolds through the trilogy. Throughout the films, there are a series of cognitive awakenings that resonate with and against Descartes's awakening in his classic thought experiment. In the terms of this chapter, this waking is also an analogy for what might be termed "the symmetry-breaking process" of becoming conscious. As the films finally explore, the question with consciousness is not whether it is essentially human or machine but rather whether it is permitted to follow its own path of becoming or if it is to be codified within a disciplinary structure of being-the-same.

Multiplicities and the Becoming of Thought

Some of the most recognizable features of Deleuze and Guattari's work—rhizomes, nomadism, multiplicities—draw upon concepts of topological geometry. As I noted above, the philosophical advantage of topology is that, unlike Cartesian spaces, it operates without reference to some external or higher unity. As such, topology becomes a mechanism for establishing a material philosophy in place of a philosophy of essences. Deleuze and Guattari draw on several mathematicians including Friedrich Gaus, Bernhard Riemann, and Henri Poincaré in developing their use of topology and related concepts such as singularities and multiplicities. As Manuel DeLanda (2002) argues, an examination of these mathematical and scientific principles allows one to understand how these theories come to describe material processes rather than simply operate as metaphors for material processes. That is, for example, Deleuze and Guattari's *A Thousand Plateaus* is not "like a rhizome" in the sense that traditional, Western philosophical text is tree-like. Instead, the book "forms a rhizome with the world" (1987, p. 11).

The same might be said of the concept of the multiplicity, which they borrow from topological geometry. In Deleuze and Guattari's terms,

> A multiplicity is defined not by its elements, nor by a center of unification or comprehension. It is defined by the number of dimensions it has; it is not divisible, it cannot lose or gain a dimension *without changing its nature.* Since its variations and dimensions are immanent to it, *it amounts to the same thing to say that each multiplicity is already composed of heterogeneous terms in symbiosis, and that a multiplicity is continually transforming itself into a string of other multiplicities, according to its thresholds and doors.* (1987, p. 249; emphasis in original)

I want to investigate two features of this definition further: the process of continual transformation according to thresholds and doors, and the multiplicity's inability to be divided without changing its nature. Since a change in nature would appear to be at least a kind of transformation, ultimately there will be an integration of these features. However, I will begin by examining them separately.

As Deleuze and Guattari's definition emphasizes, multiplicities are not fixed objects but rather material processes in continual transformation. However, this emphasis on mutation does not mean that these transformations are random. As we know in our own lives, everyday physical events are largely predictable. This predictability is a result of a feature of multiplicities termed singularities. Singularities are conceptually similar to black holes, attractors that draw in a range of potential fluctuations and bring them all to a single end point. There are numerous types of singularities, describing different patterns of attraction, but fundamentally, they each function to create degrees of symmetry within a multiplicity. DeLanda provides the example of a singularity that might constrain matter to move toward a point of minimal free energy. As such soap bubbles form spheres, with minimal surface tension, and salt crystals form cubes minimizing bonding energy (2002, p. 15). As these examples indicate, a singularity does not impart essential characteristics to matter. The soap bubble and the salt crystal are essentially different from one another. The multiplicity and singularity are conditions of possibility separate from the extensive or metric properties of the bubble or the crystal. The bubble or crystal can be larger or smaller without altering the multiplicity, which as Deleuze and Guattari note, cannot be divided without changing its nature. That is, regardless of its size, the bubble or crystal will continue to be attracted to this singularity that shapes the process of its material unfolding.

Of course, the bubble can be popped; the crystal can be dissolved. This is the type of change in nature that results from the division of a multiplicity. Again, DeLanda provides a useful example by comparing multiplicities to intensive properties (2002, p. 20). If one has a pot of water heated to 90 degrees and one divides that water in half, then one does not end up with two pots of 45-degree water. An intensive property, such as heat, cannot be divided in this fashion. However, one can create a pot of water with divided areas of heat simply by heating the pot from the bottom. In performing this everyday task, one can witness the symmetry-breaking process by which multiplicities are divided and change nature. Prior to heating, the water is in a symmetrical state. Energy is distributed equally through the liquid. As heat is applied to the bottom, the matter strives to maintain that state of equilibrium and moves through a series of states until it reaches the turbulent state of a full boil. At this point, water begins to transform to steam. In more abstract terms, the shift in intensive properties causes the singularities shaping the multiplicity to bifurcate and take on new behaviors. Spaces that were once symmetrical come to exhibit greater degrees of differentiation. As such, the process of dividing multiplicities through variations of intensive properties intersects with the mechanisms of singularities, mutating their behaviors, and leading to greater or lesser degrees of symmetry. In short, shifts in intensity result in material transformations, though they do not determine the nature of those transformations. Heat applied to water in a pot causes it to boil; heat applied to paper causes it to burst into flames (though obviously the burning point of paper is higher than the boiling point of water, so it is not simply a matter of intensity but degree of intensity as well).

One final feature of multiplicities must be considered here. As I mentioned above, conventionally conceived objects have discrete, definable boundaries. They sit in measurable relations with one another. Multiplicities, however, do not have such boundaries and instead intersect one another in zones of indetermination. This is significant, as it articulates the relationship between a continuous, topological space, a plane of consistency in Deleuze and Guattari's terms, and the multiplicities that produce the differentiated spaces we normally inhabit. As energy generates a shift in intensive properties, matter moves from an undifferentiated topological space to a more highly differentiated condition. Brian Massumi explains this evolution from an undifferentiated, undecided state to a highly differentiated one through a reference to an experiment with cognition. Volunteers had their brain waves measured by an electroencephalograph (EEG) machine. They were then asked to flex a finger at a moment of their choosing and to note the position of a dot on a spatial clock. 0.2 seconds passed between the moment of choosing and the actual flexing of the finger, *but* the EEG machine measured a marked increase in brain activity 0.3 seconds *before* the moment of choosing (2002, p. 29). From this Massumi contends, "Will and consciousness are *subtractive*. They are *limitative, derived functions* that reduce a complexity too rich to be functionally expressed" (2002, p. 29). That is, the volunteers begin in an undecided state, prior to the finger's flexing. Many possibilities exist, in a virtual state, as to when the finger may be flexed. What initiates the finger's flexing? Is it a conscious, free will? The experiment indicates that the process does not begin with a conscious choice, but rather that the choice marks only an intermediary moment in the process. In terms of the virtual-actual, the thought to flex bubbles up from an undifferentiated plane of unconscious, potential, virtual thoughts. The thought emerges in response to an energetic, intensive affect, in response to an external cue from the volunteer's environment (the experimenter's request that the volunteer initiate the experiment). The verbal request translates into energetic activity measurable on the EEG machine. After all, the spoken word is sonic energy, registered by the ear. It also carries a coded, linguistic message that is decoded by the listener, which is a process that requires the expenditure of mental energy (even though the task is not a mentally strenuous one). The decoding also initiates an affective response. This response is also energetic and idiosyncratic. Perhaps the experimenter's voice or clothing or demeanor reminds the volunteer of an old friend. Perhaps the volunteer is sexually attracted to the experimenter. In any case, these affective responses include the cue to flex a finger and, at some point, this intensive energy causes the thought to flex to emerge in a manner analogous to the way the heat applied to the bottom of the pot causes the water to boil.

Of course the analogy between thinking and boiling water is quite limited. Cognition is a far more complex, less predictable, and less deterministic process than conduction. The experimenter's request that the volunteer flex his/her finger does not compel the volunteer to do so in the way heat applied to a pot will compel the water to boil. The point is not to suggest that consciousness plays no role in thought but rather that it is not the entirety of cognition, nor even the origin of cognition. The usefulness of the analogy between thinking and boiling water is in its ability to illustrate how cognition might be understood as an energetic process in which shifts in intensity precipitate a transformation of multiplicities and lead to material changes. The experiment Massumi references suggests that consciousness marks the moment when a multiplicity of potential, virtual intensive properties becomes specific material extensive properties: the thought to flex a finger *becomes*. One might conceive of brain activity as moving through a series of symmetry-breaking intensities, finally arriving at a point where the decision is differentiated from the other potential thoughts. At the stage of highest symmetry, all thoughts, choices, and desires appear the same. As thought becomes perceptible and conscious, that is, as it becomes articulated in symbolic terms, it reaches a high level of differentiation. A thought is considered; a choice is made. One experiences the intensity of this decision as a force of will. However, prior to that differentiation, the decision and all other potential decisions exist in an undifferentiated, virtual state.

Massumi's example is significant not simply because it describes the energetic process through which intensive properties lead to transformations but more importantly because it demonstrates the role of such processes in cognition. As he puts it,

> during the mysterious half-second, what we think of as 'free,' 'higher' functions, such as volition, are apparently being performed by autonomic, bodily reactions occurring in the brain but outside conscious-

ness, and between brain and finger but prior to action and expression. (2002, p. 29)

As intensities bifurcate singularities, mutating multiplicities to unfold in new ways, they also initiate cognitive processes. While some thoughts emerge and become conscious, other potential thoughts never become but remain in a potential state as tendencies that are not actualized. This is the virtual, "the pressing crowd of incipiencies and tendencies . . . where futurity combines, unmediated, with pastness, where outsides are infolded and sadness is happy . . . The virtual is a lived paradox where what are normally opposites coexist, coalesce, and connect" (2002, p. 30). Here in Massumi's description of cognition one can see the virtual-actual loop. Virtuality is a realm of potentials that are not actualized. Those potentials exist as an irretrievable past, what we did not come to think, but from which our thoughts emerged, like bubbles surfacing on water coming to a boil. Those objects that become actual and gain extensive properties, which mark them in Cartesian space (in the case of thought, those extensive properties are linguistically defined in a rational discursive space), may be named and partially captured on a plane of reference. However, all materiality also remains in an ongoing state of flux. The body (including the mind) is both concrete and abstract, having both physical extension and an incorporeal realm of virtual potential, a topological space of multiplicities from which physical and mental extensive properties unfold.

It is finally this notion of thought as both concrete *and* abstract that becomes the trickiest. Conventionally we can acknowledge that thought is concrete in that it requires a brain that performs physical acts that can be measured. We also easily recognize thought as an abstraction, as representational and conceptual. However, it is difficult in a normal understanding of these matters to connect the concrete with the abstract. The virtual-actual does not refute that thought or the material world is both concrete and abstract. Instead it understands these concepts differently and in a manner that connects the abstract to the concrete without seeing the former as a controlling, essentializing mechanism. Ultimately multiplicities must attempt to account for this dynamic. As Massumi explains it, abstraction in the virtual-actual pertains "to the transitional immediacy of a real relation—that of a body to its own *indeterminacy* (its openness to an elsewhere and otherwise than it is, in any here and now)" (2002, p. 5). In other words, where our conventional abstractions are *determining* in that they establish essential identities for material objects, here the virtual abstract relates to an *indeterminate* plane of potential, all the heres and nows that are virtually possible but never come to be. As I have been describing, from this virtual, abstract plane, thoughts become. In the next section, I go further into the differences between an abstract, *referential* grid of Cartesian space and an abstract, *indeterminate* unfolding of topological space.

CARTESIAN AND TOPOLOGICAL SPACES

The articulation of thought in terms of a material process that unfolds according to energetic principles through topological time and space may strike some as strange, as we generally think of thought as immaterial. However, though we may not ordinarily consider it, these integral connections between subjectivity and conceptions of space and time are already apparent in the dominant notions of free-willed individuality, where the Cartesian subject is constructed to orchestrate the human body's movements through the Cartesian coordinates of three-dimensional space. Objects in Cartesian space are finite and locatable, and the rational subject functions through controlled and controllable interactions with these objects. In this model, navigating my way from my office to my classroom is a matter of my conscious mind controlling my body's movements through a fixed, three-dimensional space to preset coordinates. Think, for example, of a campus map. Each building is drawn in proportion to the others; the space between the buildings is equally representative of "real" physical, measurable distances. The map includes a legend that tells us one inch equals 100 feet (or whatever): the point is that there is a proportion, an equivalency. After some time on campus, we seem to internalize this map and the relations it represents. As Cartesian subjects, we presumably use this internalized map to navigate physical spaces. Of course the campus map also articulates ideological spaces, with different disciplines in different buildings, separate from administration or dorms or the student center. Again, the Cartesian subject is presumed to navigate these spaces in a similar fashion.

The overlay of physical and ideological spaces is neither coincidental nor limited to the campus, as exemplified in political-critical theories such as Fredric Jameson's "cognitive mapping," which seeks to account for the social conditions of space in the postmodern era (1991).

Jameson's central argument is on point here. He describes the development of social-spatial relations and capitalism in three stages: market, monopoly, and late or postmodern capitalism. The first stage is the imposition "of a logic of the grid, a reorganization of some older sacred and heterogeneous space into geometrical and Cartesian homogeneity, a space of infinite equivalence and extension" (1991, p. 410). In other words, the panoptic-disciplinary space Foucault describes. However, Jameson contends that in the Modern era, with the full development of colonialism and an increasing economic internationalization, there comes a crisis of spatial relations in the sense that individual lived experience cannot fully account for the social spaces in which one lives, spaces which are also conditioned by relations with far-off colonies. As I have been discussing, mechanical media intensifies this collapse of space, of fixed Cartesian relations. Jameson's primary concern, though, is with late capitalism, where this spatial crisis has been exponentially intensified. In effect, Cartesian distances have been subsumed within network relations. In the plainest terms, the distance between my office and the library is made irrelevant by the fact that I can access all of the library's databases and view an increasing number of materials from my computer. In more substantial terms, as has been widely discussed in mainstream media, networking and global capitalism are altering the professions that our students will seek to enter. In this situation, one impulse might be to yearn nostalgically for an era of Cartesian certainty. However, as Jameson and Foucault delineate, Cartesian space is only an historical foundation for capitalism, not a natural state. Furthermore, virtual-technological spaces continue to rely upon Cartesian coordinates, even though the spaces they measure are on a different scale.

As I mentioned earlier, the primary difference between Cartesian and topological space is that where Cartesian space is predicated upon fixed relations between objects measured upon an externally-imposed grid, topological space unfolds through deformation and symmetry-breaking transitions. Objects have no fixed shape but rather pass through shapes over time, and likewise, subjectivity unfolds through its interactions over time. Navigation becomes embodied and proprioceptive: in other words, the body guides itself in relation to the unfolding of its own movements rather than in reference to an external set of spatial coordinates. As Brian Massumi suggests, this

> has significant implications for our understanding
> of space because it *inverts the relation of position to
> movement*. Movement is no longer indexed to posi-
> tion. Rather position emerges from movement, from
> a relation of movement to itself. Philosophically, this
> is no small shift. (2002, p. 180)

In other words, Cartesian space suggests that we understand movement based upon positions: we look at a map and chart our movements based on the relationship between our current location and our
destination. Indeed, we may consult a map when we are lost or in an
unfamiliar place, but Massumi is suggesting that we do not actually
move ourselves by this logic. We do not internalize the campus map
but rather we develop an embodied sense of space based upon our
regular movement through an area. When we find our way through
our homes in the dark, is it because we have an internal map of our
furniture or is it because we can feel our way through our familiar motions of moving through the house? When we drive home from work
on "auto-pilot" and discover ourselves in our driveway with no knowledge of the trip, is it because our brains have internalized Cartesian
distances ("drive 1.2 miles from the stop light and turn left") or is it
because we have some embodied memory of spatial behaviors? The latter are examples of proprioception, of our sense of ourselves in relation
to our own bodies rather than some external grid of coordinates.

This topological approach to space does not suggest that Cartesian
and Euclidean spaces do not exist; this is not the typical postmodern
argument regarding the non-existence of reality, at least not as it is
often characterized. Instead, it is a conceptualization of how Euclidean spaces emerge. The linking of Euclidean and non-Euclidean spaces creates an infolded hinge where our proprioceptive experience of
space is doubled by our cognitive mapping of our location. Our map
of Cartesian coordinates, dominated by various landmarks, lays over
our embodied sense of direction, reinforcing the latter. Acknowledging this link is a potentially significant recognition: if one accepts the
postmodern crisis of mapping Jameson identifies, then proprioception
offers one possible strategy for expanding our ability to move through
networked spaces. The intersection of these spaces can be seen in the
mundane experience of getting lost or more specifically what we might
call getting "turned around." Typically, this might occur when emerging from a subway; our proprioceptive sense might lead us to expect to

emerge on one side of the street, only to discover that we are not where we expected. In this moment we need to access our cognitive map and re-place ourselves within it. Or, inversely,

> the first thing people typically do when they realize they are lost and start trying to reorient is to look away from the scene in front of them, even rolling their eyes skyward. We figure out where we are by putting the plain-as-day visual image back in the proper proprioceptive sea-patch. (Massumi, 2002, p. 182)

In such scenes, we find ourselves reawakening; space shifts around us (and/or we shift in space). Perhaps becoming-conscious is a similar awakening, a vector along an intensity incline through symmetry-breaking assemblages.

In the next three sections, I return to *The Matrix* trilogy where my analysis of the narrative seeks to explore further this concept of the virtual-actual, particularly how this philosophy of the virtual articulates the composition of thought and the possible relations between thought and technology. In particular, I take interest in the trope of waking, of becoming conscious. It is tempting to see (or construct) some connection between the three films and Jameson's three spatial stages (which, not coincidentally, reflect the three stages of capitalism). The connections are not as superficial as they might initially appear. Jameson admits that "'Cognitive mapping' was in reality nothing but a code word for 'class consciousness'—only it proposed the need for class consciousness of a new and hitherto undreamed of kind, while it also inflected the account in the direction of that new spatiality implicit in the postmodern" (1992, p. 418). As I will discuss, the trilogy's initial narrative, in the first film, reflects the Marxist notion of lifting false consciousness, which corresponds best with the first stage of capitalism and its corollary Cartesian coordinates. But the resulting consciousness proves to be an illusion, another ideological layer. What follows for Jameson from the Modern into the Postmodern is an intensifying sense of dislocation, as the structures that condition one's life are increasingly globalized across a power network. This is reflected in *The Matrix Reloaded* through Neo's growing uncertainty and feeling of entrapment. Ultimately, however, Jameson is in search of an evolution of class consciousness that incorporates a sense of postmodern spatiality. As I have been tracing here, that space is a topological one. In a sense, I am pursuing a similar task in articulating a virtual-actual consciousness: one that does not discount our experience with our own consciousness but envelops it in a more inclusive understanding of materiality. The final film, *Matrix Revolutions,* explores the political and ethical consequences of a topological consciousness and serves as a possible response to the task Jameson sets. Furthermore, as is significant for my own task here, this investigation elucidates the concept of the virtual-actual as a way of understanding the composition of thought and consciousness. Specifically, the films explore the situation of the virtual-technological within the virtual-actual, with consciousness serving as the body's hinge or interface between the two.

PARANOIA AND SIMULATION

As I suggested in the previous chapter, *The Matrix* trilogy provides an apt example of the perceived threat to human agency and thought represented by information technology. In a way, it is a technological update of Descartes's thought experiment: what if the world is an illusion created by an evil ~~demon~~ computer? For Descartes the question was intimately tied to concerns of madness, as both Foucault (1965) and Derrida (1978) have examined. Similarly, the uncanny encounter with media also suggests the possibility of madness, where computers shape our thoughts and present us with illusions. The impulse then becomes to uncover a means to wake up from these illusions. This impulse corresponds in many respects with the conventional impulse of critical thinking: to wake up from the false consciousness of ideology. However, much as the conditions of ideology and power in postmodernism have critiqued our faith in a critical, humanistic awakening, *The Matrix* trilogy brings the separation of technological and human consciousness under question. While at the end of the first film, we are left with the impression that Neo is indeed "the One," the complete trilogy creates a more open philosophical space. Together, the films uncover important insights in the role new media technologies play in the unfolding of subjective topologies and provide an interesting map of concepts regarding the future of new media and virtual reality, especially new subjective states that might result from combining humans and machines in the creation of virtual worlds. In other words, *The Matrix* trilogy offers insight into how one can understand cognition and agency within the twin virtuals of a technological virtual reality and a topological virtual actuality.

Here, I trace the movement from the first film's paranoid messianic hero, stuck in the simulation of revolutionary dialectic, to the topological becoming of a new consciousness suggested by *Matrix Revolutions.* The trilogy can be read as a mapping of subject production in which the subject moves from paranoid fears over his own rhizomatic and mechanistic production, through the mutation of the messianic individual into the postmodern singularity, to the multiplication of that singularity in a moment of becoming that dissipates (though does not cure) the original paranoia. As I discussed in the previous chapter, new media plays an important role in this subjective process both as material-technological means for producing these subjective effects and as a compositional means for investigating this concept. However, the passage from digital new media to topological space is not easily made. Despite the apparent mutability of virtual reality, digital spaces are rigidly defined in binary terms. Digital spaces are certainly Cartesian. Brian Massumi argues,

> Nothing is more destructive for the thinking and imaging of the virtual than equating it with the digital. . . . Equating the digital with the virtual confuses the really apparitional with the artificial. It reduces it to a simulation. This forgets intensity, brackets potential, and in that same sweeping gesture bypasses the move through sensation, the actual envelopment of the virtual. (2002, pp. 137–138)

In Massumi's Deleuzian approach, the virtual is a topological space. The only access digital media provides to topology is in the cracks between coordinates, in the proprioceptive space between and within subject and computer. It is this space that is explored in *The Matrix* trilogy.

The first *Matrix* film draws heavily upon contemporary paranoia regarding virtual reality. The film sets the scene for the trilogy by establishing the classic sci-fi plot where the machines have taken over the world and only a few humans survive to fight them. Only in this case, the machines have trapped the majority of humans inside a giant virtual reality program (the Matrix) and use their bodily energies to power their machinic civilization. The plot centers on Neo Anderson (played by Keanu Reeves), a man trapped inside the Matrix who, with the help of human revolutionaries led by Morpheus (Laurence Fishburne), comes to realize his apparent destiny as "the One": a human with the power to control virtual reality with a thought. In a Gnostic fashion, the film asserts an underlying reality hidden by the illusory Matrix. This assertion keeps the film grounded in a paranoia that moves from fearing the insertion of machines into the body to pursuing a messianic, revolutionary vision of the mind-soul triumphing over both body and machine. The film's theme of paranoia was heightened through its advertising campaign, which focused on a single question, "what is the Matrix?" The Matrix hyperbolizes the panoptic experience of modern American life, particularly since the Patriot Act. The sense of ongoing surveillance, the suspicion of everyone, and the cynicism of the jaded corporate worker all find themselves expressed in the film's paranoid viewpoint. *The Matrix* crystallizes all these fears in a scene where Morpheus reveals to Neo the nature of the world in which he has lived and confirms this initial paranoia:

> The Matrix is everywhere, it's all around us, here even in this room. You can see it out your window or on your television. You feel it when you go to work, or go to church or pay your taxes. It is the world that has been pulled over your eyes to blind you from the truth. . . . Like everyone else, you were born into bondage, kept inside a prison that you cannot smell, taste, or touch. A prison for your mind. (Wachowski and Wachowski, 1999)

Interestingly, one could substitute the word "ideology" for "the Matrix" in this passage and have a reasonable, albeit brief, definition of ideology. This suggests that while the Matrix may be primarily technological, it is also certainly ideological.

Unlike the Althusserian concept of ideology, the Matrix is described as an illusion, and one can be woken from that illusion. In this sense, the Matrix's ideological function most closely matches the pseudo-Gnostic notion of false consciousness, a world "pulled over your eyes to blind you from the truth." When Neo swallows the pill offered him by Morpheus, he is ejected from the illusory world of the Matrix into the "real" world of Zion and the human resistance to the machines. After taking the drug, Neo undergoes a reversal of the mirror stage emblematized by his transformation into a mirror-like substance. The result of his taking the pill is a radical exteriorization of his subjectivity; Neo turns inside out. He is then literally disconnected from the cybernetic mechanisms of his subjective experience, the world, as he knows it, stops, and he wakes in the machine. Within a Judeo-Christian interpretation, perhaps this moment is a baptism, a rebirth, but that would suggest that what follows, in the scene where Morpheus reveals the nature of the Matrix, is the Truth. However, as we discover later, Morpheus does not know the "Truth." Instead, Neo's drug is literally a *pharmakon:* a poison and cure. Of course, the pill is not really a pill. It is a simulation, a computer virus, downloaded into Neo's cyborgian consciousness. This non-phonic text shatters Neo's experience of self-presence. When the Matrix is viewed as simulation rather than illusion, when the textual-technological production of the Matrix is explored, a different reading can be made. The question, "what is the Matrix?" must be reexamined. It is no longer the case that one can say, as Morpheus does, that the Matrix is a lie and the world of Zion is real, that Neo's true identity is as "the One" true savior of humanity.

On one level, *The Matrix* can certainly be read as an exploration of the paranoia resulting from modern life. Jameson identifies the use of computer technology to understand contemporary psychological and ideological conditions as a characteristic of a genre he terms high-tech paranoia:

> in which the circuits and networks of some putative global computer hookup are narratively mobilized by labyrinthine conspiracies of autonomous but deadly interlocking and competing information agencies in a complexity often beyond the capacity of the normal reading mind. Yet conspiracy theory (and its garish narrative manifestations) must be seen as a degraded attempt—through the figuration of advanced technology—to think the impossible totality of the contemporary world system. (1991, p. 38)

Jameson explains that the paranoid belief in grand plots responds to the postmodern inability to produce a cognitive map of real global conditions. In *The Matrix* these paranoiac elements are heightened, as the enemies are the machines themselves rather than some human agent behind the machines. In short, the film organizes a genuine concern about the effects of technology around this paranoid plot that machines are taking over and, in doing so, consoles our inability to understand the complex interactions of humans and technology in the real world. This complexity is reduced to a single conflict, humans versus machines, which is reduced again to the classic narrative, man versus machine, or more specifically, Neo versus the machine's Agent Smith. However, despite this tendency to reduction in popular entertainment, Jameson notes the value of technology in serving as a "representational shorthand for grasping a network of power and control even more difficult for our minds and imaginations to grasp: the whole new decentered global network of the third stage of capital itself" (p. 38). Many of the central authors of cyberpunk have incorporated explorations of transnational corporate capitalism into their novels, through establishing various corporate entities as antagonists or creating elaborate corporate cultures as the backdrop for narratives.

The Matrix, however, has a different take on this theme. In the absence of human corporations, the machine world itself is presented as a corporate entity. The machine's agents appear in the standard dark-suited, masculine corporate uniform, and the "vampiric" nature of capitalism is literalized in the machine's draining of the human body's electrical power. In an odd literalization of Marx's description of capitalism's interaction with labor as a purely subjective force, here human labor is reduced to its basic bioelectrical form. In return, humans are fed fantasies that keep them content and passive, that is, except for the few anomalies, like Neo, who begin to question the nature of their reality. Here, however, the focus shifts from a global-cultural scale to an embodied-subjective one: rather than focusing on the means of global ideological control, Neo offers insight into the potential implosion of those control mechanisms in the production of the subject. That is, while the techno-ideological fantasies of the Matrix are stable in its Cartesian virtual reality as it is programmed, the intersection of the digital with the body creates a topological-virtual space as digital space folds into subjective space. This shift corresponds with the replacement of Cartesian coordinates with proprioception that I discussed earlier. *The Matrix* does not, cannot, produce an accurate Cartesian-style map of global capitalism, which would appear to be what Jameson is pursuing; however, it may be possible to investigate the multiplicities of proprioceptive navigation that allow us to move through such spaces.

As Massumi has described, Cartesian and topological spaces intersect at a hinge or interface, an assemblage that undertakes the process of intensification between the different levels. In the movement from the digital-geometric production of the Matrix to the experience of the Matrix within the bodies and minds of the attached humans, an implosive process occurs in which digital information is folded into the analogical intensities of the body. After all, the body's senses do not accept digital code as such; instead, the senses register intensities, shifts in sound waves, light waves, pressure, temperature, and so on. The interface with the Matrix is at the base of the skull, so the download bypasses the sensory organs and taps directly into the brain's processing of sensory information. However, the information that the brain receives is also analog; it is bioelectrical. Though the specifics of the technology are not discussed in the film, one must assume that the interfacing technology translates the digital information of the Matrix into bioelectrical, analog information that can be read by the brain. Furthermore, the technology must work both ways; it must be able to translate the brain's biochemical and bioelectrical information into digital information so that the user can interact with the digital environment.

The feasibility of such a technology is not really the issue, though it is not unlike the technology Vannevar Bush imagined interfacing with his typist. In fact, digital information is translated into analog information on a regular basis when MP3 files become audible sound, DVDs become viewable movies, or computer operating systems become graphical user interfaces. The only difference here is that the digital information is being sent directly into the brain rather than through the eyes and ears. Technologically, this is a substantial, perhaps insurmountable, difference. Philosophically, the same principle is at stake in both instances: some interface/hinge must exist to move information between the systems. One does not have to turn to the computer to see this. It is already visible in a simpler digital technology, the book. The book is digital in that its information is coded rather than being transmitted in shifts in intensity. Of course, this information is also stored analogically, in the changes in intensity that make letters visible on the page. The eyes register these shifts but the brain must interpret the symbols. "Through the letters, we directly experience fleeting visionlike sensations, inklings of sound, faint brushes of movement. . . . In the experience of reading, conscious thought, sensation, and all the modalities of perception fold into and out of each other" (Massumi, 2002, p. 139). Massumi's underlying argument here is that it is not possible simply to replace analog experience with digital, as the notion of a Matrix-like virtual reality might suggest. The analog and the digital exist in concert with one another, "though there is always an excess of the analog over the digital, because it perceptually fringes, synesthetically dopplers, umbilically backgrounds, and insensibly recedes to a virtual center immanent at every point along the path" (Massumi, 2002, p. 143). That is, like proprioception, analog experience moves through topological space, shifting and mutating; it is never a fixed location like a digital code. It should also be remembered that it is not only humans that are analog; at their base, computers function by analog shifts in voltage intensities powered by electrical currents. Within Deleuzian-topological spaces all materiality is composed of intensities.

However, the apparent "superiority of the analog," to use Massumi's phrase, does not mean that digital codes cannot come to dominate psychic and social spaces. The cultural dominance of digital information, which creates the exigency for the arguments for embodiment articulated by Hayles and others, inspires the paranoia driving *The Matrix,* but it also lays the foundation for the critique of simulation by theorists such as Baudrillard. Baudrillard's *Simulation and Simulacra* was an obvious inspiration for the film (and, in fact, makes a brief appearance at the beginning of the film). In *The Matrix Revisited,* a documentary on the making of the movie, Keanu Reeves mentions that the Wachowskis required him to read Baudrillard before allowing him to read the script. In Reeves's words, the Wachowskis see Baudrillard's discussion of simulation as an investigation of the decay of meaning (imagine Keanu Reeves explaining Baudrillard—a postmodern moment Baudrillard himself could be proud of). This is conveyed within the Matrix through a preoccupation with distorted reflections (in Morpheus's sunglasses, in rear view mirrors, bent spoons, etc.), images of a decaying city, and a general moral decay among the Matrix's virtual citizens (particularly in comparison with the brave revolutionaries of the Nebuchadnezzar, the rebels' ship, and their distant utopia, Zion).

In a line from the script, though excised from the film itself, Morpheus explains to Neo, that "[a]s in Baudrillard's vision, [his] whole life has been spent inside the map, not the territory" (1998): a line in reference to Baudrillard's "The Precession of Simulacra." Beyond the

Gnostic, messianic, paranoid belief in a secret, hidden reality, beyond Descartes's radical skepticism and hypothetical evil genie, beyond the sophomoric question of "how do we know reality is Real?" lies the problem of simulation. Morpheus misinterprets Baudrillard here: the Matrix is not simulation; it is dissimulation, a lie. Or at least so it seems to Morpheus, who believes that the world of Zion is reality and that Neo is the savior of Zion, the One. However, if one views this from a Baudrillardian perspective, Morpheus's planned revolution makes no sense. One cannot wake up from simulation into reality. Simulation exists because there is no reality, and in a simulated environment, history cannot be propelled forward into a new condition. Revolutions only function within the dialectics of history. Whether the struggle is class-based or between humans and machines, simulated revolutions simply participate within the existing program.

This tension between simulation and revolution extends through the film. In another edited line from the screenplay, this one from Neo's closing speech, he speaks to the "Source," the machines behind the Matrix:

> I believe deep down, we both want this world to change. I believe that the Matrix can remain our cage or it can become our chrysalis, that's what you helped me to understand. That to be free, truly free, you cannot change your cage. You have to change yourself. (Wachowski and Wachowski, 1998)

The revised line in the film is more threatening and promises direct confrontation: "I will show [the humans] a world without you." Neo's unrevised sense of metamorphosis resonates with Baudrillard's belief that

> one must not resist this process by trying to confront the system and destroy it, because this system that is dying from being dispossessed of its death expects nothing but that from us: that we give the system back its death, that we revive it through the negative. (1994, p. 24)

Neo's statement suggests that change might occur within the context of the machine. His own internal transformation demonstrates this: the Matrix can be a chrysalis for exploring new modes of subjectivity.

However, Neo's transformation does not resolve the tension between the competing worldviews surrounding the film. When brought back to life by Trinity's kiss, Neo gains access to the informational patterns beneath the illusory world of the Matrix. The paranoid might say that Neo realizes the Truth about his reality and gains amazing powers through his access to that secret knowledge. The Cartesian, revolutionary, dialectical position sees Neo as a rational mind separable from the illusions of reality that takes command of the Matrix's mode of production and asserts his Will. In a Baudrillardian view, Neo implodes into the cool seductive space of simulation. His power is his objectification, his becoming the "One."

CHOICE AND FREE WILL

However, Erik Davis points to an earlier scene as the mark of transformation. It occurs when Neo returns for the first time to the Matrix after learning its digital nature.

> Realizing that he no longer sustain his normal round of identifications, [Neo] asks Trinity what it all means. "That the Matrix cannot tell you who you are," she responds. If you hit the pause button right there, before the film fills in this space of not-knowing with Neo's emerging identity as a Christ-hero, then you are at the empty heart of the subject. (Davis, 2002, p. 24)

Indeed, as we discover in *The Matrix Reloaded,* a program named the Architect has orchestrated the prophecy of the One and the entire struggle between the machines and the people of Zion. Is this realization of simulation then the secret knowledge that needs to be realized? Is there knowledge that can provide us with heroic agency? Is this when Neo wakes up? If so, then this is simply a return to paranoia.

Hints of this post-paranoiac position appear earlier in *The Matrix Reloaded,* where Neo comes to terms with the role of consciousness in making choices. Philosophically speaking, one of the film's key scenes occurs when Neo questions the Oracle about the significance of her prophetic powers. We learn that the Oracle is not a human trapped in the Matrix, but rather a renegade software program. This is a significant realization, as it suggests that the conflict here is not between humans and machines but rather between instrumental reason, with its limit-case in fascism, and some unrealized alternative, which promises and threatens some post-human future. The Oracle explains that we are not here to make choices but to understand the choices we have already made. Of course, this does not mean that freedom does not exist; only that it is not "ours." This articulation of choice reflects Massumi's description of experiments in cognition: the conscious mind neither initiates nor completes choices. Rather than interpreting this revelation as asking us to understand our own Calvinist predestination, one might view this as an articulation of the preconscious, material, though topological, processes involved in the production of desire, thought, and choice. This suggests that the conscious mind serves a feedback, evaluative, revisionary function, where the interpretation of prior choices ultimately informs future decisions. The conscious awareness of a choice occurs as part of the decision-making process but is not itself that process.

However, this is not a complete answer to Neo's question, which is really about free will. If the Oracle knows what Neo will do, is there any free will in the system? From where does will originate? Once again, one encounters this now classic postmodern question about agency. In *Reloaded* this question comes under investigation in the climatic encounter between Neo and the Architect. The Architect explains that there have been many Zions and many Neos in the past and that they exist for the purpose of "balancing the equation" that underlies the Matrix. The suggestion here is that thought, not simply consciousness, but the entire process, is calculable. Surrounded by screens, Neo is presented with his own multiple potential reactions to the Architect's revelations. This scene dramatizes an underlying problem in Cartesian thought made palpable through cybernetics. In the intersection of Cartesian space and the Cogito, there is a necessary calculation. The mind directs the body through Cartesian space by calculation; thought is calculated and thus calculable. This same calculability allows Turing to conceive of his Universal Machine and the Turing Test and spurs the worries of Wiener and other cyberneticists. But the calculations are incomplete. As in Cartesian philosophy, God must ultimately secure the rational mind's representations; in other words, God serves a foundational, cybernetic function. For the Architect, the One is a mathematical version of this function; for the people of Zion, he is likewise a Christ-like martyr whose myth provides meaning to their lives. However, the narrative denies both of these options in turn for an alternate understanding of consciousness.

Reflecting the Eastern sensibility of the film, Erik Davis compares this alternate consciousness with a test the Sixth Ch'an Patriarch presented to his students.

> Show me your original face. What original face? The face you had before your parents were born. That is, before you tried to find yourself in the Symbolic Matrix of identification and signification, a "before" that does not lie in some foundational past but in the bottomless pit of the passing present. (2002, p. 27)

In other words, consciousness and pure subjectivity must be separated from the identity that gives them meaning within the Symbolic realm. Thinking must be separated from the "I" who names itself the thinker. Of course, identity is always asserting itself as the "thinker of thoughts" in its recognition of the external world. That is, we tend to experience the seat of our identity, that which calls itself "I," as the site of thoughts. However, as I have been discussing in this chapter, thought emerges from a virtual, topological space. The virtual-actual is the "bottomless pit of the passing present" Davis references. However, the thinking process results in the production of identity, creating the "I" who recognizes the thought. In short, though our conscious identity is not the producer of thought, it covers the absence of a clear origin for thought. Identity operates as a simulation that covers the virtual, undecided state from which thought emerges.

The virtual-technological space of the Matrix serves this function on a cultural rather than an individual, conscious level. That is, as the first film suggests, we may be tempted to view the Matrix as an illusion obscuring the reality of the world of Zion, but *Reloaded* reveals that Zion is also part of the program, part of the simulation. From the Architect's view, the digital precedes the material. However, this precision is purely conceptual. It is a perspective built into the Architect's programming. Clearly the machines behind the Matrix, like their human counterparts, are material and rely upon material resources to survive. Indeed, their reliance upon human batteries is the entire premise of the conflict. However, it would be a mistake to presume the material precedes the digital either, even though historically the material world must exist in order for the Matrix to be created. Instead, both material and digital emerge from a less differentiated space. Neo reaches into this space when he wills the destruction of the sentinels in the physical world at the end of *Reloaded*. This leaves us speculating on the nature of the relationship between the embodied consciousness of humans, the hardwired cognition of machines, and the digital world of the Matrix they share.

More generally, our conscious experience of the material is always already a simulation. It is not the world as it "really" is but an apprehension and construction of the world through sensory data, embodied cognition, and technological-symbolic networks. However, our consciousness is also not an illusion. As autopoiesis and distributed cognition would have it, the "real world" is of little use to us, particularly in daily life. We rely upon our successful evolutionary adaptations that filter and process materiality. Most of us would much rather deal with the simulated (inter)face of a computer than try to communicate with the "real" material, voltage exchanges of computer circuitry. Similarly, our reality, including our consciousness, provides us with a pragmatic interface for the world. All of these—the material world, our sensory receptions, and the conscious, simulated environment—emerge from a common topological virtuality into a material existence where no one is more or less real than the others and no one is more or less free-willed than the others. One cannot "wake up" by shifting from one set of recognitions to another.

Machinic Enslavement

Matrix Revolutions does not provide any easy answers to the dilemmas of consciousness and will raised in the *Reloaded*. One can read Neo's final sacrifice as a messianic gift of renewal. In fact, at the end, the people of Zion celebrate him as their prophesized savior. However, the viewer realizes this is a misrecognition. Neo has not sacrificed himself to save Zion. Nor has he surrendered himself to the cool, cynical seduction of his simulated martyrdom as the Matrix's Architect would have it. Instead he taps his own indeterminacy, his own embodied topological becoming, as a means of avoiding the catastrophic implosion of the Matrix. Perhaps this is a move beyond Baudrillard toward a more active Deleuzian subjectivity, or perhaps it is an expression of a Nietzschean *amor fati,* a fatal strategy in Baudrillard's terms, in which the surrender of the ideals of *resentiment*—liberation, justice, freedom, and so on—guides one into the post-human, post-subject environment.

Ultimately, rather than providing an answer, *Revolutions* suggests that Neo is asking the wrong questions when he focuses on issues of choice and destiny. Waking up is not about finding out the Truth, and the imperative for human consciousness is not to have the ability to make choices freely. In the place of these concepts, one uncovers a topological materiality where degrees of freedom exist in various combinations as multiplicities and singularities interact and transform. The danger lies in the imposition of a fascistic logic of control upon these operations; a danger personified in the Agent Smith program. Neo comes to this realization at the beginning of the final film, where he finds himself in the limbo space of a "subway station." Neither in the Matrix nor the physical world, the subway is a way station, a border crossing where machine entities escape the tyranny of efficiency that is the machine world. In the depiction of the refugee family of applications, the Wachowski brothers present oedipalized, bourgeois familial affiliations among machinic consciousnesses. As strange as this may seem, the films have already presented machines with a range of emotions and human traits from Agent Smith's disgust to the Merovingian's lechery to the Oracle's grandmotherly affection. Are such emotions digitally simulated, covering the absence of subjectivity? Or are they *virtual,* emergent phenomena of the material process of becoming conscious? While there is no answer, the films present no suggestion that the programs' emotions are any less real than those of the humans. In this moment, it appears the Neo understands what he must do, that his battle is not against the machines but rather against machinic enslavement.

Deleuze and Guattari define machinic enslavement in relation to the Marxian concept of surplus labor, noting that under the conditions of late capitalism,

> Surplus labor, capitalist organization in its entirety, operates less and less by the striation of space-time corresponding to the physiosocial concept of work. Rather, it is though human alienation through surplus labor were replaced by a generalized "machinic enslavement," such that one may furnish surplus-value without doing any work (children, the retired, the unemployed, television viewers, etc.). Not only

does the user as such tend to become an employee,
but capitalism operates less on a quality of labor than
by a complex qualitative process bringing into play
modes of transportation, urban models, the media,
the entertainment industries, ways of perceiving and
feeling—every semiotic system. (1987, p. 492)

This machinic enslavement addresses everyone, from those human
batteries caught in the Matrix to those of us sitting in theaters watching the films. The viewers, the "real" humans, are batteries too, fueling a transnational economy. However, Deleuze and Guattari's point
is that machines are integrated into this circuit as well once they begin
to produce surplus value, and then "capital reaches its 'absolute' speed,
based on machinic components rather than the human component
of labor" (p. 492). What is at stake, finally, is symbolic behavior itself. The surplus value produced by capitalism is purely symbolic and
spreads from the marketplace across culture. All symbols, every semiotic system, becomes integrated into the capitalist equation. When the
very act of becoming conscious produces such values, consciousness
itself becomes a battery fueling surplus labor to the capitalist system,
just as the human body's regular functioning powers the machine
world of the Matrix.

However, the process is never that simple or complete. The transport into the symbolic realm can never be finalized. What is captured
in the coordinates of a digital-symbolic system is only the trace of consciousness passing. Perhaps this could be enough (to be profitable), but
it is not enough for the logic of machinic enslavement. The terminal
violence of machinic enslavement results from its impetus to translate
everything into its logic. What happens here, rather than an ongoing
process of becoming conscious, is a continual repetition of the same.
This desire for a repetition of the same is dramatized in the *Matrix*
trilogy in Agent Smith's ability to replicate himself. Ultimately, in the
final conflict, Neo faces a Smith who has transformed all the beings of
the Matrix into Smith copies. Deleuze and Guattari find this suicidal
impulse at the heart of fascism. Smith's desire to transform everyone
into versions of himself mimics the Nazist goal of pure racial identity.
The Nazi desires to make everyone the same, to match the body to the
symbol of the body, and to eliminate others. But no body can match
the symbol. Smith desires not only the destruction of the Matrix, but

the destruction of the human and machine worlds as well, which logically includes himself.

For Deleuze and Guattari, fascism is the result of the State's attempt to envelop topological space, to control what everything *becomes*. All the mechanisms of machinic enslavement, the production
and capture of a variety of affects and symbolic surplus values constitute a mode of fascism as they operate within the smooth spaces of desire. In other words, everything from military campaigns to television
entertainment, ethnic cleansing to educational toys, becomes a mode
of fascism. While this may seem overstated, Brian Massumi notes,

> There is nothing extraordinary about fascism. It is
> normality to the extreme, an exacerbation of the con-
> stituent tension of identity, an acceleration of the vis-
> cous actual-virtual circuit peculiar to the process of
> social induction. Fascism is social Reason, and Rea-
> son is its own revenge. (1992, p. 117)

Smith, the replication of Smiths, represents the fascist in all of us, what
we become within the symbolic logic of Reason, but what in fact we
can never become except through accepting the pure destructive and
ultimately suicidal drive of fascism: to become what we believe is our
"true" self through the destruction of our bodies, only to discover that
the "true" self is merely a seductive simulation, a marketing ploy.

If one thinks of cyberpunk as Jameson does, as an attempt to deal
with the "sublime" encounter with global technocapitalism, then the
Matrix emerges as a surprisingly effective map. The map begins with
the paranoid, ideological conflict between the "master" machine civilization and the "slave" human culture. Neo plays the messianic role
for them both. In their conflict, both struggle to control the topological, virtual space between the digital world of the Matrix and the
embodied, material world. However, this virtual space emits two attractors: one is fascistic, represented by Agent Smith; the other, represented by Neo, is mutative. In their climactic battle, Smith's attempt
to assimilate Neo causes both their deaths, with the apparent result
that the Matrix is saved. But this is a strange victory. Neo has sacrificed himself to save the Matrix and to win peace between Zion and
the Source, but what can be made of such a peace? What, if any, understanding can ever be built between the humans and machines? In
Revolutions's conclusion, the Oracle and the Architect meet in a park

like two, ex-Cold War warriors, East and West. Neither expects the peace to last. The only optimistic answer here is that Neo does not sacrifice himself for the humans but for the Matrix, for the border zone where machine, body, and symbol collide. More pessimistic: this is a final reassertion of Baudrillardian simulation. The machines do not create the simulation. This would be a paranoid claim. Simulation is a condition under which both humans and machines operate. To imagine machinic conscious as somehow free of the problems of human conscious is to return once again to the Cartesian mind, free of the influences of the material world. Consciousness, regardless of its embodied form, requires symbolic behavior and the misrecognition of the self that is identity. None of us understands who we are. Even the Oracle cannot see beyond decisions she fails to understand. Consciousness is part of thinking, part of the negentropic, nomadic function of virtual space. Thought may be put to the service of the state, as it is when it becomes identity, and it may be turned to fascism. However, thoughts, as the "products" of thinking, are traces of a process that is only partly symbolic. Thus consciousness, with its reason and its Cartesian world, may be a simulation of the world, but beneath it exists a virtual, topological space that is neither real nor simulated from which the world we consciously inhabit emerges.

Virtually Autonomous

The Matrix trilogy resonates with the issues raised by the digital technologies that produced it. As with Kittler's deconstruction of media technologies discussed in the previous chapter, the films only serve to deepen the problem of human subjectivity. However, it is also possible to read Kittler in conjunction with Massumi's analysis of the digital and analog. As Massumi argues, the digital's access to the virtual occurs only through its intersection with the analog, such as at the point where it interfaces with human senses. In this space, there is a hinge into topological space. Kittler points to an additional analog space in the hardware itself. As such, the digital is enveloped by the analog, which remains in excess of digital-computational power. In the end, the journey through the digital is perhaps longer than expected, the passage from digital to virtual passing through the uncertain terrain of the analog. New media presents the interpenetration of information and materiality, with its multiple resultant effects processing and replication upon an imaginary self already uncannily doubled by film.

Paranoia is understandable. However, the digital is enveloped by the analog. As exemplified in Neo, the digital must pass into the analog, must mutate into affect, to enter the body. In part, this is Manovich's transcoding, but there is more taking place than the translation into cultural values; this is an embodied, sensory experience first and foremost. But before the intense VR user interface of the Matrix can pass into Neo's senses, it must first descend into the analog waves of silicon hardware. The pro*gram* (echoing Derrida's exploration of the gram) is written to insert some determinacy or control in the otherwise indeterminate analog interface between human and machine. The program is intended to produce the feeling of self-presence within the Matrix, but it leaves a trace, an uncanny, perhaps even schizophrenic, sensation that one is other than oneself. Neo articulates this sensation in a single question, "what is the Matrix?" In this question is the potential for autonomy. In Neo's case, that autonomy arises through the shock of being woken from the Matrix. The paranoid response to Neo's "awakening" is a messiah-complex, or what Freud terms an "omnipotence of thoughts" (1996, p. 165). However, one might reject the notion that in VR one will be able to achieve one's desires with a thought. Instead, like Neo, one comes to recognize autonomy as occurring through interactions with the machine in the circuit between the digital and analog.

While the process of cognition articulated within the virtual-actual may not provide us with the comfortable, albeit illusory, notions of rational, free-willed thought native to humanism, they manage to incorporate the operation of the body, the unconscious, and the material world, including technology, into the production of thought without falling into the paranoia of mind control or suggesting that subjects are entirely without agency. Ultimately, what we find instead is a continuous environment composed of differentiating, mutating multiplicities that give rise to our bodies and our thoughts. Our consciousness is part of this system. It is not responsible for it. It is not the "author" of thought or volition. However, neither do external forces determine our consciousness. Instead, thoughts and consciousness and subjectivity unfold through the processes of multiplicities, in a continual process of becoming. In this way, the virtual-actual provides a philosophical point of departure for interacting with media and information networks in a manner that does not force us to choose between human will and computer control.

7 Virtual Composition

At the outset of the previous chapter and earlier in the introduction, I argued that contemporary theories of embodied and distributed cognition, built upon developments in media composition and information networks, have significant implications for rhetoric and composition. Furthermore, I have suggested that these same processes are already transforming both compositional processes and the university culture in which we work. The first six chapters have worked to establish a material, historical, and theoretical context for these transformations. In this chapter, I now turn specifically to describe how the two virtuals challenge and reshape our conventional notions of authorship and composition. Fundamentally, this reshaping is a matter of understanding writing as a topological, cognitive process of unfolding that integrates multiplicities of networked technologies into the production of media. The result is a compositional process that brings into question values of intellectual property (and the properties of intellectual work) foundational to a print-based marketplace of ideas, including both copyright and plagiarism. Copyright and plagiarism may seem tangential to the issues of new media rhetoric I have discussed here, but their centrality in public discourses regarding composition and technology requires that they be addressed. That is, since copyright and plagiarism are the primary cultural domains where new media compositional practices are being defined, they are issues that cannot be ignored. The questions raised by the virtual compositional practice I will describe not only have implications for media corporations waging copyright battles with their own consumers but also for our classroom and scholarly work, which are founded upon the same values of originality and authorial ownership.

Copyright began formally in England in 1710 with the Statute of Anne, nearly 250 years after the invention of the printing press. In the period prior to the printing press, the copying of texts was labor intensive. In addition, since few copies of most books existed, control over copies could be exercised by controlling access to the few significant libraries. Gutenberg's invention did not cause an immediate widespread effect as the number of printing presses grew slowly. In addition in England, access to printing was controlled through the government and the printing guild. During this time, the right to make copies and ownership over copies was attributed to publishers, not authors. It was only with the 1710 Statute that authors were given copyright. Even then, it took several decades of common law decisions to establish this right firmly. This law formed the basis of modern copyright law in the United States. Significantly, the Statute did not extend copyright privileges in perpetuity but rather for a limited period of time (14 years, extendable an additional 14 years if the author were still alive). Quite clearly, the proclaimed purpose of copyright was then, as it is now, to enable the commercialization of intellectual labor. However, as Lawrence Lessig (2004) points out, the commercial culture and intellectual property created by this law has traditionally been situated in a broader "free culture," in which citizens tell stories, sing songs, tape-record television and music, without being perceived as infringing upon commercial culture. Copyright was created to protect commercial enterprise, and the activities of free culture were not perceived as a threat to that enterprise. Until now. As Lessig argues,

> for the first time in our tradition, the ordinary ways in which individuals create and share culture fall within the reach of the regulation of the law, which has expanded to draw within its control a vast amount of culture and creativity that it never reached before. (2004, p. 8)

Lessig's observation about copyright law complements the more general observation, made by Fredric Jameson and others, that late capitalism is typified in part by the expansion of a capitalist logic of marketplace exchange to all sectors of a culture. The law insists that everything I write is copyrighted. I need not take any action for my work to become my property. On the contrary, if I wish to not copyright my work and to make those wishes known to others, I would have to advertise this fact. Lessig's organization, Creative Commons (creativecommons.org), helps writers, artists, and others share their work by quickly producing legal language that defines which rights the author/owner wishes to retain. In the words of the organization, "some rights reserved." While Creative Commons is helpful and potentially revolutionary in creating a forum for the sharing of intellectual work, it does not alter the fundamental shift in the cultural condition of composition. All compositions are presumed to be commercial properties; they all have a putative exchange value; and hence they are all both protected by copyright and potentially liable for copyright infringement. While the presumption of copyright might be viewed as a protection, for most compositions, from garage band mixtapes to first-year composition essays to many academic essays and books, there is little, if any, practical commercial value. Instead, copyright simply becomes a form of commercial censorship, restricting the ability of citizens to make free use of their own culture for noncommercial ends. In this respect, copyright laws have come full circle, to the purposes to which they were put by the Council of the Star Chamber in sixteenth-century England, when proto-copyright laws were used to prevent the publication of heretical works (Patry, 2000).

Fundamentally, the premise of intellectual property is that intellectual works contain original material that is the product of the author's creativity. In a sense, the text is a property of the mind and viewed as both an extension and exteriorization of private, individual thought; as I discussed in Chapter 2, this articulation of the relationship between thought and writing comes directly from Plato. Copyright then is the commodification of thought. The same premise is at work in our determinations of plagiarism, where again the expectation is that unless information is cited, it is the product of the author's creativity *or* common knowledge. The last sentence would be an example of the latter; no one would expect me to cite where I learned what plagiarism is. However, some teachers might expect their first-year composition students to make such a citation. The point is that common knowledge is relative to the author and the community in which s/he writes. A similar gray area exists in copyright where, in addition to criminalizing the wholesale copying of intellectual property, there is a prohibition against *derivative* works. As Lessig points out, there is a long history of artistic accomplishment that might be identified as derivative works. He calls this "Walt Disney creativity" (and does so ironically, as he contends that Disney's desire to protect its intellectual property, Mickey Mouse in particular, is a primary influence in contemporary copyright law). Clearly Disney draws on works in the public domain, like fairy tales, much like Shakespeare derived many of his plays from existing works. Lessig terms this "Rip, mix, and burn," and suggests, "there are some who would say that there is no creativity except this kind" (2004, p. 24). I would take this one step farther and suggest that there is no cognition except this kind. Our thoughts are not a site of creation or originality, except in the sense that one might pick any point in a recursive process and argue that it is the beginning of something. However, once this distributed cognitive process is acknowledged, we can no longer claim ownership over thought or text on the basis of originality. This does not mean that individuals do not labor to produce media for which, at least within our current marketplace system, they deserve recompense. It simply means that we need a better understanding of the compositional process on which to base exchange, whether in the marketplace or the classroom.

This chapter elaborates on the compositional process Lessig terms *rip, mix,* and *burn.* The terms are direct references to the practices of copying and mixing music. One "rips" music from its original context (e.g., on a CD you bought at a store), "mixes" it with other content, and then "burns" it onto another CD as an "original" composition. The topological unfolding of thought is a similar process in which cognitive content is "ripped" from materiality via sensory organs, "mixed" with other content including memory, and "burned" into language at the conscious level. Much like the selection process in which one chooses songs to rip for mixing onto a CD, sensory information is also selective, though obviously not consciously selective. That is, our sensory organs pick up a certain band of light and sound; our attention is brought to some objects and not others. In this chapter, I am going to argue that the compositional process, like the topological thought process in which it participates *and* like the technological process of rip, mix, and burn in which it *also* participates, functions in a similar way. I am then going to return to this issue of copyright and plagiarism and reinterpret these concerns from this new perspective on composition.

While rip, mix, and burn refer specifically to the production and dissemination of computer music files, here I will explore these as more abstract processes. Ripping is a process of copying, quoting, or citing. It is the slicing of material from one context and its insertion into another. As I will discuss, this process creates conditions for the spread of *contagions;* that is, by ripping two or more pieces of media open and inserting them into one another, one creates the possibility for information to flow from one into the other causing mutation. This is akin to the process by which multiplicities mutate, which I discussed in the previous chapter. In this way, ripping leads into mixing, whereby the contagion spreads from the immediate site of the rip through the intersecting media. This *proliferation* typifies the mixing process as the multiplicities mutate and unfold in a fractal-like pattern. Eventually this proliferation slows down and the multiplicity returns to a relatively stable state; the mixing is done. At this stage, the composition is burned. The burning process is one of *involution*, that is, one both of shrinking but also involvement. Literally, the file size shrinks through a process of data compression. Also the burned file can be made accessible on the informational network, where the process may be reiterated. It is certainly possible to view the burned file as a finished product that might be copyrighted. However, technically the process can be stopped at any moment and the existing text copyrighted; notes I write on a cocktail napkin are copyrighted. In compositional terms, the burned file is simply a site for ripping in an ongoing iterative process.

In the next three sections I examine these compositional processes—ripping, mixing, and burning—and their associated effects/affects—contagion, proliferation, and involution. Specifically, I take up Gregory Ulmer's use of the saprophyte (or mushroom) as a mechanism of ripping-contagion, Deleuze and Guattari's rhizome as mixing-proliferation, and Derrida's hérrison (or hedgehog) as burning-involution. By linking these concepts the text articulates intersections between technical and theoretical discourses, allowing their singular affects to spread through one another, resulting in a mutated composition: that is, the text pursues its own ripping, mixing, and burning.

The compositional process I am describing is the same whether one is producing an experimental video or an office memo. It is not a deterministic process and is completely abstracted from the content of the composition, much like the multiplicities I described in the previous chapter are separate from the materiality that unfolds from them. That is, just as a singularity that draws materiality into states of lowest energy might unfold both soap bubbles and salt crystals, these compositional processes might unfold, in a non-deterministic way, into a wide range of media depending upon the other materials and multiplicities with which they intersect in the compositional process. That said, understanding the operation of these multiplicities opens the opportunity to engage strategically with their affects. In addition, this compositional process of ripping, mixing, and burning allows us to rethink how we teach composition and how we might incorporate new media into it.

RIPPING.CONTAGION.MUSHROOMS

The uncertainty of the effects of mushrooms is well known. One mushroom of a certain variety might be benign while another of the same variety could be poisonous. In a biological ecology, the mushroom serves to break down certain complex structures (such as trees) that cannot be consumed by many other biological organisms. That is, the mushroom constitutes a certain actualization of trees. A tree might become a fire, a log house, furniture, or a book; it might also become fodder for mushrooms. Mushrooms help to break down the wood so that it might fertilize other plants. In agricultural environments, biological saprophytes are grown under careful conditions to produce benign mushrooms such as those found in supermarkets. In the wild, however, some mushrooms might kill you. Or, like psychedelic mushrooms, might produce ineffable effects. In his essay, "The Object of Post-Criticism," Ulmer employs the concept of the saprophyte or mushroom to explore how unpredictable intensities accrete within media. In doing so, he seeks to invent a new critical, composition approach based on the practice of quotation.

Much like the mushroom, the compositional saprophyte breaks down (digests, interprets, or actualizes) textual matter. That is, it injects itself into an existing composition and rips material from it, digesting the content for its own uses. In this conceptual space, the dangers associated with the biological saprophyte relate to the problem of translation, precisely the difficulty of the *pharmakon*. As Ulmer notes, "the mushroom turns out to be the best emblem yet for the '*pharmakon*,' modeling what Derrida calls (by analogy) 'undecidables' (directed against all conceptual, classifying systems)" (1983, p. 104). Ulmer employs this indeterminacy to oppose unproblematic translation or exchange. Texts are interconnected; clearly they are references for one another in countless ways. In their hyperconnectivity, they approach a virtual and unmapped space. However, at the site of intersection between two texts, at the point of quotation, it becomes possible to study the process of exchange. Unlike the exchanges of traditional translation, here there are no fixed rates. Instead, these exchanges are gifts, information offered to the other with the ethical awareness of an always-already existing interdependency. Ripping files requires that files be openly shared across a network. It works best when there are few, if any, caveats on sharing, beyond perhaps asking that new material also be made accessible. In the forest, trees and mushrooms share points of connection that allow one to flow into the other. Similarly, electronic files share formatting information, which allows entry into their data, the mixing of data, and the composition of new media. Of course, there are limits to this mixing. One cannot easily transform an image into a music file (though such compositions are not impossible). There are related common practices that shape the mixing of print compositions. Genre, for example: the inclusion of research material in a work of fiction is different from that of an academic essay. Nevertheless, the process of ripping participates in the unfolding of the composition.

Of course, ripping is anathema to the marketplace-factory logic of the traditional classroom, which insists upon consistent interpretation and exchange (for grades) and thus cannot accept the notion of ripping from a shared collection of data, without a payment being made, without an acknowledgement of debt (a citation). In technical terms, university network administrators go to great lengths to ensure files are not shared by students and are not ripped from the network. Ripping is practically the definition of plagiarism. Yet, ripping is also integral to the composition process and thus unavoidable. Fortunately, writers can rip much from non-proprietary sources: sensory information and memory for example. In addition, there is the indeterminable pool of "common knowledge," to which one appears to gain greater access with greater education. In copyright terms there is also public domain, but even this material is subject to plagiarism. Indeed, not only are the copyrightable features of a text subject to plagiarism but the alleged information contained "within" the text, however represented, must also be cited. That is, one must acknowledge a debt to a text for information produced through embodied cognitive processes that were in some way connected to the experience of interfacing with this text. Following this logically, what sentence would not be indebted to other, indeed all, media spinning out indeterminably in a web of interconnection? Needless to say an arbitrary limit is placed on this obligation.

However, while the limit is arbitrary and shifts depending on author and context, it is not without purpose. Specifically, identifying the problems of copyright infringement and plagiarism, a remedy of payment or indebtedness/citation, establishes a discourse that can control and occlude the operation of ripping as composition, an operation that opens onto the aporia of symbolic behavior, cognition, and the impossibility of intellectual property. That is, establishing a focus on the problems of plagiarism (e.g., how to catch plagiarizers or stop illegal file-sharing) occludes the more intractable issues of originality, creativity, and the compositional process. Secondly, the limitation of ripping serves as an attempt to limit the dangers of the contagions spread through the ripping process that mutate media and dislodge the notion of authorial originality and control. As John Logie observes, since composition courses are the primary place where students learn about the integration of others' work into their own compositions, "the principles embedded in the pedagogies of composition classrooms are likely at the heart of most college graduates' perceptions of copyright and intellectual property" (2006, p. 131). Logie argues that first-year composition's hyper-concern with plagiarism undertakes ideological work in the name of a decidedly protectionist perspective on the issues of authorship and creativity.

Even when the proper citing procedures are observed, a quotation's mutative potential remains. This is fortunate since the contagious potential of ripping provides composition its creative energy. The danger of digesting the quotation is the same as that of eating the mushroom: one never can know with certainty that it isn't poison. Each new rip can include unforeseen implications for the composition. That is, even with the best security systems, errors persist and viruses proliferate, though they might not always be visible. As Derrida writes,

> It is the sustained, discrete violence of an incision that is not apparent in the thickness of the text, a calculated insemination of the proliferating allogene through which the two texts are transformed, deform each other, contaminate each other's content, tend at times to reject each other, or pass elliptically one into the other and become regenerated in the repetition, along the edges of an overcast seam. Each grafted text continues to radiate back toward the site of its

removal, transforming that too, as it affects the new
territory. (1981, p. 355)

The allogene, like the mushroom, provokes a reaction in the text. Each
additional graft both remarks the territory of the text and its periph-
eral traces and returns back upon the previous text to rewrite that as
well. The montage may appear seamless as a result of a careful editorial, rhetorical process, but one can still uncover the edges between the
grafts. It is at those edges, the asymptotic approach of one text to another, that one finds the growth of saprophytes: deforming, distorting
feedback that connect textual structures with the larger media ecology. Conventionally, quotations provide a largely nutritionless (con-
tentless) flavoring. They are "supportive" material, subsumed with the
governing logic of the text, under the author's control. Seen from this
compositional process, however, ripping initiates a mutative unfolding
of the text as the "allogenes," the affective energy, of the rip spreads
through the emerging media composition.

MIXING

As those allogenes recede from the point of grafting, they come to
encounter other rips within the media composition. Here the process
of mixing begins. The mix is not a melting pot. A music mix does
not devolve to a continuous monotone. The rips maintain their het-
erogeneity while establishing relational points between one another.
In musical terms, these relations might reflect intersecting rhythms
or tones, themes or melodies, instrumentation or vocals, and so on.
Images might share perspective, hue, saturation, lighting, subject matter, or mood. Of course, points might be established across media as
well, as happens regularly on a website. Sometimes those connections
reflect well-defined, ideological connections, like an American flag
on a patriotic website or discursive conventions, like photojournalistic
images of an event covered in an adjacent news article. Connections
might be of a more personal, but still culturally recognizable, indeed
clichéd, dimension, like a mix of love songs handed from one lover to
another. As I suggested above, the mixing of media may rely upon formal relationships. However, these only represent potential apprehensions of mixing, modes by which the mixing process is put to cultural
work. None are necessary constituents of the mixing process itself.

Instead, the mix articulates the heterogeneous unfolding of a topological space. This unfolding points to one of Deleuze and Guattari's most recognizable concepts, the rhizome. Where the saprophyte articulates one point of interface, the rhizome maps the emergence of a constellation of interfaces, like mushrooms proliferating across the forest floor. As Deleuze and Guattari explain, our understanding of the rhizome has been diminished by the predominance of arboreal thinking, the classificatory logic that seeks to limit the potential of media and information mixing together. However, rhizomatic and arboreal thinking are not oppositional any more than topological and Cartesian geometry are opposition. Instead the rhizomatic incorporates the arboreal as one mode of connectivity. The tree establishes one pattern of growth, but the mushroom grows on the tree and spreads its spores out across the forest. Once one goes in search of saprophytes, they are, like mushrooms in the forest, easy to find. Similarly, once one seeks out rhizomatic connectivity and patterns, one can witness their unfolding in almost any situation. If mixing describes the process by which ripped material comes together, the rhizome describes the mode of connectivity, with the result being the proliferation of contagious material . . . infectious beats on the music mix.

With the rhizome, the saprophytes' interconnectivity becomes hyperconnectivity:

> there is no longer a tripartite division between a field of reality (the world) and a field of representation (the book) and a field of subjectivity (the author). Rather, an assemblage establishes connections between certain multiplicities drawn from each of these orders, so that a book has no sequel nor the world as its object nor one or several authors as its subject. (Deleuze and Guattari, 1987, p. 23)

As with the translation between languages, in conventional rhetoric there exist standards and protocols for establishing relations between these fields. There are firm borders: where one ends another begins, even though there may be a certain circularity so that the world informs the author who produces the book that depicts the world, etc. Though obviously in this formula both the author and book are a part of the world, they exist as separate, separable objects. And the book, as an act of representation, makes more or less accurate statements about the world; it takes the world as its model. However, since the rhizome has no beginning or end, it necessarily results in different relationships between material, subjective, and textual machines. The rhizomatic approach to writing can be difficult: "it's not easy to see things in the middle, rather than looking down on them from above or up at them from below, or from left to right or right to left: try it, you'll see that everything changes" (Deleuze and Guattari 1987, p. 23). From this perspective one is always already in the middle.

The association of the rhizome with new media is a common one, as the hyperlink suggested the non-linear quality of the rhizome. However, the argument was always less convincing in practice than in theory. That is, if one visits popular websites such as Amazon or CNN, one will find a primarily arboreal logic governing connectivity. And while, as I have noted, arboreal logic is one form of connectivity that may emerge from a rhizomatic mix, it certainly does not address the potentials raised in theories of hypertext. On such sites, information is organized and linked by familiar categories—books, music, videos or national news, international news, sports, and so on. The mixing of media (image and text) on each individual page is similarly arboreal in its predictability. That said, the more recent emergence and growing popularity of XML and database technologies offer some interesting rhizomatic possibilities, in particular with the use of free-form tagging on websites such as del.icio.us and flickr.com.

Del.icio.us is a website that permits what it terms "social bookmarking." At its base, the site allows users to share Web bookmarks with one another. When a user enters a new bookmark, s/he includes a URL, a brief description, and a series of "tags," which s/he believes describe the site. As such, if I were to bookmark my own blog, I might use the tags "blog," "new media," "rhetoric," and "higher education." These free-form tags are then searchable in the database. Thus, for example, I could look for all the websites tagged with new media and blog or new media and rhetoric. I could then look at one of those sites and see what other tags other users used to describe those sites. I can also see tags the computer recognizes as commonly associated with the ones I'm searching. For example, new media might be associated with Web design. That is, sites that users commonly tagged with the term new media were also commonly tagged with the term *Web design*. Flickr.com offers a similar capability for sharing photos, except in this case one is tagging images rather than bookmarks. The result of this is an unfolding rhizomatic web of interconnectivity. Undoubtedly, just as with multiplicities, there are a range of singularities that might be at play, drawing users to employ common tags or bookmark similar sites. Some of these singularities might have to do with current events (which cause people to look for, and bookmark, common websites for common reasons) or with the selection process that creates the community of del.icio.us users (which might tend to include a disproportionate number of particularly Web-savvy users who in turn may disproportionately represent a particular demographic). It would be an error to imagine that the mixes that form rhizomes are free of ideology. Instead, they result in an indeterminate unfolding of ideological forces.

As Clay Shirky (2005) writes, tagging suggests an alternate ontology than conventional cataloguing. Arboreal, conventional catalogues, like those in libraries, assume a universal perspective, in which all subjects may be incorporated. However, not all the subjects constructed for the library cataloguing system in the mid-twentieth century continue to be appropriate. For example, what is one to do now with a category like "East Germany"? Shirky notes two significant aspects of catalogues that make them inappropriate for understanding Web content, both of which are addressed by tagging. First, cataloguing systems are not designed to organize content but to organize books (in which the content is published). As physical objects, books can only be organized in one way (a book can only be in one place in a library). Electronic files can be organized on the fly. Though they also may have only a single physical address, that address is not significant in determining how the files can be organized for viewing. It is as if the library books could fly off their shelves and appear before a user in any order the user wished. Second, and more importantly, catalogues are *ad hoc* systems of organization; cataloguers must try to approximate what the future content to be catalogued will be, as well as the manner in which users will search for the material. The success with which library cataloguers have been able to do the latter is in inverse proportion to the amount of library skills instruction students require. Tagging, on the other hand, is an organic *post hoc* method: tags develop with use.

I am not interested here in arguing the pros and cons of different cataloguing systems. However, Shirky's account of tagging's ontology resonates with my earlier discussion of topological ontologies: rather than assuming objects have "essences" (which become catalogue subjects), objects unfold and their traits of expression become potential sites for connection. This mixing of heterogeneous objects in a conductive manner (where one idea conducts you to the next) is, after all, at the root of com-positioning, meaning literally to position adjacently. Undoubtedly objects can obey some logical rule in their positioning, or some set of discursive expectations, but those behaviors would be secondary to composing itself, which points to a more general practice of connectivity. Beginning with the practice of ripping, it should already be apparent that a composition incorporates heterogeneous material; as such, the experience of a "unified" or "logical" composition is an ideological one achieved through rhetorical means. That is not to say that being unified or logical are "bad" qualities of writing. I am making some effort to be unified and logical here; these are effectively necessary qualities of texts under the ideological and discursive conditions in which I am writing. Rather than making a judgment, I am simply observing that the composition process of ripping indicates that all texts acquire their apparent unity through a process of occlusion, which, of course, becomes the basis for deconstruction—uncovering the discontinuity of a text and using it as a basis to destabilize a text's argument.

BURNING

With ripping and mixing one already has a significant part of the compositional process. Information is ripped from the network of distributed cognition (media, sensory information, memory, etc.). As these rips emerge through cognitive processes into consciousness, they spread their affects, their contagion, as thought unfolds. The rips, or their ripples, intersect one another, as tagged points of conduction, and form a rhizomatic, compositional network. They mix together to produce a heterogeneous accumulation of interconnected media. However, I have yet to account for the final part of the process, burning. As I noted earlier, in the practice of producing a mix of music on a CD (from which the phrase "rip, mix, and burn" comes), burning is the step in which the music files are recorded onto the CD so that the files can be shared. Whereas a working media file, whether a piece of music or video or image, keeps the various rips separate (in layers for example in *Photoshop*) so that those pieces can be individually edited, a burned file flattens the layers. This is analogous with the difference between a printed paper turned in for a class and the word-processing file from which the paper came. Before the file is burned or printed, the compositional process is ongoing; changes might still be made. After burning, changes might still be made to the working media file, but they would have to be re-burned.

Generally speaking, in technical terms, a burned file is a compression of the working media file. That is, the file size is literally smaller. Though this is not always the case, particularly when producing for the Web (where large files mean longer download times), one makes an effort to reduce file size as much as practically possible. Obviously this means they contain less information than working media files. This process of "lossy compression" means that noise is added into a file as information is removed. For example, a GIF image reduces file size by limiting the number of colors used to build the image; the smaller the palette, the smaller the file. However, reducing the number of colors results in noise, in that areas of an image that were once differentiated now become the same. Making choices about compression is always simultaneously a matter of cybernetics, rhetoric, and aesthetics: how much information can be removed, how much noise can be added, before the message becomes unintelligible? Cybernetics might provide us with a mathematical answer. Here, however, the burning process is part of composition; the purpose of burning is not to create a file equivalent to the unburned file, or even necessarily to approximate it, but to be other than the unburned file, to mutate.

Burned files are generally not as easily editable as unburned ones: note, for example, the difference between editing a *Word* document and a printed essay or a PDF file. However, while the burned file is not as easily editable, it is far more accessible via a network. This accessibility is not only a result of its compression but is, in fact, the purpose of burning. For example, "burning" (though that's not the term conventionally used) a *Photoshop* document (a PSD file) as a JPG image file allows that file to be viewed via a Web browser and makes the image accessible to users who may not own *Photoshop*. JPG files—ripped, mixed, and burned files in their own right—can then become part of other compositions: websites, *PowerPoint* slideshows, print documents, and other multimedia. As composition is an iterative process, there is no endpoint. By habit we might view burned files as final products, as these are the ones we typically look to exchange (for grades or tenure or money). However, within the context of composition, burned objects are simply the site of ripping; compressions are simultaneously rips as well. In effect, in the process of burning, information is ripped from the mixed media file into a new composition, with which the working media file maintains a rhizomatic connection.

Analogous to the compression of data in the burning of media files is the compression of sensory data entering the brain and the compression of data in our cognitive processing of texts and other media. This compression is recognizable in the writing process. As one writes, words appear on the screen or page. There is no simple way to separate the articulation of particular words from other parts of the cognitive process of composition; that is, the process is iterative and recursive in each moment. Each event in writing, each word, emerges from a rhizomatic network of proliferating, contagious affects produced from data ripped from the network. That data enters cognition through a process of compression but then unfolds, spreading outward with potential. Each word then is a burning: the apprehension and compression of a topological event of affective unfolding. As compression, each word is a noisy, partial capture. This is not "error," nor is it a problem with writing to be solved or avoided. It is instead an integral part of composition, which allows for the transmission of data across the network. Who would want or need to have access to the layers of thought that are compressed into each word? Only one who imagined that clear and distinct thoughts appear from nothingness in a final, unproblematic form could also imagine that a language could exist to communicate such thoughts. However, our minds do not function in this way and neither does our language, which is obviously an integrated part of cognition.

If ripping spreads contagion with indeterminate effects (like eating a strange mushroom), and mixing proliferates that contagion along a rhizomatic network, then burning engenders a process of involution, an inward turning and shrinking, much like Derrida's *hérrison* (hedgehog) balling up defensively. Derrida presents this concept in an exploration of poetry. While poetry might seem distant from a conversation on ripping, mixing, and burning, Derrida's approach to poetry raises a common issue in his work, translation. Peggy Kamuf notes

> the risk of this loss in crossing over from one language to another, or already in the transfer into any language at all, causes the *hérrison* to roll itself into a ball in the middle of the road and bristle its spines

> . . . If indeed the poetic bristles with difficulty, this
> very mechanism of turning in on itself for protec-
> tion from the rush of traffic is also what exposes it to
> being rubbed out. (1991, p. 221)

Technically, burning is a translation from one file format into another.
However, in my broader use of the term here as a compositional process, burning is the transfer into language. As such, it is a point where
the indeterminate, virtual topology of thought becomes actualized as
specific words. This is an involution, a compression, an *in*folding of
possibility.

The *hérrison*'s involution is also a protective gesture, a resistance to
the gesture of determination, of the reduction of possibility. Of course,
as Derrida points out, on the highway of translation, the gesture is an
ill-fated one: the machines of translation will come along soon enough
and flatten possibility. Nevertheless, here Derrida insists is where one
finds poetry, turned inward and unaware of its imminent demise, and
that, as such, one must resist the impulse to translate the poem; one
must "not let the *hérrison* be led back into the circus or menagerie of
poiesis" (1991, p. 233). Instead he looks to the poem as

> a certain passion of the singular mark, the signature
> that repeats its dispersion, each time beyond the *logos,*
> a human, barely domestic, not reappropriable into the
> family of the subject: a converted animal, rolled up in
> a ball, turned toward the other and toward itself, in
> sum, a thing. (1991, p. 235)

In this sense, the process of involution might be separated from the
process of translation or interpretation. As I mentioned before, burning files alters them and makes them accessible in a variety of applications. In this sense, it makes them available for translation into a
new setting. However, one cannot imagine burning as a transparent
process that leaves the file unaltered or opens its "truth" for everyone
to see. At the same time, involution is unavoidable. As Derrida suggests, all one might do is approach the poem as singular, as "a thing."
In connecting to this thing, the compositional process begins anew:
another connection, another contamination.

ELECTRACY: CREATIVE AFFECTS

Ripping, mixing, and burning present a topological approach to composition in which one can articulate a process, replete with mechanisms, but do so without reducing writing to a discrete set of practices. That is, unlike invention, arrangement, and revision, ripping, mixing, and burning are not steps, not even recursive steps. Nor are they deterministic in their products in the sense that invention is where ideas are produced, arrangement is where those ideas are organized, and revision is where "correction" or clarification occurs. Instead, they describe the unfolding, the composition, of thought as it moves from a virtual, undecided state and becomes articulated in the conscious as language (an unfolding that includes the material, technological act of writing). Gregory Ulmer's "textbook," *Internet Invention: From Literacy to Electracy* (2003), pursues the com-positioning of a multiplicity of material-symbolic things, ripped, mixed, and burned into a heterogeneous rhizome of connectivity. I place textbook under question here, since the text, while marketed by the publishers as a textbook, does not serve the traditional functions. It is instead a nomadic, hypertextual production (despite its printed form) filled with the esoteric knowledge (i.e., theory) usually reserved for "experts" only. Ulmer's text extends on the theme of navigation by relating an anecdote regarding Albert Einstein. At the age of eight, Einstein received the gift of a magnetic compass. The memory of this gift was forever vivid for him, as "in retrospect [he] recognized the symbolic value of the compass gift since he of all people became the one to explain the physics of the electromagnetic field that caused the action of the needle" (Ulmer, 2003, p. 21). This anecdote becomes a starting point for a project that arcs through the text, the production of a website, a "widesite," in which students investigate their own sources of creative energy and their relationship with institutions of what Ulmer terms the "popcycle" (essentially the primary ideological apparatuses of our society). Where the compass charts the currents of electromagnetic energy across the surface of the earth, Ulmer's widesite charts affective currents in the intersection between the body, the conscious, and institutions. The widesite experiment, if successful, produces a tool for affective-proprioceptive attunement whereby the writer can navigate affective currents. The widesite operates as a compass, locating the pull of the popcycle, but like the compass, which does not require the user to go north but provides orientation for moving any direction, the widesite enhances the user's cognition of cyberspace.

Ulmer describes the widesite project as going in search of an understanding of "electracy," which essentially serves a role for new media that is analogous to the role literacy serves in print media. The primary assignments in the project carry the students through what Ulmer terms the "popcycle," which includes the primary ideological institutions of American culture: career, family/home, entertainment media, and history/community/school. At the core, the widesite project asks students to search the Web for images that evoke strong memories and feelings about their experiences with these institutions. The final assignment then asks students to build an emblem from their imagery that captures some commonality between the images. Ideally, this emblem will serve as a type of compass that helps the student-composers understand how media and institutions orient their state of mind. That is, the emblem maps the cultural, media mechanisms by which our unfolding experiences become organized as subjective positions.

As the assignments ask students to deal with the particularities of their lives and encounters with the "popcycle," I believe a personal example will best explain how the widesite functions. The following example traces my own path through Ulmer's widesite project. The particular materials of the project, my life experiences, are not especially relevant (except perhaps to me). However, the example presents the *singular*, which, like the singularities that form multiplicities, are mechanisms that affect the unfolding of materiality. As such, this example can be apprehended in several ways: as a document of my ideological interpolation; as a creative "expression" of my life; or as an investigation into the singularities that orient the unfolding of my consciousness. The first two are familiar approaches to autobiography or memoir. The final approach demonstrates how the example is *not* about my life, the material, but about the composition method and the mode of literacy/electracy to which it points. Only here can one grasp how a new media, rip/mix/burn, pedagogy can extend the teaching of cultural studies and post-process composition.

The example begins with one of the popcycle assignments relating to entertainment media. The specific language of the assignment is quite general and benign: "make a website documenting the details of a movie or TV narrative some part of which you still remember from your childhood years (K-12 years)" (Ulmer, 2003, p. 127). However,

Ulmer then goes on to provide two chapters of dense theoretical prose that makes this apparently simple task seem nearly impossible. At the core, however, the task is to analyze through image the way in which one comes to an identity through a process of identifying with image and culture. For example, in carrying out this assignment with my students, I selected the film *Star Wars. Star Wars* was a huge part of my life when I was seven and eight years old. This choice happens to resonate well with *Internet Invention,* which uses the mythic narrative structure of Joseph Campbell's *The Hero with a Thousand Faces* as one of its multiple framing mechanisms (Campbell's book was also a direct inspiration—one might say diagram—for Lucas's story). In Ulmer's textbook, the heroic narrative proceeds along with the completion of the various assignments. Ulmer describes the narrative moment associated with the entertainment assignment as the point where "the subject is presented with a problem or challenge that will change his/her destiny. The subject experiences fear of the unknown or fear of outside forces. The wise one: a mentor gives guidance and support to the subject" (p. 126). I focused my site on two particular scenes in *Star Wars*—one at the beginning of the film and one near the end—that resonate with this description. The first is the scene where Luke stands looking out over the deserts of Tatooine at sunset after his droid, R2-D2, has run off. The second is the climatic moment of the film where Luke turns off his targeting scanner and chooses to rely upon the "force" to destroy the Death Star (Ben's voice insistently ringing in his head, "Use the force, Luke!").

Ulmer devotes much of his discussion of entertainment to the practice of impersonation (Elvis impersonation in particular). Certainly I was guilty of this as a boy, literally impersonating Luke Skywalker for one Halloween, but also acting out the role of the Jedi hero, much like most children imagine and role play. While various accoutrements (e.g., the light saber) are necessary for the impersonation, just like the lip curl is necessary for impersonating Elvis, what is ultimately at stake is the *feeling* of being Luke, a feeling I can still manage to summon watching those films now. It is a feeling of resolution, of making the choice to step into a world of danger, an adult world. However, it is also the decision to rely upon one's embodied understanding, one's instincts, such as when Luke destroys the Death Star. In short, what occurs here for me is my own singular, embodied encounter with a piece of media that interpolates me into an ideological narrative of masculine values and identity. And yet, the experience cannot be wholly captured upon this ideological plane of reference.

Gary Cooper in *High Noon* serves a role for Ulmer that is similar to that of Mark Hamill in *Star Wars* for me. Ulmer notes,

> Other commentators described Cooper's gest as that of *thinking,* which is the quality that might have prompted Strasberg's observation: "One cannot imagine John Wayne philosophizing about his lot as one could Gary Cooper. Though Cooper's hero was a man of fewer words than Wayne's, his silences were more than hiatuses between 'Yup' and 'Nope'—they were the interval in which he confronted himself" . . . . Cooper had a knack, it was said, of "turning momentarily into a totem—but a *thinking* totem." In my remake, he is thinking about Derrida. (1994, p. 211)

On the ideological level, Cooper's hero, similar to Skywalker, teaches us how to "be a man." I won't make any claims about Mark Hamill's acting in comparison to Cooper's. However, in the first scene I mention above, Luke stares out toward the horizon. It is a formal gesture built into the classic heroic narrative. Conventionally, one might construe this gaze as an attempt to peer into the future, to place oneself against the horizon of possibility.

However, just as Ulmer imagines Cooper thinking of Derrida, in my widesite, Luke's gaze is not to the horizon but is instead a "haptic" one:

> no line separates earth from sky, which are of the same substance; there is neither horizon nor background nor perspective nor limit nor outline or form nor center; there is no intermediary distance, or all distance is intermediary . . . There exists a nomadic absolute, as a local integration moving from part to part and constituting smooth space in an infinite succession of linkages and changes in direction. It is an absolute that is one with becoming itself, with process. (Deleuze and Guattari, 1987, p. 494)

For Deleuze and Guattari, haptic vision references sight that does not fix objects in a plane of reference, against a horizon, but rather absorbs their materiality and unfolding process. Haptic vision causes us to fold ourselves into the image rather than separate writer and audience as subjects separate from the media object. Perhaps if Ulmer's Cooper is thinking of Derrida, my Luke is thinking of Deleuze.

Either way, the widesite I created ends up focusing on images of desert horizons. Interestingly, Lucas's desert planet Tatooine is in a binary star system: the sunset features two suns. This connects with my later website on history/community/school, where Ulmer asks students to make a website that documents an "exemplary story from your community." I chose the detonation of the atom bomb at Trinity Site, a place I visited while in graduate school. The visit was memorable because of the surprising absence of there being anything to see. Aside from a monument, all evidence of the explosion was gone: the crater had been refilled and the trinitite (the green glass created by the intense heat of the explosion melting the desert sand) had long ago been taken away by curious souvenir hunters. So here was my own binary, my own second sun, to match Lucas's Tatooine. This conduction continues as the codename for the test detonation was "Trinity" (as in Trinity Site), and thus two becomes three. Trinity obviously references the Christian Trinity of three-who-are-one, which in turn reflects fundamental mythical structures of the type on which Luke Skywalker, and later Neo Anderson (in *The Matrix*), are based. The reason why the tests were called "Trinity" remains unknown. However when asked, Oppenheimer said,

> "Why I chose the name is not clear, but I know what thoughts were in my mind. There is a poem of John Donne, written just before his death, which I know and love. From it a quotation: 'As West and East / In all flatt Maps—and I am one—are on, / So death doth touch the Resurrection.'" ("Hymn to God My God, in My Sicknesses"). Oppenheimer continued, "That still does not make a Trinity, but in another, better known devotional poem, Donne opens, 'Batter my heart, three person'd God;—.' Beyond this, I have no clues whatever." (Trinity Test, 2005).

In any case, Trinity certainly references the Christian god.

> In contradistinction to Donne's confession and submission, I bring a slogan to my wide image, "I have

nothing to admit," the title of one of Deleuze's essays (an element that appears earlier in my Career website). In it, Deleuze concludes,

> The problem is not one of being this or that in man, but rather one of becoming human, of a universal becoming animal: not to take oneself for a beast, but to undo the human organization of the body, to cut across such and such a zone of intensity in the body, everyone of us discovering the zones which are really his, and the groups, the populations, the species which inhabit him. (1977, para. 10)

So what is captured in this scene? A double sunset fracturing the desert horizon; a moment tempted by self-judgment in which one is asked to "be a man," to place oneself against the horizon of the future, and submit to God; but instead, there is this refusal—"I have nothing to admit"—and a haptic gaze. The purpose of the gaze is to break away from interpolative demands, to search in the event of becoming for fissures that "undo the human organization of the body." Finally, I must add one final element. Trinity Site, now a national monument, is only open to the public on the first Saturday of April and October each year. My trip to Trinity Site was on April 1st. I take this not entirely coincidental fact as emblematic. My vision is like that of the traditional Tarot image of the Fool, stepping off blindly, with insouciance, into the void. The Fool initiates the journey of the Tarot's Major Arcana. Perhaps young Skywalker is also akin to the fool, staring outwards (with haptic vision) and not realizing where his next step is about to take him.

The entertainment discourse project begins as a cultural studies investigation into the way in which a popular film participates in the formation of identity by passing along subjective traits to young viewers. However, the widesite project invites students to rip apart such media compositions and infuse them with other affects. The image of Luke Skywalker staring across the desert might still evoke the excitement of an impending journey but it is no longer one toward a ready-made identity. Instead there is an opportunity for experimentation and risk. Compositions such as the one I describe above do not necessarily come quickly or by chance: the composition of a rhizome requires experimentation to discover what will cause the proliferation of information. Nor is the wide image an answer. It does not reveal the "truth" about me. It is not a confession: I have nothing to admit. Instead it is a tool, a compass-like device, which orients my responses to media in relation to the unfolding of my thoughts and the articulation of my subjectivity. As such, it is a tool that provides further critical insight into my affective responses to future media; it produces a critical electracy analogous to my critical print literacy.

RHYTHM SCIENCE

Ulmer's widesite project opens up opportunities to develop both compositional practices of rip/mix/burn that produce creative understandings and articulations of data and critical faculties for engaging in the ideological functions of discourse. Furthermore, the project creates the possibility for an unfolding of thought, for the emergence of an unpredictable becoming. Points can be captured from this unfolding, as I have done here, but the learning takes place in the movement. Clearly one would not expect a student to construct a site (or describe it) in a manner similar to mine or Ulmer's. However, the access to a theoretical discourse is ancillary to the project. A critical pedagogy may take on the task of teaching such concepts, and *Internet Invention* would offer the opportunity to do so. More importantly, the project demonstrates how a rip/mix/burn composition might produce conditions in which students can use cultural-analytical tools on their own experiences. Of course, the critical pedagogue can reassert a goal of a particular ideological brand of critical awareness, but such is not necessary here. Instead there is an engagement with the unfolding of cognition into subjectivity, the space where individuals and groups are articulated as such. Undoubtedly the discourse used to apprehend this unfolding is ideological, but the process itself is material and subject to a different mode of power.

This ideological component is already clear in *Internet Invention*. Ulmer parallels the historical development of new media literacy (electracy) with the emergence of a new syncretic culture that combines the previous Western syncretism of Greco-Roman and Judeo-Christian culture with the values of Afro-Caribbean culture. This combination reflects the cultural development of the Americas in the twentieth century as well as the consequences of the contemporary global economy.

> It is ironic, or paradoxical, or lucky—depending on
> one's point of view—that at the very moment when
> the Western dream of transcendence of the body pro-
> duced a technology (VR) capable of leaving behind
> the filthy 'meat' of the flesh (wetware) to realize the
> omnipotence of the mind, that the African body
> emerged in our behavior in a way that inverted the
> VR hierarchy in favor of the embodied flesh. (Ulmer,
> 2003, p. 303)

In short, Ulmer's text suggests important connections between the
philosophical issues surrounding new media literacy and consciousness and the aporia of globalization. In this, his project resonates with
those of Katherine Hayles and others who emphasize the potential
of embodiment as a concept for countering the potential dangers of
technology.

Ulmer is also not alone is sensing the connections between rip,
mix, and burn composition and globalization. Paul D. Miller (a.k.a.
DJ Spooky, that subliminal kid) has articulated these connections in
his work. He provides a narrative exemplifying this admixture of the
technological and the global in the unfolding of composition:

> I was in Tokyo and doing a show with an old Japa-
> nese friend of mine, Dj Krush, and some new folks
> on the block, Anticon, young white kids from Middle
> America. They were doing a collabortion with Krush,
> a piece called "Song for John Walker"—the suburban
> kid who joined the Taliban. Needless to say, the back-
> stage vibe was all about dialogue and we were all just
> kicking it. Krush's wife walked in and handed him
> a samurai sword before his set, and everyone in the
> room was . . . ummm . . . kind of silent. In a moment
> like that, the strangeness (strange-mess) of global cul-
> ture, hip-hop, and of operating as a Dj on a global
> level crystallized before my eyes. We all just sat there
> and paused for a second. It really felt like a still from
> a video art installation. Krush doesn't speak English,
> and we have communicated mostly with beats over
> the years. The show was a benefit for Afghani war
> orphans at Tokyo's Liquid Room in the Shinjuku dis-

trict, and well . . . you just had to feel the oddity of being in a room with some white Americans talking about a lawyer's kid who read Malcolm X and defected to a terrorist organization and a Japanese kid who prayed with his family and was into Shinto Buddhism chants before he went on stage to do turntable tricks. A scene like that doesn't fit into any normal categorization of hip-hop that normal America wants, and it never will. That's the joy of being able to see how this stuff is unfolding in a real way across the globe. It's almost exactly a social approximation of the way Web culture collapses distinctions between geography and expression, and it's almost as if the main issues of the day are all about how people are adjusting to the peculiarity of being in a simultaneous yet unevenly distributed world. (2004, pp. 104–5)

Miller/DJ Spooky struggles here to describe the feeling of this odd cross-cultural scene. The connections between Krush, Anticon, and Spooky are particular, in their communication via beats. There is also some intersection over politics and social action, in their interest in John Walker and their participation in the Afghani benefit. However, from this point they unfold in unexpected directions. As Miller points out, "normal America" already has its aesthetic values and discursive expectations for hip-hop, and they don't include Buddhist chanting or songs about the Taliban. Nevertheless, he finds himself in this scene, which strikes him as a "still from a video art installation," because it evokes this feeling, this "peculiarity of being." The difficulty in describing this moment does not come simply from cultural difference. As unusual as the scene may be, it falls well within the cultural imagination; that is, the coming together of American and Japanese culture *is* part of what "normal America wants." The struggle instead comes from Miller's sense of the creative potential of the moment, in his desire to capture a zeitgeist and a vision of futurity: here, in this scene, Miller believes he finds the emergence of a future that is spreading.

Internet Invention takes on a similar project and method. In seeking "electracy," Ulmer lays out a project for uncovering the future of rhetoric and composition. Like Miller's rhythm science, the "widesite" project in Ulmer's textbook looks to combine cultural elements with embodied feeling, though Ulmer focuses more on image, where Miller's primary interest is sound. As Ulmer contends,

> the language apparatus is a prosthetic memory—an artificial memory that augments and extends the power of living organic human memory. And each apparatus has its own way of performing this supporting function. This power of a photograph *to stimulate involuntary personal memory* is the point of departure for an electrate institutional practice. (2004, p. 44)

Here Ulmer is drawing on Barthes's concept of the *punctum* to articulate a new conceptual framework for electracy that is structured upon feeling and state of mind. Through the widesite project, students collect images and compose websites that "stimulate involuntary personal memory" with the goal of uncovering/composing an image that summons a creative state of mind. Ulmer's reference to memory clearly evokes Derrida's *pharmakon* and the saprophyte from Ulmer's essay twenty years earlier: in theory, the widesite is the right "mushroom" for bringing one into the compositional event, the site of creativity. The images are clearly particular to the producer, evoking his or her idiosyncratic memories regarding encounters with primary cultural institutions (family, school, entertainment, etc.). Miller finds such a moment and feeling in this scene. However, like the consumption of psychedelic mushrooms, the experience is somewhat ineffable.

In short, what both Ulmer and Miller suggest is that composition is guided by affect, by feeling or intuition. This suggestion might be mistaken for typical Romantic experience of inspiration. As Brian Massumi notes,

> It is not that. First, because something happening out of mind in a body directly absorbing its outside cannot exactly said to be experienced. Second, because volition, cognition, and presumably other 'higher' functions usually presumed to be in the mind, figured as a mysterious container of mental entities that is somehow separate from body and brain, are present and active in the now not-so 'raw' domain. (2002, pp. 29–30)

That is, the affect does not come here from within the mind of creative genius, but instead results from the proliferating contagion of material ripped from a network of distributed cognition. That said, it is decidedly difficult for us to conceive of creativity outside the discourse of individual genius, particularly while holding onto the concept of affectivity. However, in Ulmer's case, affect works much like a compass, a navigational tool leading us toward a promising outcome. As Deleuze and Guattari note, "you don't know what you can make a rhizome with, you don't know which subterranean stem is effectively going to make a rhizome, or enter into a becoming, people your desert. So experiment" (1987, p. 251).

Affect guides this experimentation by acting as an attunement to the emergence of the rhizome, much like the compass needle tunes itself to magnetic waves. Deleuze and Guattari describe the rhizome as unfolding on a "plane of consistency," which intersects the multiplicities composing the rhizome. Here again they refer to geometric shapes, noting how shapes of one dimension are cut from shapes of higher dimension: the square is cut from the cube; the circle is cut from the sphere, etc. Thus multiplicities of different dimensions can intersect through the composition of a plane of consistency, the sites of contagion from which material is "ripped." The contagion proliferates across the plane, intersecting, rhizomatically, with other ripped sites. This proliferation is a wave or vibration that combines with other contagions, as I noted before, to create harmony, dissonance, counterpoint, and so on. Affect then is an attunement to these vibrations, a means of mapping the unfolding of the rhizome. As with DJ Spooky, it all comes down to being able to feel the beats, to a rhythm science.

BURNING COPYRIGHT

Unfortunately, our dominant model of creativity, manifested in copyright and intellectual property, not only fails to account for the topological unfolding of composition but also threatens to constrain intellectual work. As I discussed earlier in the chapter, copyright laws were developed to encourage and protect intellectual work, essentially by restricting the legal means by which work can be copied. It is largely impossible to restrict the flow of information derived from intellectual work, except by keeping that work secret; the purpose of copyright has always been to limit the accessibility of information by placing firm limits on who has the right to publish and distribute copyrighted material. The practice worked because the mechanisms of publication and distribution were expensive and centralized in a relatively few number of publishers. Now, obviously, anyone with a computer and an Internet connection can publish and distribute information at levels of quality that rival those of corporate publishers. In short, in the past, the practice of composing works was technologically separated from the practice of publishing and distributing them. As such, copyright laws, which effectively limited the latter, did little to affect the former, except when the composer chose to publish those works widely. Now composition and publication can be nearly simultaneous events, as they are with blogging. The result being that laws designed to promote intellectual work now hamper it.

As Lawrence Lessig notes,

> capturing and sharing content, of course, is what humans have done since the dawn of man. It is how we learn and communicate . . . digital 'capturing and sharing' is in part an extension of the capturing and sharing that has always been integral to our culture, and in part it is something new. (2004, p. 184)

What is "new" in new media composition is the exponential increase in our information processing capacity, our access to data, and our ability to disseminate our compositions. Lessig's primary concern is that copyright laws are currently being enforced in such a way as to dissuade creators from making use of the potential advantages of new media composition. Even in cases where a creator may be making legal use of copyrighted material (and remember *all material* is copyrighted), the cost of a legal defense is often in itself enough of a deterrent. The result is that only the wealthy and corporations can make use of this compositional technology, as only they can afford to pay for copyright and/or defend themselves in the courtroom. Again, copyright functions by preventing access to intellectual work. However, in this case this lack of access hampers future intellectual work, essentially protecting intellectual work by making that work nearly impossible.

This intractable situation affects the writing classroom as well, though in a different way. As I mentioned earlier, our notion of copyright shares its concept of intellectual property and originality with our definition of plagiarism. Though studies have indicated that incidents of plagiarism *have not increased* with the availability of the Web, awareness of the issue certainly has ("Plagiarism Epidemic, Media Epidemics," 2004). Ironically, Web databases like Turnitin.com, which keep copies of student work to check against future students, may infringe on student copyright to do so. As with Lessig's argument, the flow of information seems to benefit those with power. Not surprising. I can assure you that Turnitin.com would not get away with making copies of MP3 files as it does with making copies of student papers, even though both are equally protected by copyright law. The overlap between copyright and plagiarism is in the perception that composition occurs through an act of individual, internal, creative will. From this perspective, the ease with which information may be ripped, mixed, and burned from the Internet points to an act that is contrary to true creative composition, which is internal. Thus, any use of the Internet would contravene creativity, just as any use of the library might. This perception results in the practice of some professors insisting that students *not* use the library, because the professor wants to hear the students' "own thoughts." Indeed, having access to information is apparently such a threat to original thought that many professors have eschewed formal writing assignments altogether, opting instead for in-class writing exams (how they will deal with wireless access to information is another matter).

If these perceptions and practices were not so widespread and potentially detrimental to learning, they would be rather humorous. After all, does it really make sense that professors should be discouraging students from doing research, whether in the library or online? Given the extensive bibliographies that follow any academic publication, do we really believe that doing research is counter to producing "original" work? Again, the point is not that copyright infringement does not occur or that plagiarism is not an unethical practice. Instead, the point here is that the "legitimate" compositional process is not different in kind from the infringing of copyright or plagiarizing. Each is a practice of ripping, mixing, and burning. However we finally adjudicate these issues, there will need to be recognition that creative work relies upon our ability to make use of existing cultural information. As always, the difference between ethical and unethical use is one of degree and context.

In short, it should be clear that while the advent of new media has offered us new modes of composition, tremendously greater access to information, and the power to publish our work, what is perhaps more significant is the opportunity cybernetics and media have offered us to rediscover our cognitive processes, including our compositional methods. While the developments of cybernetics and media have caused worry regarding their implications for our valued notions of individuality and freedom, parallel concepts of the material unfolding of thought offer us new ways of understanding these embodied experiences. Of course, this is not to say that we should not be concerned about the ideological power of media or the influence of the instrumental logic of technology in shaping our culture or the technological invasion of our privacy and regulation of our behaviors. Instead, the work I have described here has gone in search of a different way of understanding the intersection of human bodies and technologies that does not fall back upon the binary of freedom or slavery. In its place, I have described a more integrated network of embodied and technological cognition from which cognition and consciousness unfold. The composition of consciousness is much like the composition of text in that it is a process of ripping, mixing, and burning.

In Chapter 8, I investigate the pedagogical implications of the virtual-actual and rip/mix/burn composition. To a certain extent I have already begun that investigation in my discussion of Ulmer. If our conventional notions of the writer are founded upon our concepts of thought and consciousness, certainly our pedagogies are as well. After all, how can one teach students without a concept of how students think and learn? Furthermore, as I will investigate, teaching is hinged upon a theory of space-time, perhaps best exemplified in the cliché of the "teachable moment." In the next chapter I revise this phrase into a concept of "event pedagogy" that takes up the topological unfolding of space, time, and thought as the material site of learning.

8 The Pedagogic Event

The process of rip/mix/burn indicates how composition operates as an unfolding of cognition that incorporates a network of technologies and media. Rip/mix/burn is not simply about *new media* composition; it is an understanding of writing enabled by new insights into cognition and generated through the development of cybernetics and digital media. As an experimental writing practice, rip/mix/burn emerges from a long line of experimentation going back to Modernist collage through the Black Mountain School to John Cage, William Burroughs and beyond. Notably, all of these experimenters developed writing practices in response to the developing technologies of their time. In short, developing experimental writing techniques through new media technologies is hardly a new idea, and for the modern history of rhetoric and composition (since the 1960s), there has never been an absence of inventive writing practices to explore in the teaching of writing. However, in an academic context, the constraints on discursive practices have less to do with how we might be able to imagine composition than they do with other institutional values and interests. I addressed one aspect of this issue in the previous chapter in my examination of copyright and plagiarism. As I discussed there, the values of originality and ownership are integral to the marketplace exchange of compositional products as commodified intellectual properties. Rip/mix/burn casts doubt on the traditional principles of authorship in a manner that would be problematic for the academy. It would clearly be difficult for academic institutions to forego their ideological commitments to intellectual property, particularly as higher education becomes an increasingly capitalist and entrepreneurial endeavor. As I investigate in this chapter, the difficulty of teaching rip/mix/burn composition, of developing a pedagogy that operates within the material topological unfolding of thought across a network of distributed cognition, lies not simply in articulating how such a pedagogy might function but more broadly with the challenges such a pedagogy would bring to the general operation of discourse in the university.

While plagiarism works as an excellent site for investigating the potential implications of the compositional process I have been describing, it is only one small aspect of the broader practice of pedagogy. Much like traditional perspectives on composition, pedagogies, both inside and outside composition, tend to have a cybernetic function. That is, a course is established with preset goals, and pedagogy is the practice of steering the course toward reaching those goals. In a traditional, lecture-driven course, this practice is relatively easy to see. The professor gives a series of lectures that provide discrete pieces of information; each piece is an incremental step toward the end point. In a student-centered classroom, the type that has become commonplace in composition, the goals are just as specific, even though they are achieved by different means. For example, the syllabus establishes a series of assignments that have specific expectations. The students are expected to make progress toward becoming "better" academic writers. In doing so, the students are expected to learn to employ "the" writing process. Even in a post-process composition classroom goals exist in terms of developing student awareness of the social-discursive contexts in which they write.

Indeed, it is difficult to imagine pedagogy without a goal, nor would I suggest that pedagogy can, conceptually speaking, be understood separately from a goal. Even if we were to imagine a classroom without predetermined assignments or content, in which students could do or say anything, the very fact that we take a room full of people and identify it as a classroom with a pedagogy would implicitly suggest that there was some goal, some expectation, that these students would learn something. Even if the particular thing they learned were not predetermined, there would still be a goal of learning in and of itself. In other words, the simple act of naming an activity as pedagogical situates that activity within a certain ideological context, particularly when that naming coincides with the location of that activity in a college campus classroom. This recognition is part of the impetus for post-process composition: in order to understand (and thus perform) academic writing, it is necessary to recognize that it is fundamentally "pedagogical" in nature. This means that conventional academic writing is cybernetic and intended to reach predefined goals—goals that are determined by the instructor, not the student.

In this context, the student's body and cognitive processes are simply instruments in the pedagogical navigation of the course. In Maturana and Varela's terms, the student is an *allopoietic* system, a system whose cybernetic functions are subordinated to another system, much like the cybernetic functions of my car are subordinated to my desire to get to the store. Of course, students are generally more resistant than automobiles when they sense they are being mistreated. Furthermore, in conventional terms at least, faculty bear an ethical, professional responsibility to their students. The students subordinate themselves to the professor's directions—attending class, completing assignments, submitting themselves for evaluation, and so forth. They exchange their subjective, cognitive labor for a grade and credits. However, they also expect to learn, to be led to a particular point, to cover a range of territory or subject matter. This is an expectation bred into students through years of classroom experience.

In post-process composition and cultural studies pedagogies, these expectations come under critique. Rather than seeing education as an apolitical, neutral delivery of objective information, this perspective looks at teaching as an institutional, ideological operation, whose primary function is to produce and manage student subjectivity. This operation can also be understood as cybernetic: pedagogy steers students to a predetermined point by locating and identifying students and mapping out the territory through which the course will move. Cultural studies pedagogues are well aware of this cybernetic process of interpolation as it operates broadly throughout the culture and insist on making it visible to students. Lawrence Grossberg argues,

> If political struggles are won and lost in the space
> between people's everyday lives and the material pro-
> duction and distribution of values and power, in the
> space where people and groups are articulated, both
> ideologically and affectively, to social identities, cul-
> tural practices, and political projects, then it is here
> that pedagogy must operate. (1994, p. 19)

To which I would add that pedagogy already does operate here, that all pedagogy is fundamentally a process by which people and groups are articulated as such. One might even go so far as to suggest that the content of a pedagogy and its relative success or failure in reaching pedagogic goals is ideologically negligible in comparison with the function the classroom serves in producing and managing subjectivity. That said, course content is generally integrated into this ideological process.

As Grossberg suggests, critical pedagogy seeks to intervene in this process. However, critical pedagogues face numerous challenges in terms of ideological resistance from students, other faculty, their institutions, mainstream media, politicians, and the culture at large. In part this is to be expected when confronting the dominant ideological values of a culture. That said, part of the problem here lies in understanding the relationship between ideology, subjectivity, pedagogy, and embodied cognitive processes. Pedagogy has an undeniable cybernetic function, but cybernetics does not have to be viewed as a process of external control and navigation across a predefined grid of points. Instead, it can be articulated as a proprioceptive process of becoming where pedagogy's abstract mechanisms shape cognition in a non-deterministic way. As I discuss in this chapter, this pedagogical approach draws on an alternate understanding of the "teachable moment" as a pedagogical event. Briefly put, rather than imagining a course as Cartesian space-time, as a series of orchestrated points/moments, I describe a course as an unfolding that cannot be reduced to simple points. Clearly "course" has multiple meanings here: a class, a path of navigation (as in charting a course), and a flow (the river coursed down the mountain).

PEDAGOGIC COMMUNICATION

In undertaking this investigation, it becomes clear that the rip/mix/ burn compositional method does far more than bring intellectual property under question (as if that were not enough). In challenging the traditional relationship between conscious thought (as the site of originality) and text (as a reasonably transparent, though sometimes vexed, means of communicating thought), one quickly runs into the fundamental values supporting the university. Derrida explains,

> all teaching in its traditional form, and perhaps all teaching whatever, has as its ideal, with exhaustive translatability, the effacement of language, meaning *both* the *national* language *and,* paradoxically, an ideal of translatability that neutralizes this national language. Nationalism and universalism. What this

institution cannot bear is a transformation that leaves intact neither of these two complementary poles. It can bear more readily the most apparently revolutionary ideological sorts of "content," if only that content does not touch the border of language and of all the juridico-political contracts that it guarantees. (1991b, pp. 262–3)

Derrida's critique of translation speaks directly to the importance of the technological processes I have been discussing. While we may typically think of translation as the act of moving between two human languages, translation also pertains to the cybernetic, technological process of communication. Of course, Derrida goes farther than this to suggest translation is always already there in the entry of thought into its "original" language. Here, Derrida contends that the university's power is based upon its claim to produce verifiable knowledge about the world. This claim occludes the role rhetoric plays in the formation of that knowledge, as well as the social and political nature of its discourses, under a value of transcendent rationality. The university is less concerned with the actual meaning that a text might communicate (i.e. its "content") than it is with regulating the means, the technology, of communication, which Derrida terms "the concept of translation." While there are clearly many different professional, disciplinary means for verifying the content of academic discourse, Derrida suggests that the university does not need to be greatly concerned with academic contents that are critical of its operation, provided that those critiques do not undermine the transparency of communication that allows academic knowledge to become an exchangeable commodity.

For example, a cultural studies course might introduce students to theories that challenge the mainstream notions of race and gender. Such a course may bring into question university practices, and certainly there have been occasions when such courses have provoked a response from administrators. However, for the most part, such a course is safely insulated within a pedagogic program that understands these critiques as a content contained within a liberal education (e.g., at my college we have a general education category titled "Prejudice and Discrimination"; however radical the content of courses in the category may or may not be, their inclusion in the curriculum is not problematic). Such courses are perceived as simply representing another piece of information that the students should acquire in their development.

This process is perhaps even clearer in the case of Derrida himself. In American universities, Derrida has largely been contained within literary studies as little more than an interpretive word game in which students "deconstruct" this or that literary text. There is little, if any, sense that Derrida's work might constitute a critique of the normal functioning of pedagogy (e.g., assigning and grading essays) or curricular structures (e.g., the division of writing from literature, literary periods, etc.), let alone the notion of using his methods to attend to university culture (a subject assumed to be outside of one's specialization). Instead, we reserve interpretive indeterminacy only for literary texts. Otherwise, we view texts as logocentric, adhering to the belief that the text can translate authorial conscious (which is presumed to be the originating site of information in the text) to the audience.

Based on this belief, and through a mastery of academic discourse, university subjects, students and professors alike, are expected—albeit with different levels of success—to produce and communicate their thoughts. Academic discourse assumes itself to be sufficient to the "Truth." What it fails to communicate is either false or inconsequential. This concept of academic discourse sustains the identity of the university as a place that "gives rise only to the production and teaching of a *knowledge* [savoir], which is, of knowledges [*connaissances*] whose form of utterances is not, in principle, performative but theoretical and constative" (Derrida, 2002, p. 218). That is, the university believes that the knowledge it produces and teaches can be proven true or false. This theoretical/constative knowledge is differentiated from "performative" knowledge, by which Derrida means knowledge that does work. This binary maintains the difference between pure and applied science, between the study and making of art, or even the study and practice of law. Each of the latter represents a performance, a doing, or the making of an *oeuvre,* a work. By establishing this boundary, the university seeks to insulate itself, to create independence from the demands of the marketplace and other "real world" institutions. This separation is clear in the traditional division of professions from other kinds of labor. Professorial activity is not meant to be "work" in that it comes from a different motive: a pledge the professor honors and a faith in the knowledge he or she professes.

However, in the contemporary university, there are many faculty engaged in performative practices. Indeed, the production of marketable works is the hallmark of the growing academic capitalism in which we see partnerships between industries and universities. Pedagogy is also taken up in this: in student participation in applied research, in the shifting emphasis from liberal education to training, and in the capitalist logic of efficiency that determines course and program offerings. One wonders to what extent this traditional image of the university ever materially existed in practice. Certainly American universities have been serving commercial, industrial interests for more than a century (though admittedly the intensity of the involvement of corporate America in higher education has raised considerably—and continues to increase—over the past twenty years or so). Thus, while on the one hand, the proclaimed neutrality and transparency of constative knowledge may no longer be tenable, the performative points to even greater problems as it draws professorial activity into the capitalist marketplace of labor. This is especially the case with post-process composition, cultural studies, and other "engaged" or critical pedagogies, which reject the proclaimed objectivity of the constative and the commodficiation of the performative. Instead, critical pedagogy argues for the intellectual freedom attached to abstract, constative knowledge *and* the right to produce performative, though non-commercial, works (to engage in social change through professorial activities in research, teaching, and service).

Here is where the problem arises, at least from the perspective of those critical of such pedagogies. As performative discourses, pedagogies seek to regulate the outcomes of their performance. If pedagogy is ideological, as cultural studies would contend all pedagogy is, then the performance must include some degree of coercion. In conventional terms, pedagogy keeps from being coercive only because its content is objective, constative knowledge. If both performative and constative discourses are ideological, then the classroom becomes a site where professors lead students to accept an ideological viewpoint. This is the complaint traditional humanists make about a course that they claim tries to convince students of a Marxist or feminist perspective (a complaint echoed by the conservative proponents of the "Academic Bill of Rights"). However, the same may be said of a course that seeks to convince students of the literary value of Shakespeare or the practical value of engaging in "the" writing process. In short, here one can see the collapse of the distinction between constative and performative discourse under the pressure of cultural critique on one side and capitalist market pressures on the other. What is required then is a means to pursue professorial activity without recourse to constative knowledge and without falling into an ideological marketplace. If, as I mentioned earlier, pedagogy cannot be separated from goals, even if the goal is simply "learning," that goal or point can be abstract and non-deterministic in the unfolding of pedagogic activity. From this perspective, learning becomes much like the activity of rip/mix/burn I have described, an activity in which consciousness unfolds through an injection of contagious data into a network of distributed cognition, followed by a proliferation of that contagion unfolding rhizomatic potentialities or virtualities, which are then reduced through a process of involution into the actualization of thought in the conscious mind. In this approach, pedagogy describes the multiplicities, the mechanisms, involved in the process, as well as strategies for engendering this experimental learning activity.

THE "TEACHABLE MOMENT"

In moving beyond the constative and performative, Derrida identifies the event, which he insists "must not only surprise the constative and propositional mode of the language of knowledge (S is P), but also no longer let itself be commanded by the performative speech act of the subject" (2002, p. 233). As I have suggested, Derrida eschews the performative because "what takes place, arrives, happens, or happens *to me* remains still controllable and programmable within a horizon of anticipation or precomprehension, with a *horizon,* period" (2002, pp. 233–4). Put simply, while the concept of performance moves academic knowledge beyond the realm of the "purely" theoretical and constative, it still denotes actions whose results can be predicted. That is, the performative remains cybernetic. To perform is not to move beyond the "horizon of anticipation," and as such not to move beyond the capture of ideology. Unlike performance, the event supposes "an *irruption* that punctures the horizon, *interrupting* any performative organization, any convention, or any context that can be dominated by a conventionality" (2002, p. 234). As the term "event" suggests, moving beyond the constative and performative depends on a particular approach to time.

In the calculus of cybernetics, time is divided into a series of points. In inventing calculus, Newton imagined a clock marking out time across the universe. Contemporary physics continues to build theories around the existence of time, as Stephen Hawking's concept of "imaginary time" suggests (though some physicists, Peter Lynds in particular, suggest that time may not exist). In effect, time is divisible into units or points through which motion can be plotted. In this manner, activity becomes measurable and predictable. This is the time of performative pedagogy, where pedagogy is a cybernetic equation that plots the passage of activity through a series of points (teachable moments) to a predetermined destination. Much like the regularization of physical space upon the abstract grid of Cartesian coordinates, time becomes regularized and abstracted in increasingly smaller units. However, just as one may describe a topological unfolding of space from the virtual into the actual, one might describe a topological unfolding of time. Deleuze and Guattari describe these two modes, the time of the event and the time of measure:

> *Aeon:* the indefinite time of the event, the floating line that knows only speeds and continually divides that which transpires into an already-there that is at the same time not-yet-here, a simultaneous too-late and too-early, a something that is both going to happen and has just happened. *Chronos:* the time of measure that situates things and persons, develops a form, and determines a subject. (1987, p. 262)

In the virtual present of the *Aeon*, consciousness does not exist as such but is rather always in a process of becoming. The event, which Deleuze and Guattari term the haecceity (after the medieval Scottish philosopher, Duns Scotus), is the spatiotemporal hinge where the always already past of immanent non-being passes through the plane of consistency, with its intensive, affective becomings, and verges toward its partial capture within a plane of reference as a subjective form. That is, as I describe in Chapter 7, cognition emerges from a sea of potentiality, virtual thoughts that are simultaneously potential and impossible in that they will never be realized, never become actualized as thought. This is the always already past of the virtual. Thought becomes actual and material through the compositional process of rip/mix/burn undertaken on the plane of consistency, where it unfolds as affectivity, as feeling and sensation. As thought becomes language it becomes captured, partially, on the plane of reference; thought becomes located and identified on a grid of possibility.

As the unfolding of thought indicates, *Aeon* describes the time of becoming. Rather than attempting to identify stages or points of composition or pedagogy that lead to a destination, the time of *aeon* offers insight into motion or activity itself. As Deleuze and Guattari continue, it is not a matter of choosing between *aeon* and *chronos,* instead,

> we must avoid an oversimplified conciliation, as
> though there were on the one hand formed subjects,
> of the thing or person type, and on the other hand
> spatiotemporal coordinates of the haecceity type. For
> you will yield nothing to haecceities unless you real-
> ize that that is what you are, and that you are nothing
> but that. (1987, p. 262)

The relationship between *aeon* and *chronos* is analogous to that between their plane of consistency and plane of reference. We move within the consistent space-time of *aeon,* but in the process of apprehension, of thought becoming symbolic language, we become articulated on a plane of reference. Again, here is where institutional pedagogy does its work, as Grossberg noted, in the articulation of people and groups as such, in the capture of bodies in the measured coordinates of referential time and space.

Teachers and students, as subjects, do not populate the event's plane of consistency; such subjects are instead figures on a plane of reference. However, the bodies and cognitive processes from which these subject positions are captured do unfold within topological space-time. The challenge lies in describing the composition of thought within *aeon* as learning. The pedagogic modes and concepts associated with teachers and students will only return us to the plane of reference: a different articulation of pedagogy is necessary. While, as Derrida indicates, the event exists in excess of predictability, this does not mean that the pedagogic event cannot be conceptualized, though the conceptualization will clearly be different from our normal approaches to teaching. In *Difference and Repetition,* Deleuze articulates pedagogy through the analogy of the swimmer:

> The movement of the swimmer does not resemble
> that of the wave, in particular, the movements of
> the swimming instructor which we reproduce on the
> sand bear no relation to the movements of the wave,
> which we learn to deal with only by grasping the for-

mer in practice as signs. That is why it is so difficult to say how someone learns: there is an innate or acquired practical familiarity with signs, which means that there is something amorous—but also something fatal—about all education. (1995, p. 23)

Deleuze's example recalls Rodney Brooks's discussion of the complexity of an ant's gait across a sandy beach (see Chapter 3): the complexity of the motion does not lie within the ant but in the intersection of the ant's proprioceptive, distributed cognition with the environment. The signs of the swimmer become embodied in the student to become emergent properties in the context of the wave. Of course, swimming instruction is a clearly cybernetic pedagogy, where the goals are quite easy to identify. However, even in this teachable moment, once the student enters the water, there is a significant mutation of the signs communicated by the instructor. Such mutations should be recognizable to those who teach writing. Perhaps one possible insight here is that composition instruction cannot possibly account for the complexity of writing, but such an accounting is not necessary. What is necessary are strategies for interfacing with the wave and allowing the text to unfold.

In the conventional classroom, we focus our pedagogic practice on our operation as subjects using symbolic systems (speech, text, other media, etc.). Critical pedagogy has carefully critiqued the ideological function of this practice and sought to imagine means by which teaching can not only make such functions visible to students but also open spaces for greater freedom or agency. Henry Giroux and Stanley Aronowitz (1993) have identified the discontinuity of ideological power; that is, the existence of spaces or discourses that are not so fully regulated. Yet the difficulty always seems to fall back upon the process of subjectification itself. That is, as a critical pedagogue, even if one finds a relatively open space and can create an opportunity for students to move out from under the careful management of their thought undertaken by ideology, the students as subjects often cling to the psychological and emotional ties that have been built between them and the dominant ideology. Short of some coercion (which is the accusation often leveled against critical pedagogy), the means to move students into a potentially new ideological perspective are elusive.

While on the subjective level, identity remains closely tied to ideology, in the space-time of topological *aeon*, the material unfolding of

cognition encounters a different operation of power. It is crucial to remember that such spaces are *not* "pre-ideological" in any way. Indeed,
under the auspices of Deleuze's "control society," ideological technologies enter into the production and management of affect. For example,
department stores experiment with various scents that help put their
customers in a "buying mood." Any type of anti-depressant or anti-
anxiety medication constitutes a similar ideological intervention into
affect. The entire field of aesthetics as a management of desire, connecting design with cognition, points to the intersection of ideology
with material, cognitive processes. In fact, one might take this further,
as Brian Massumi does, and suggest that ideology "no longer defines
the global mode of functioning of power. It is now one mode of power
in a larger field that is not defined, overall, by ideology. This makes
it all the more pressing to connect ideology to its real conditions of
emergence" (2002, p. 42). This is what I am effectively suggesting
here: that one might think of ideology as the operation of power on the
plane of reference where subjects are captured, but another mode of
power can be aligned with ideology, one which operates on the plane
of consistency to shape desire and cognition. Again, this seems to be
where Grossberg is suggesting critical pedagogy must operate—in the
topological spaces where cybernetic mechanisms intervene to shape
the unfolding of thought toward predictable activities that can be easily captured upon an ideological plane of reference.

As such, the concept of event pedagogy does not open up some
"free" space but instead allows for the development of critical strategies
to address the material operation of power. However, this has been a
difficult step for cultural studies to take. The problem cultural studies
encounters in dealing directly with the body and cognition reflects the
broader crisis in the humanities I have been discussing here. Unwilling
to accept (and rightly so) the notion of unmediated access to "reality"
or the purity of individual experience (what Massumi terms "naïve realism" and "naïve subjectivisim" respectively (2002, pp. 1–2)), cultural
studies turns to a cultural theory based upon mediation (textuality). In
this model, materiality is not directly accessible. Instead, materiality is
always already shaped by discourse, and hence by ideology. Likewise,
all experience is always already ideological. This model bears a close
relationship to what develops from the field of cybernetics, or at least
what many cyberneticists feared they were describing: that human
thought and experience with the world is mediated by information

processors, including media technologies. In both models the traditional humanistic potential for free thought and agency evaporates; the ability to make social change disappears before the instrumental logic and ideological power of the postmodern mediascape. In each case, the subject is largely detached from the body. Perhaps this is simply a continuation of Cartesian duality, except in these cases the cybernetic subject is formed through abstract information processing, and the ideological subject is formed through disciplinary-discursive management. In cultural studies, the attempt is made to create some opportunity for resistance or subversion through articulating how each subject constitutes a unique combination of cultural identities (gender, class, sexuality, and many other preferences). However, as Massumi asks, "How does a body perform its way out of a definitional framework that is not only responsible for its very 'construction,' but seems to prescript every possible signifying and countersignifying move as a selection from a repertoire of possible permutations on a limited set of predetermined terms?" (2002, p. 3).

Massumi's question is somewhat rhetorical as he undertakes a project to re-understand the role of the body, of movement and sensation, in relation to ideology, a project that is related to, though far from wholly continuous with, other recent theorizations of embodiment such as those by Mark Hansen and Katherine Hayles. These differences aside, the underlying point here is not to view the body as free from ideology but to understand materiality as a space where power operates but under different terms than those that describe discursive, representational ideology. Ultimately, the purpose of pursing such a theory is to establish experimental strategies for unfolding thought to produce an event of consciousness, the arrival of a thought that was not merely improbable but altogether impossible to think within ideological constraints. How does the ideological subject respond to that? Such events are not necessarily rare. Indeed, there is no thought that passes simply and wholly onto the plane of reference. However, we have been taught to ignore the excess. Through the experimental pursuit of the intensification of this effect, particularly in media compositions, one produces contexts that require subjectivity to shift. The subject still remains a referential point on a grid; it will never be anything but that. The criticism of the subject is *not* that it is representational, but that ideology works to manage cybernetically the subject positions we inhabit, to limit subjectivity and its expressions. However, the shape of the subject does change as the result of material conditions. We regularly acknowledge this, for example, in the emergence of new patterns of subjectivity with the coming of disciplinary-industrial culture. Here, the notion is also to mutate subjectivity, but in a non-deterministic, unpredictable manner by experimenting with the embodied and materially networked processes of cognition and media composition: the result, hopefully, being the production of new affects and a virtually present consciousness that demands new modes of subjectification.

In pedagogic terms this means moving away from constative and performative discourses, which precisely seek to use media to produce predictable thoughts and subjects. Instead the pedagogy of the event focuses on the motion, the activity, of communication and cognition (the activities of learning) and not on the achievement of specific points or goals. In focusing on the material, embodied activity of learning to write, the concept of "process" is reinvigorated by stripping process from its ideological attachments to the static author who is always already in control and defines the text as the making of a series of points. (I term the author "static" as s/he exists as an abstract consciousness separate from the body and its motions.) In doing so, one can articulate process in connection with the post-process understanding of discourse and ideology. Rip/mix/burn composition describes the material unfolding of thought and media, and cultural studies describes the articulation of thought and media on a plane of reference. Event pedagogy then inserts itself experimentally into the material unfolding of thought and media, where people and groups are articulated as such.

Inventing New Media Pedagogy

New media pedagogy, because it still remains largely uncharted and undisciplined territory, offers a number of such experimental opportunities. However, this does not mean that traditional expectations and issues regarding literacy instruction are not immediately ported into the new media classroom. Technical instruction, like that in new media, can easily shift into a training exercise, reflecting the most pedantic instructional models. And certainly, the most palpable pressures for such training come from student expectations: students show up to a new media course to learn how to make Web pages. In short, there is no need for the teacher to establish a goal for the course; the students arrive with a goal. This is simply an indication of the effectiveness of ideological indoctrination. While students (and perhaps their parents and some college administrators) might push for pragmatic, how-to job preparation, other faculty might push equally hard for the expectation that a new media writing course, as a course in the humanities, adhere to a general humanistic vision of the liberal arts and not become a "training" course. In short, though the means for teaching new media, and the particular contents of such courses, remain fairly open, such courses quickly become a site for re-enacting some of the oldest concerns in rhetorical instruction, particularly this concern that courses in new media sacrifice humanistic content in the name of career preparation. This concern is essentially a reincarnation of a debate between rhetoric as a set of skills and rhetoric/philosophy as a mode of intellectual investigation that goes back to Plato's arguments against rhetoric in *Gorgias* and *Phaedrus*. From this longstanding debate, we develop two conflicting perspectives—one which views rhetoric as a communication skill for the delivery of knowledge and another which views rhetoric as a critical, philosophical method itself. This binary should ring familiar, as it is a re-enactment of the division of constative and performative discourse that governs the traditional university: rhetoric as communication is a performative discourse, and rhetoric as philosophy (or cultural studies) is a constative discourse.

However, new media also provides us an opportunity to move beyond this to a new understanding of rhetoric. While such changes may be slow in higher education, new media is already bringing about a transformation of professional discourses, which suggests that training in instrumental, transactional, technical writing, or even the traditional argumentative structures of academic discourse, may no longer be as valuable as they once were. Instead, there is a growing belief that the American professional workforce of the future will need to be more adaptive, visionary, and creative—attributes that relate more to an experimental approach to pedagogy. Jon Udell, writing for the O'Reilly Network, picks up on this shift in the values relating to professional preparation and goes so far as to suggest that the future of first-year composition will be characterized by the production of multimedia documents, which he terms "screencasts." Udell sees screencasts as being rhetorically different from traditional genres of professional writing related to software development, which might be divided into technical or support documents and marketing or sales materials. The purpose of the screencast will be to connect end-users with the design-ers of new technologies and applications. Udell writes,

> the rate-limiting factor for software adoption is in-creasingly not purchase, or installation, or training, but simply 'getting it' . . . We haven't always seen the role of the writer and the role of the developer as deeply connected but, as the context for understand-ing software shifts from computers and networks to people and groups, I think we'll find that they are. ("The New Freshman Comp," 2005, para. 15-16)

In short, as information technologies become increasingly about social uses (e.g., wikipedia, del.icio.us, flickr), there is an increasing need for writers who can communicate the social dynamics of a technology; that is, someone who will be able to work with developers in helping to articulate and communicate their vision. As Udell continues,

> *The New York Times* recently asked: 'Is cinema stud-ies the new MBA?' I'll go further and suggest that these methods ought to be part of the new freshman comp. Writing and editing will remain the founda-tion skills they always were, but we'll increasingly combine them with speech and video. The tools and techniques are new to many of us. But the underlying principles—consistency of tone, clarity of structure, economy of expression, iterative refinement—will be familiar to programmers and writers alike. ("The New Freshman Comp," 2005, para. 23)

Udell's vision may still sound very much, in principle, like the traditional values of technical composition, plus the addition of new media, in that he makes reference to values like consistency, clarity, economy, and refinement. However, there is a deeper transformation taking place in the coming together of media and the identification of a new purpose and new audience, specifically in Udell's suggestion that screencasts need to help their audience "get it," to see the social value of a new application. "Getting it" is not particularly a matter of rationally communicating the various features of an application (as technical documentation would) or even selling those features or some feeling a company hopes to associate with an application (as marketing or advertising media would). Instead, Udell describes an emerging genre that seeks to demonstrate to potential users the ways in which a new application might fit into lives and allow them to make better use of the increasing amount of media available to them. For example, it is not enough for the developers of blogging applications to provide technical documentation or to produce advertising for their service. They need to communicate to potential users how a blog will allow them to participate in a community of readers and writers. This participation gets more specific as one thinks about particular types of bloggers: educators using blogs in the classes, professional writers who want to make money from their blogs, companies using blogs for internal communication or to communicate with clients or market products, and other individuals who simply wish to keep a diary or share a personal interest or viewpoint. Of course, the audiences become even more specific than that (e.g., addressing the use of blogs in first-year composition courses). A screencast for blogging in composition would include video, audio, and text that would demonstrate how you might easily set up a blog to share information with students, to have students comment on readings or distribute and comment on drafts of more formal writing assignments; it might also discuss how giving students the experience of producing their own blog creates an opportunity for investigating how discursive practices and a sense of audience develops in a new medium. Whatever the particular content of the screencast, the basic point is that it requires a new rhetorical, compositional approach in which writers and developers strive to help their potential users see how a new application fits into a larger picture of their information habits.

This shift away from instrumental reason is echoed elsewhere in the rethinking of professionalizing education. Richard Gabriel, a Distinguished Engineer at Sun Microsystems, has argued that software engineering programs should pattern themselves after MFA programs in creative writing. In particular, Gabriel references the system of mentoring, the community of writers, and the curriculum of ongoing practice, reflection, and revision in the context of workshops, conferences, and other coursework. He recognizes that

> in software as in writing, there are people whose work is 'doing the thing'—writing and designing programs—and such people do this work every day. They hope to be good at it and to be able to improve

over time. They have pride in what they do and are
satisfied or not with each project they do. To them
what they do feels more than craft, includes engineering and science, but still feels like more. ("Master
of Fine Arts in Software," 2001, para. 3)

Gabriel is articulating the need for software engineering programs to
develop a reflective and broader vision of the process of composition,
one that does not focus solely on the grammar of coding or other
practical issues but, as Udell is suggesting, aids software designers to
develop an ability to "get it" and communicate their understanding to
others. In many ways this is much like an MFA program that assists
writers in developing a critical understanding of their own writing.
That is, it is one thing to have some native sense of when one's writing
is or isn't working; it is another matter to develop the critical ability to
explain why a piece of writing does or doesn't "work."

Business guru Daniel Pink makes a similar argument, suggesting

in a world upended by outsourcing, deluged with
data, and choked with choices, the abilities that matter most are now closer in spirit to the specialties of
the right hemisphere [of the brain]—artistry, empa-
thy, seeing the big picture, and pursuing the transcendent. ("Revenge of the Right Brain," 2005, para.
5)

Pink, who has been proclaiming, "The MFA is the new MBA," reflects
this broader shift in our understanding of how humans interact with
information and information technologies. Going back to Aristotelian
categorization or the organization of libraries or academic disciplines
or even the nested folders or directories of early computers, the primary emphasis has been on so-called "left-brain" thinking. In order to be
a professional of any kind, one needed to be able to organize information and access structured bodies of information according to pre-existing principles. As I discuss in the previous chapter in relation to del.
icio.us and the practice of tagging, the growing body of information
with which we now work no longer submits itself effectively to categorization. This is already clear in the popularity of Google as a navigating mechanism. Similar strategies are now being applied to computer
operating systems (e.g., "Spotlight" in Mac OS 10.4 "Tiger"), which
has led some computer experts to speculate that we will soon see the

end of folders as a method for organizing files (Christopher and Faden 2005). In response to this general shift in the way we produce, store, and circulate information, Pink, Gabriel, and Udell are each arguing for the need for education to prepare a workforce that can work in these cognitive spaces. In this context, the "left brain" activities are not unimportant: undoubtedly, the workplace will still require texts that are well-organized, logical, clear, and so on. However, these activities are relatively less important, whereas the ability to think creatively, to put together information in surprising ways, and to operate in a more embodied, intuitive mode that does not require a firm structure are all dramatically more significant.

The reference to MFA-type programs likely emerges because such programs are the most common models of writing beyond composition instruction. Pink, Gabriel, and Udell do not think of technical writing programs, which they may view as too "left-brain," as positivistic and mechanical, though such programs are not necessarily that way. And though Udell discusses composition, it is primarily to suggest that it should be radically revised to focus on screencasting. Much like technical writing, composition is largely viewed as rational and positivistic, often centered on the mechanics of paragraphs and sentences. However, despite their endorsement, the MFA is not entirely the right model either. MFA programs in creative writing can be quite anti-technological, much in the same way as many traditional English departments (though again there are exceptions). In this resistance, one might recognize the willingness to cede, partially, the domain of the "left brain" to the technological. Perhaps, the argument goes, humans and machines share a capacity for logical information processing, but the domain of the "right brain," creativity, remains purely a human trait. As such, to recognize the role of technology in shaping "creative ideas" requires once again encountering the ideological boundaries of human identity. It is not simply technology that is at stake here, but the "technological way of thinking" that is associated with technical writing and, to a lesser extent, with rhetoric. So while there may be traits of the MFA that would be integral to the education desired here, they would need to mutate in some significant ways to be integrated with technology and business.

To imagine a program that can develop these compositional practices, it is necessary to dispense with the opposition of poetics and creative writing against rhetoric and technical writing. It is also necessary to move beyond knee-jerk prejudices regarding technology while retaining an *informed,* critical understanding of new media. A program such as the type Udell, Gabriel, and Pink describe would then combine aspects of creative writing, composition, and technical writing programs to include:

- a mentoring system similar to the MFA in which students develop close working relationships with faculty;
- a community of writers, students, and faculty, who share their work with one another in performance, in workshop, in the hallways, on blogs, etc.;
- "creative writing" courses, which offer opportunity for experimentation, for practicing poetic language, for thinking about character (psychology or affect) and narrative, for crossing genres, and for addressing audience in unexpected ways;
- courses in poetics and rhetoric as the underlying theories and philosophies of writing, which is something often absent from creative writing courses that tend to naturalize the writing process (and here I'm *not* thinking about the conventional rhetorics of a first-year composition handbook, not a pragmatics or how-to of process and audience-awareness, but an encounter with the aporias of symbolic behavior—again, the point is to develop creative, conceptual "right-brain" practices);
- courses in other professional genres—technical writing, business writing, and so on—that are not taught in the traditional positivistic manner, but rather in the context of creative writing and rhetoric/poetics;
- and, of course, coursework in new media, the practical but also its aesthetics, poetics, and rhetorics, which is not to say that technology isn't infused throughout this curriculum, but that one also has to have a place where students experiment with the media.

The result, ideally, of such a curriculum is a student who is a confident, practiced writer; who understands his/her creative process; who has developed a productive writing practice for him/herself; who has composed and performed work in multiple "creative writing" genres; who has internalized some sense of rhetorical and poetic; who has experience writing in workplace genres and bringing a more creative, "right brain" perspective to them; and has a strong foundation in working with new media.

How might such a program conform to the concept of an event pedagogy? As I mentioned earlier, it is impossible to discuss pedagogy without discussing goals on some level; simply to say that someone will learn something—that is, to say something is pedagogical—already constitutes a goal. I have just articulated a programmatic approach to writing instruction that might suggest a number of potential goals. However, the goals are quite abstract, as Udell, Gabriel, and Pink have described them: the ability to grasp "the big picture," to conceptualize on a large scale, and to be creative in one's ability to combine information and produce something new. In the terms I have been employing, the capacity to rip, mix, and burn information on this scale is not something that can be taught in a positivistic, step-by-step manner. The process does not operate in that mode but rather through a topological unfolding that one learns, through practice, how to navigate—not through the use of some external logical grid, but rather through proprioceptive sensibility, feeling one's way. Though one might say broadly that the "goal" of such a program and pedagogy would be the development of the ability to practice composition in this fashion, it is not a goal to which students can be led in a programmatic fashion. Instead, the purpose of the curriculum is to provide students with the material context in which opportunities for both experimenting with writing practices and reflecting critically upon such practices are facilitated. The idea is ultimately for students to develop individual strategies for entering into a compositional practice.

Ultimately, the question for professional writing programs and new media education is *not* how to balance the demand for "right brain" professionalization with critical humanism, but rather how to dispense with the binary altogether. That is, it is possible to come to see an education that prepares students for their professional lives as simultaneously developing a critical understanding of culture and ideology. Just as event pedagogy might intersect productively with the market-driven notion of a right-brain professional, drawing energy from these market interests without simply subsuming itself to market demands, event pedagogy finds a productive, mutational relationship with cultural studies and post-process composition studies. As I mentioned in the previous section, this relationship begins with the virtual-actual offering cultural studies a means to investigate the body that does not fall into the trap of naïve realism and subjectivism. The new media pedagogy I am describing does not imagine an objective reality that corresponds to thought and language and permits the transparent communication of information. That is, it is not the world of homeostatic cybernetics. Likewise, it does not found composition on the creative originality of the author, on the purity or insularity of subjective experience. That is, it is also not the world of autopoietic cybernetics. Instead, the virtual-actual offers a means for mapping and intervening—critically, experimentally—in the intersections between materiality, ideology, culture, information, technology, bodies, cognition, consciousness, and subjectivity. The right-brain professional interest in "getting it," in seeing the big picture, in operating on an affective/empathic level requires developing a critical and practical understanding of the larger operation of media and information. Investigating professional communication in these terms simultaneously opens a critical space for investigating the ideological components of media. After all, if one is to see the "big picture" and learn how to convey such an understanding to an audience on an affective level, would this not require a strong insight into the ideological mechanisms of media? What could be a better way to educate students about culture and ideology, particularly within the context of a writing curriculum, than to investigate directly the compositional methods by which corporate ideology is disseminated?

As the next chapter investigates, such a curriculum is emerging at a crucial moment when the academy appears poised for a potentially dramatic transformation, moving from a supportive but ancillary role in the economy to becoming another aspect of the marketplace. Chapters 7 and 8 have identified potential sites of opportunity for new media savvy rhetoricians to investigate this transformation. Challenging intellectual property through rip/mix/burn composition opens up new possibilities for cultural production and knowledge outside the boundaries of what is officially sanctioned; event pedagogy provides an understanding of how teaching practices can avoid simple capture within the representational logic of an institutional curriculum and offer an opportunity for learning to unfold in unpredictable ways. Drawing on this work, the final chapter explores more broadly how these understandings and practices of new media rhetoric and composition might point to a post-disciplinary, academic community better prepared to meet the technological and ideological challenges of a globalizing, information culture. In that chapter, I discuss how the notion of the right brain professional resonates with the "limited flexibility" that characterizes the ideal corporate worker within the broader, late capitalist environment Deleuze terms the "control society." However, as I have suggested here, I will also contend that within the virtual-actual, beneath the articulation of the corporate worker, there remain experimental, compositional, and pedagogy strategies that offer some hope for the university to remain something more (or at least other) than a simple servant of corporate interests or another extension of the capitalist marketplace.

9 Whatever Discipline

Copyright's expansion signals the growing importance of proprietary knowledge in our information economy. Clearly information technologies have played a significant part in the development of this economy, and much of the particularly sensitive proprietary information in our culture relates to computer hardware, software, and the various media they deliver. As I discuss in Chapter 8, this model of proprietary knowledge, which builds upon traditional notions of individual authorship and intellectual property, is poised to have a growing influence upon the shape of higher education. This influence potentially extends from teaching and research to administration and is closely tied to our uses of technology. It also brings its marketplace values with it. That is, it suggests that academics increasingly make their choices about the research they pursue and the curriculum they deliver based upon the market value of that knowledge, a market value that is in part determined by consumer (i.e., student) preference and in part by corporate demand. As I discuss in the previous chapter, one of the more common concerns about the influx of new media into higher education is the way in which such a curriculum threatens to devolve into training in a range of proprietary applications at the cost of a liberal education. The critique of the university's shift toward corporate logic has become a significant concern, and the increasing use of technology has been one of the more salient effects of that shift.

In cultural studies and in post-process composition studies, the critique of our information society, and the role of the academy within it, focuses primarily on the level of ideology and discourse, on the production and management of subjectivity. As effective as such analysis can be, one of the ongoing challenges of these pedagogies lies in the articulation of a compositional process that can move outside the instrumental logic of the corporate university. That is, the conventional writing process approach (and its even more traditional antecedents) view writing as a cybernetic process of targeting and control orchestrated ultimately by the original, creative thoughts of the author. This perspective on composition remains consonant with notions of authorship, originality, and intellectual property that founded copyright law nearly 300 years ago. In short, conventional composition is the production of proprietary, copyrighted media. These productions are then exchanged for grades, credits, and, ultimately, degrees. Later, one might exchange academic compositions for tenure and promotion. While Chapter 9 explores experimental means for meeting this challenge, currently the operation of writing pedagogy, in composition and across the curriculum, serves largely to reinforce capitalist practices of intellectual property and commodity exchange.

This academic market has traditionally run parallel to, but separate from, the capitalist marketplace. As Sheila Slaughter and Larry L. Leslie (1997) argue, since the sixties and seventies, the decline in general federal bloc grants to research universities, combined with budget shortfalls at the state government level, has resulted in these universities turning to the private sector for funding. This trend has come in combination with shifting values in terms of both research and teaching, with an increased emphasis put on research with market applications. That is, where in the past, scientists may have received support from the Pentagon to conduct research they hoped might have military applications, which might then also prove commercially viable (Eisenhower's military-industrial complex), now federal funding pursues university-corporate sponsorships that aim primarily at commercial products (which is not to say that military research is not also ongoing). Likewise, in terms of curriculum, increasing pressure exists to prepare (train) students specifically for entry into the corporate workforce. Given the continually changing demands of the workforce, especially in relation to technology, one encounters an ever-evolving curriculum. This includes training in industry-specific software applications. As a result, both research and curriculum are now closely tied to proprietary commercial products, if they are not indeed such products themselves.

This transition is easiest to see in fields where the process has been functioning the longest. For example, as Slaughter and Leslie note,

> Before the 1980s, biology was a basic science whose faculty were concerned primarily with performing research for the National Science Foundation and au-

> thoring papers for scholarly conferences and journals
> . . . By the mid 1980s, most full professors of mo-
> lecular biology held equity positions (they were given
> stock in return for their expertise) in spinoff compa-
> nies (small corporations based on products develop in
> university or government laboratories). (1997, p. 6)

Other salient examples would include computer science or application programs and business programs, where students might receive
direct instruction in technology and practices employed by major corporations. Such effects are less direct in most humanities programs.
However, the result has been a decline in traditional humanistic
programs and increased pressure to "professionalize" the humanities
through developing new curricula, often with a technological emphasis.

As critics of higher education note, the influence of capitalism on
higher education is long-standing and widespread. It includes busi-
nesspeople who serve as trustees; influence through donations given
to universities in the form of endowed chairs, programs, centers, and
buildings; partnerships for research; partnerships for student services from food and clothing to technology and finance; and curricular
partnerships including internship programs. The depth and breadth
of this phenomenon is beyond the scope of this text. However, clearly
there is no simple or broad means to address it. Higher education has
always fundamentally served the interests of the state that supported
it. That said, academics have generally held views that placed them
on the cultural periphery. As Noam Chomsky says rather matter-of-
factly,

> democracy or not, the integrity of the university
> and, in fact, its social role, depends on its function-
> ing as basically a subversive institution. That is, rais-
> ing questions, challenging received ideas, seeking to
> gain truth and also understanding in any domain,
> and that usually does lead to a subversive character.
> (White p. 200, 442)

As should be quite obvious, the role of the university is to question
cultural knowledge, values, practices, and assumptions, to produce
knowledge through research that offers new perspectives and opportunities for action, and to teach students similar critical skills. None of

this is new. What is new is this changing relationship between corporate and academic culture. Perhaps from the corporate perspective it is difficult to not view higher education as another marketplace to dominate, just as corporate interests have come to dominate much of the public sector. From this perspective, the "leasing of the ivory tower," to borrow Lawrence Soley's phrase (1995), is part of the broader process in which one sees a reversal from the situation in which corporations are created to serve the interests of the state to one where the state serves the interests of corporations.

While technology has been viewed as complementing the corporate takeover of higher education, it does not necessarily need to play this role. While the critique of the corporate role in academia, including the function of technology, is crucial to the long-term project of articulating a role for higher education in late capitalism, it is also necessary for us to investigate critical uses of technology in imagining what the future of the academy might be. As I have been arguing here, it is necessary for us to understand that we think *with* technology, not before, after, against, or despite it. This does not obviate our responsibility to investigate the recursive relationship between technology and human cognition. In fact, it heightens the necessity of such an investigation. In this chapter I make no pretension to offering a quick solution to the challenges that face us. While the past eight chapters suggest ways we might rethink our understanding of composition and pedagogy in the context of new media, they do not do so in a way that points to a particular practice.

Below I explore the current situation in higher education in the context of Deleuze's concept of control. Control expands on Foucault's disciplinary society to account for more subtle, micropolitical ideological mechanisms. In university terms, I discuss this in the rhetoric of excellence that has become commonplace on campuses (a phenomena observed by Bill Readings, among others). As I see it, excellence and control facilitate the development of a degree of flexibility perceived as integral to the emerging economy. This flexibility can be found in university management, in curriculum development, in the professional development of faculty, and certainly in the preparation of students for the corporate workforce. Fundamentally, flexibility is the result of the careful, cybernetic modulation of information and desire. Flexibility demonstrates the ways in which cybernetic technologies have played an integral role in the development of new ideological mechanisms, much like industrial technologies were indispensable to the panoptic powers of a disciplinary society.

While control represents an extensive system of ideological power, it is far from omnipotent. As I have been examining throughout this text, cybernetic technologies rest upon a virtual-actual space of indeterminacy, and it is within that virtual-actual space that cognition is composed. As such, I suggest that one possible response to the emergence of Deleuze's control society within higher education is to focus on the singularity of composition and pedagogical events as I have been describing them. I discuss this in terms of Giorgio Agamben's concept of "whatever," the notion that we might accept events as whatever they are rather than simply apprehending them against some preexisting points of reference. This means setting aside the common complaints of student discipline or literacy or maturity to examine the aporia of the virtual-actual that lies beneath them. It is in those events that learning and composing unfold, and it is there that I suggest our future exists.

EXCELLENCE AND CONTROL

A part of this understanding is recognizing how information technologies have altered the practices of power and ideology from those typically identified in Foucauldian analyses of disciplinary institutional discourses. A good example of this changing operation is the "rhetoric of excellence" within higher education. Today, excellence is used widely in university discourses to describe overall missions and visions as well as shorter term, more strategic goals. Universities seek to promote excellence in terms of faculty research, student services, and teaching. One of the more salient results of this rhetoric has been the development of centers for excellence in teaching and learning at universities around the nation. Most of these have appeared in the last 20 years, though some, such as those at Stanford and Harvard, go back as far as 1975. It is not coincidental that such centers develop over the same period that sees the emergence of our post-industrial economy. A perusal of the centers' websites reveals strong rhetorical similarities in their missions, goals, and programs—not unlike the similarities one finds visiting English department websites around the nation. For example, Stanford's Center for Teaching and Learning describes its mission as being, "[i]n its broadest terms . . . to promote excellence in teaching at all ranks and excellence in student learning inside and outside the classroom" (2006), and Harvard's Derek Bok Center for teaching and learning writes that the university's "continuing support of the Center reflects a commitment to the belief that excellence in research, teaching, and learning are compatible at the very highest level" (2007). Aside from this general commitment to teaching "excellence," most centers see the integration of new technologies into the classroom as a significant part of their mission. Often this results in close institutional ties with their universities' instructional technology centers and the promotion of pilot programs involving electronic pedagogy. The emergence of these centers, however, is only an indicator and not the cause of the rhetoric of excellence.

Instead, the emergence of the rhetoric of excellence is part of a larger cultural shift Deleuze observes from Foucauldian disciplinary societies into new "control societies."

> Factories formed individuals into a body of men for the joint convenience of a management that could monitor each component in this mass, and trade unions that could mobilize mass resistance; but businesses are constantly introducing an inexorable rivalry presented as healthy competition, a wonderful motivation that sets individuals against one another and sets itself up in each of them, dividing each within himself. Even the state education system has been looking at the principle of "getting paid for results:" in fact, just as businesses are replacing factories, *school* is being replaced by *continuing education* and exams by continuous assessment. It's the surest way of turning education into a business. (1995, p. 179)

Deleuze's description of "rivalry" sounds very distant from the rhetoric of excellence, which emphasizes academics working together across disciplines in pursuit of a common goal. This emphasis on collaboration is echoed in new corporate rhetorics that describe the contemporary workplace as a "team environment" founded on creative participation. Of course, the notion of team is meaningless without "healthy" competition, and within this rhetoric, it is only "natural" that competition might emerge between teams. Likewise, the pursuit of excellence is predicated upon a certain striving where individuals, and their departments, are recognized (and sometimes compensated) for their "excellence." This competition results in the familiar practice in American public education of schools "getting paid for results" measured by standardized testing. More importantly, Deleuze's language contextualizes the rhetoric of excellence within the larger cultural shift from "discipline" to "control." The notion of discipline is familiar to pedagogic institutions, many of which reached their modern form during the rise of disciplinary power during the nineteenth century. There are academic disciplines, the disciplinary action of the teacher in the classroom, and the self-discipline attributed to successful students. Each of these disciplines represents a focusing mechanism imposed upon the subject, or as Deleuze terms it, a mold into which the subject is placed. As such, discipline requires the notion of free will: we choose discipline because discipline is good for us. Otherwise, it would be hopelessly coercive. Control, however, does not require this fiction as it does not impose upon the subject, but rather participates in the production of subjectivity itself. Rather than a mold, Deleuze sees control as a modulation, a modification of desire and experience that participates in the unfolding of thought. Of course, control does not erase discipline, but rather adds to it, extending power into new spaces.

The ideological advantage of control over discipline lies in its potential flexibility. This is implicit in the shift from a mold to a modulation. Despite the stereotypical rigidity of computer logic, information technologies permit a high degree of flexibility as we fine tune production and management processes. In turn, the new economy requires more flexibility from workers in terms of training, labor practices, cultural requirements, and ideology. In effect, the introduction of cybernetic mechanisms into the economy (e.g., computers and robots) have necessarily altered the type of work required by humans, just as mechanical industrialization did a century or more before. It may not be the case, as cyberneticist Norbert Wiener feared, that we have come to view humans as cybernetic machines (though perhaps that has happened as well), but in working in the context of a computerized, automated, information economy, the human worker must be flexible enough to interface with the technology and respond to input as the computer does. Of course, this flexibility has its limits. James Berlin observes "the standards voiced by corporate leaders call for workers who are at once creative and aggressive in identifying and solving problems and submissive and unquestioningly cooperative in carrying out the orders of superiors" (2003, p. 52). This call resonates with the demand for "right-brain" thinking discussed in the last chapter. This, then, becomes the primary mandate for university curricula, the production of limitedly flexible workers. Ideologically, this limited flexibility fits comfortably with the mainstream, liberal agenda of most universities: the inculcation of awareness and appreciation of cultural difference and the ability to cooperate with "others." For example, the housing of "multiculturalism" or "diversity" within specific, required general education courses testifies to the university's desire to promote limited flexibility. Workers must be able to function with "others" in their midst, in their relative professional class, but they should not be encouraged to identify with the problems of others in any substantial way that might lead them to employ their creative, aggressive problem-solving skills *against* the post-Fordist economy. Nor is there any inherent desire among the majority of students to make such identification. Trained to recognize the fluidity of their own identities, students are prepared to deconstruct and reassemble their selves in order to fit into the modulations of the new economy. They must be prepared for a life of continuing education, for a workday without boundaries (realized through the telecommunications that turn the home and even the car into potential workspaces), for migration on a global scale as they move through and between transnational corporations, and for the cultural and ideological differences they will face as they move through these spaces.

Ultimately flexibility becomes translatability: the ability of the student-subject to be translated seamlessly into the virtual economy. All other parts must be excised. Kroker and Weinstein (1994) would understand this subject as a "recombinant sign," as a series of elements that can be broken down (digitized) and reassembled as needed. When the subject becomes modulated into a virtual version of herself, she can then be transmitted to other nodes in the economic network. This process may sound like the worst type of discipline—an irredeemable infringement upon her free will—but it is not that at all. Instead, it is the careful shifting of desires. One needs not be suspicious or fearful of computers; they are helpful tools, as a course in the computer classroom will illustrate to you. The helpful pedagogue will ease the transition into being a computer user, and the university and their corporate partners will provide loans for the purchase of a computer. Becoming a proficient computer user will open more career options for the future and increase earnings potential, and once one has learned the basics, it becomes easier and easier to update computer skills as new applications emerge. As a graduate, the proficient computer-user will be more valuable to his or her employer, who can shift the new employee into a range of different work situations. This pedagogic process is not an imposition of power but rather an exercise in flexibility. The student recognizes the need to be flexible in order to be successful, to be open-minded, to be willing to try new experiences; the teacher must be flexible to respond to the expectations of students as consumers and the changing practices of the university; and the university must be flexible to meet the demands of its new workplace and the new virtual economy.

Of course, this flexibility is really not about being flexible at all, but rather about adjusting the body to meet the demands of virtual technology, just as the discourses of biopower adjusted the nineteenth-century body to the demands of industrialization. The rhetoric of excellence transforms this process of adjustment into a virtual, aesthetic experience, one from which pleasure might even be derived. Where the panopticon observed the body as a whole and discipline forced the whole body to fit into molds, virtuality dissects the body at a pre-subjective level, and control modulates its elements. At the beginning of the modern university, pedagogy may have been a transcendental experience through which one came to a realization of the Truth. In virtuality, however, pedagogy is an immanent experience that happens to and through the body, via desires and technologies. The flexible, excellent university changes programming like television networks do—in response to the preferences of its consumers and other stake-holders—and modulates consumer desire through its own pedagogic technologies. The university requires the rhetoric of excellence to undertake these practices, as the late capitalist logic of profit cannot be made to apply directly to the academy (at least not yet). That is, academic institutional values prevent decisions from being made solely on monetary grounds; other values must be incorporated into the process if the university is to maintain its cultural function. However, these values must be made fungible; they must be integrated into a commodified system of exchange. This is because the shift from panoptics and discipline to virtuality and control allows for more extensive micromanagement and an apparently seamless integration of desire into the institution. In order for control to be able to function on this level, it must be able to divide content into arbitrary units (much like labor is divided into money and media is divided into digital bytes).

In short, the university is transformed from a site of discipline, where students are molded into particular kinds of people, into a site of control, where students are matched to a series of modulations reflecting and shaping their desires. These modulations take the form of virtual commodities that student-consumers purchase. I write "virtual commodities" for while some of the university's products are fairly tangible—a degree, certified knowledge or expertise, comfortable dorm rooms, convenient parking—many are more subjective, more closely tied to desires or cultural status. In this manner they are similar to the affects or attributes promised to the consumer of a particular beer or the wearer of a particular sneaker or the driver of a particular car. The subjective commodities of being "the" college student, and eventually, "the" college graduate are the university's best selling points.

WHATEVER DISCIPLINE

However, while control introduces cybernetic principles and power into the topological unfolding of thought, it can only function to the degree to which those unfolding thoughts can be apprehended on the plane of reference. That is, control can only serve to try to limit the mutative potential of becoming. By identifying and analyzing these strategies of control it becomes possible to incorporate them into further mutational experiments. Extending on the example above, the university may seek to modulate student desire to become a flexible, computer-literate corporate worker, but, as I discuss in Chapter 8, Ulmer's *Internet Invention* demonstrates how the cybernetic mechanisms put in place by the university to ensure this modulation might be ripped from their context, mixed in new combinations, and burned to produce an alternate mode of relating with media. That said, the pedagogic event does not provide specific guidelines for behavior or method; it does not reveal how to resist control or excellence. A pedagogic event is not a teaching practice but rather the material space in which pedagogy occurs. Without a clear method or response, the question remains in our discipline and others: how to respond to technology? How to respond to growing corporate influence?

The excellent university, with its flexible, market-driven logic, has its own ideas for how the humanities might develop. Of course, faculty in English Studies and the rest of the humanities have different ideas (and ideas that conflict with one another). Clearly in our own discipline, internal conflicts abound between and among traditional literary studies, rhetoric and composition, cultural studies, and other areas. In part these conflicts turn on concerns that are specific to our discipline. However, much of our disagreement is also conditioned by the larger academic and cultural shifts I have been describing here. As such, the past decade has seen the infusion of technology and the proliferation of professionalizing curricula in English departments. For some, this may appear to be a solution and potential future for English Studies; for others, it is further evidence of the growing crisis in our discipline. Victor Vitanza, writing specifically about the future of rhetoric and composition, suggests another possibility:

> Perhapless, there are two possibilities here: "We" can start teaching writing precisely as the university needs it taught. Or "we" can attempt "to teach" writing the way "we" want. But there are, let us not forget, third (interval) wayves. And therefore, "we" should ask: What is it that writing wants? I suspect that "writing" does not want what either the uni-versity thinks it needs nor what "we" think we want. ("Abandoned to Writing: Notes Toward Several Provocations," 2004, para. 8)

Though we can devise means to critique and resist the excellent university and its increasing coziness with corporate interests, it would be naïve to imagine that higher education will not continue to serve the interests of the state as it always has. On the other hand, it would be a gross oversimplification of ideology to imagine that academic institutions can simply control pedagogy. Similarly, even if we were to imagine some highly unlikely future where our discipline had some consensus over what "we" want to teach, undoubtedly that consensus would be shaped by institutional contexts.

The fundamental error here is imagining that pedagogy can (or should) be about control, about producing predictable results. It is an error that overlooks that composition and pedagogy are distributed, material-cognitive processes that unfold in fundamentally indeterminate ways. Can anyone really imagine that the 20 or 30 or more students sitting in a classroom are really experiencing equivalent cognitive processes? Certainly, we can do many things with discipline and control to steer subjects in a particular direction, to require similar results on tests, and so on. However, none of that really affects the material processes of thought and composition. For the most part, we simply ignore this or cover over this aporia with problems, such as "students are undisciplined" or "students can't write." Perhaps, as Vitanza suggests, one way to respond to the challenges of the excellent university, as well as our intra-disciplinary struggles, is to forego these dialectics and the problems they announce and not forget these "third (interval) wayves." To examine the virtual-actual unfolding of composition and pedagogy, as I have been doing in this book, means to interact directly with the material processes underlying our disciplinary practice. This in no way means that we should ignore the ideological operations of higher education but rather that we might more productively understand ideology through an examination of the materiality of thought and language.

In part, approaching composition and pedagogy through the virtual-actual means recognizing that each compositional or pedagogical event occurs singularly. In its singularity, the event must be accepted for "whatever" it is (to borrow Giorgio Agamben's term). In recognizing the singularity of the event for whatever it is, Agamben argues "Singularity is thus freed from the false dilemma that obliges knowledge to choose between the ineffability of the individual and the intelligibility of the universal" (1993, p. 1). From this perspective, one does not situate writing or new media (or rhetoric and composition as we name these things in disciplinary terms) as a discipline or as a sub-discipline (i.e. in a situation where rhetoricians must fight for recognition); one does not situate a discipline, called whatever, as a servant, as loyal opposition, or as some more critical or revolutionary force in relation to the excellent or corporate university; and finally one does not situate a discipline or a university or academia in general as a cultural force that serves or opposes or vies to influence or direct the state. Of course, these are all ways we discuss discipline, just as we might discuss writing or teaching in these terms—as practices through which we submit/are submitted to power, grab for and make use of power, and serve or oppose power. However, the pedagogic event opens insight into how pedagogy is not what (we think) it is, just as cognition and consciousness are not what (we think) they are in subjective terms. In the unfolding, topological process of becoming, we never become what we are. Whatever discipline introduces a similar concept. It asks us to accept the aporia of thought that makes a pedagogy of control impossible and to set aside the problems (of student discipline, literacy, maturity and so on) with which we obscure that aporia. Furthermore, it suggests that we invest in this aporia, in the "whatever" of human thought and subjectivity, as the best, indeed the only, site of composition and learning.

The notion of whatever may appear apolitical; however, Agamben sees

> the novelty of the coming politics is that it will no longer be a struggle for the conquest or control of the State, but a struggle between the State and the non-State (humanity), an insurmountable disjunction between whatever singularity and the State organization. (1993, p. 85)

Or as Félix Guattari puts it,

> the future of contemporary subjectivity is not to live indefinitely under the regime of self-withdrawal, of mass mediatic infantilisation, of ignorance of difference and alterity—both on the human and the cosmic register . . . Beyond material and political demands, what emerges is an aspiration for individual and collective reappropriation of the production of subjectivity. (1995, p. 133)

In this sense, the struggle against the corporate university, and its use of new media and information technology to produce an infantilizing spectacle of control, takes place in the moment of the event, at the site where whatever "our" singular becoming will (never) be is shaped, managed, and organized. Writing, and new media composition as what writing becomes, offers a practice for entering into this space. Writing, as that object-technology-practice that is always already outside of/prior to the emergence of concepts, reminds us that consciousness is a material unfolding through a network of distributed cognition. Corporate culture may indeed come to shape the logical organization of the university (as if there were a time when the university did not serve the state), but with such topological processes of knowledge production at its foundation, discipline can never be anything except *whatever* it is.

The practices I have described here undoubtedly can be turned in part to serve dominant ideological interests; they can also be employed to serve critical perspectives. All writing and media have always been recruited in this fashion. However, cognition and composition have always also held out the possibility for the unpredicted: rip/mix/burn always promises the spread of the *pharmakon* with unforeseeable results. Here is the power of the singular, not to reproduce its singularity in a process of becoming-the-same (to make you agree with me) but to initiate another singular becoming (into whatever being). As Vitanza notes, "Neither the uni-versity nor you can stop this bacterial-viral-crystaline infection from sp.reading to y.our students. 'It' comes not from some foreign, devil*u*sh notions about writing and community; rather, 'it' comes from within 'writing' itself! Hahahahahahaha. To write is to infect" (2003, para. 14). Vitanza's playful observation resonates with the dangers Derrida notes the critique of translation presents to the university (see Chapter 8): writing challenges the transparent circulation of constative knowledge and undermines performative discourse with its indeterminacy. One does not have to go in search of "difficult" texts to see this; it exists in the most mundane, bureaucratic rhetoric. Each singular student with a "problem" demonstrates the indeterminacy of written college policies, an indeterminacy that invariably results in the production of further, indeterminate text and ultimately an arbitrary decision/judgment. The problem, of course, hides this aporia of indeterminacy from sight; the simulation of order runs on with the singular student as the exception that proves the rule. However, whatever being insists each one of us is singular, and the coming community of whatever being proves the empty and arbitrary nature of rule and judgment.

This is what the university cannot withstand, the revelation of the emptiness of signs, even though this is precisely the condition that the corporate society of the spectacle brings about. Contemporary politics, Agamben argues,

> is this devastating *experimentum linguae* that all over the planet unhinges and empties traditions and beliefs, ideologies and religions, identities and communities. Only those who succeed in carrying it to completion—without allowing what reveals to remain veiled in the nothingness that reveals, but bringing language itself to language—will be the first citizens

of a community with neither presuppositions nor a
State" (1993, p. 84).

The urge to resist this experiment, to cling to traditions, is understandable; it is the appearance of cultural conservatism everywhere, from those insisting upon traditional humanistic curricula in universities to religious fundamentalism around the world. The experiment is devastating. And yet, the task, as Agamben describes it, is to complete the experiment, to bring language to language, and to articulate a language of the singular. It is a task that appears impossible, except that writing already is singular, that new media composition is a material process of unfolding rather than a controlled simulation of thought.

ENDIT

This book began with Derrida's question, "Where is to be found the communitary *place* and the social bond of a 'campus' in the cyberspatial age of the computer, of tele-work, and of the World Wide Web?" (2002, p. 210). It is a question of technology and of the future of higher education, but more fundamentally it is a question of space and time and community. The "university without conditions," as Derrida terms the institution he investigates, must deconstruct the cybernetic simulation of knowledge, individuality, and institutional community in order to allow the unfolding of the event, the unpredictable, even impossible, becoming of the materiality of distributed cognition. Only through such a process, as unlikely (indeed impossible) as it may be, will the humanities move beyond its allegiances to enlightenment and modernity and participate in the coming community of singular beings, whatever they may be.

Writing and new media offer means for pursuing the coming community and university without conditions. Clearly it is not necessary for these technologies to lead in this direction. In fact, one might say it is impossible for them to do so, but, of course, impossibility is precisely the point here—the impossible present of the event. One cannot follow a line or follow directions into becoming a writer (though perhaps some directions might serve a heuristic purpose). One writes into a space of writing that is produced through writing, just as one thinks into a space of thought that is produced through thought. Or as Blanchot writes, "one writes only if one reaches that instant which nevertheless one can only approach in the space opened by the movement of writing. To write, one has to write already" (1982, p. 176). Writing is, in this sense, an act of sorcery: a pact made with a demon at an aporetic crossroads in which the contagion of thought is passed on. After all, Thoth and Hermes, the patron gods of writing and literature, were also the gods of magic.

> If the writer is a sorcerer, it is because writing is a becoming, writing is traversed by strange becomings that are not becomings-writer, but becomings-rat, becomings-insect, becomings-wolf. . . . Who has not known the violence of these animal sequences, which uproot one from humanity, if only for an instant, making one scrape at one's beard like a rodent or giving one the yellow eyes of a feline? A fearsome involution calling us toward unheard-of becomings. (Deleuze and Guattari, 1987, p. 240)

Perhaps we can begin to understand such accounts of writing not as poetic metaphors or mystifications but instead as attempts to articulate the material processes by which thought and composition emerge from the virtual-actual.

To the contrary of our common concerns, new media technologies need not lead us away from our animal heritage by fulfilling some fascinating fantasy of transcendence. Instead tapping away, forming letters on a screen, might remind us of our Paleolithic heritage, our ancestors marking indecipherable symbols on cave walls; the waves and radiation of the computer might recall the ethereal *chora*; and our passage through cyberspace might resemble the disappearing wake of the original "cybernauts" navigating the seas of ancient Greece. Like our ancestors, we face a not so dissimilar informational and social crisis, our comfortable social networks and ways of knowing challenged by new demands. And perhaps beneath these problems we have invented to shield ourselves, we will find the same *aporia*.

The problems and potentials of new media, information, and globalization surround us in the contemporary academy. They represent issues that we must address for many reasons, not the least of which being that they constitute a cultural force that will transform higher education. Ironically, though, at this apparent moment of capitalism's engulfment of global culture, at the cusp of realizing transcendent virtual reality and consciousness, and the achievement of rational science and the technological way of thinking, cybernetics opens an aporetic fissure in the will to virtuality. Modern art and media disrupt our fascination with uncanny presentations of the body we have sought to suppress. And contemporary philosophy articulates new concepts to wrench open that fissure and dramatically undo the virtual prognosis pronounced as our future. As Derrida warns, "If the impossible that I'm talking about were perhaps to arrive one day, I leave you to imagine the consequences. Take your time but be quick about it, because you do not know what awaits you" (2002, p. 237). Derrida's words remain apt here. As always, the future demands action, forever diverging from the present. However, we can persist only in the impossibility of the event and must seek to articulate our thoughts and actions upon that slipping ground.

References

Adorno, T. & Horkheimer, M. (2002) *The dialectic of enlightenment: Philosophical fragments.* Stanford: Stanford University Press.

Agamben, G. (1993). *The coming community* (M. Hardt, Trans.). Minneapolis: University of Minnesota Press.

Arnold, M. (1993).*"Culture and anarchy" and other writings.* Cambridge, UK: Cambridge University Press. (Original work published 1869)

Baudrillard, J. (1983). The ecstasy of communication. In H. Foster (Ed), *The Anti-Aesthetic: Essays on Postmodern Culture* (J. Johnston, Trans.) (pp. 126-134). Seattle: Bay Press.

Baudrillard, J. (1988). *America* (C. Turner, Trans.). London: Verso.

Baudrillard, J. (1993a). Game with vestiges. In M. Gane (Ed.), *Baudrillard live: selected interviews* (R. Gibson and P. Patton, Trans.) (pp. 81-95). London: Routledge.

Baudrillard, J. (1993b) Forget Baudrillard. In M. Gane (Ed.), *Baudrillard live: selected interviews* (pp. 99-127). London: Routledge.

Baudrillard, J. (1993c). *Symbolic exchange and death* (I. H. Grant, Trans.). London: Sage.

Baudrillard, J. (1994). *Simulacra and simulation* (S. Faria Glaser, Trans.). Ann Arbor: University of MI Press.

Barber, B. (1992). Jihad vs. McWorld [Electronic version]. *The Atlantic Monthly.* Retrieved May 10, 2005 from http://www.theatlantic.com/doc/prem/199203/barber

Berlin, J. (2003). *Rhetorics, poetics, and culture.* West Lafayette, IN: Parlor Press.

Benjamin, W. (1968). The work of art in the age of mechanical reproduction. In H. Arendt (Ed.) *Illuminations* (Harry Zohn, Trans.) (pp. 219-253). New York: Harcourt.

Blanchot, M. (1982). *The space of literature* (Ann Smock, Trans.). Lincoln: University of Nebraska Press.

Bolter, J. D. (2001). *Writing space: Computers, hypertext, and the remediation of print.* Mahwah, NJ: Lawrence Erlbaum.

Brooks, R. A. (1991). Intelligence without representation. *Artificial intelligence journal, 47,* 39–159.

Brooks, R. A. (1997b). From earwigs to humans. *Robotics and autonomous systems, 20*(2–4), 291–304.

Brooks, R. A., Breazeal C., Marjanovic M., Scassellati B., & Williamson, M. (1999). The cog project: Building a humanoid robot. In C. Nehaniv (Ed.), *Computation for metaphors, analogy, and agents* (pp. 6-12). New York: Springer.

Brooks, R. A. & Stein, L. A. (1994). Building brains for bodies. *Autonomous Robots 1* (1), 7–25.

"Bullet Time Walkthrough." (2003). *The Matrix Trilogy*. Retrieved July 15, 2003 from http://whatisthematrix.warnerbros.com

Bush, V. (2001). As we may think. In R. Packer and K. Jordan (Eds.), *Multimedia: from Wagner to virtual reality* (pp. 135-153). New York: Norton.

Campbell, J. (1972). *The hero with a thousand faces*. Princeton, NJ: Princeton University Press.

The Center for Teaching and Learning. (2006). Center for teaching and learning – General information. Retrieved May 13, 2007, from Stanford University Web site: http://ctl.stanford.edu/General/mission.html

Christopher, A. & Faden, M. (2005) Tiger tweaks could kill folders. *Wired. com, 9*. Retrieved June 10, 2005 from http://www.wired.com/news/mac/0,2125,67774,00.html

Clynes, M. E. & Kline, N. S. (1995). Cyborgs and space. In C. H. Gray (Ed.), *The cyborg handbook* (pp. 29-34). New York: Routledge.

Davis, E. (2004). Synthetic meditations: Cogito in the matrix. In D. Tofts, A. Jonson, & A. Cavallaro (Eds.), *Prefiguring Cyberculture: an Intellectual History* (pp. 12-27). Cambridge: MIT Press.

DeLanda, M. (2000). *A thousand years of nonlinear history*. New York: Zone.

DeLanda, M. (2002). *Intensive science and virtual philosophy*. London: Continuum.

Deleuze, G. (1977). I have nothing to admit. [Electronic Version] Retrieved June 5, 2005 from http://bush.cs.tamu.edu/~erich/misc/nothing_to_admit

Deleuze, G. (1983). *Nietzsche and philosophy* (H. Tomlinson, Trans.). New York: Columbia University Press.

Deleuze, G. (1988). *Foucault* (S. Hand, Trans.). Minneapolis: University of Minnesota Press.

Deleuze, G. (1995). *Negotiations* (M. Joughin, Trans.). New York: Columbia University Press.

Deleuze, G. (2000). Having an idea in cinema. In G. Flaxman (Ed.), *The brain is the screen: Deleuze and the philosophy of cinema* (pp. 14-19). Minneapolis: University of Minnesota Press.

Deleuze, G. & Guattari, F. (1983). *Anti-Oedipus: Capitalism and schizophrenia* (R. Hurley, M. Seem, and H. R. Lane, Trans.). Minneapolis: University of Minnesota Press.

Deleuze, G. & Guattari, F. (1986). *Kafka: Toward a minor literature* (D. Polan, Trans.). Minneapolis: University of Minnesota Press.

Deleuze, G. & Guattari, F. (1987). *A thousand plateaus: Capitalism and schizophrenia* (B. Massumi, Trans.). Minneapolis: University of Minnesota Press.

Deleuze, G. & Guattari, F. (1994). *What is philosophy?* (H. Tomlinson & G. Burchell, Trans.). New York: Columbia University Press.

Deleuze, G. & Parnet, C. (1987). *Dialogues* (H. Tomlinson & B. Habberjam, Trans.). New York: Columbia University Press.

Derrida, J. (1976). *Of grammatology* (G. C. Spivak, Trans.). Baltimore: Johns Hopkins University Press.

Derrida, J. (1978). *Writing and difference* (A. Bass, Trans.). Chicago: University of Chicago Press.

Derrida, J. (1981a). *Dissemination* (B. Johnson, Trans.). Chicago: University of Chicago Press.

Derrida, J. (1981b). *Positions* (A. Bass, Trans.). Chicago: University of Chicago Press.

Derrida, J. (1991a). Che cos'é la poesia? In P. Kamuf (Ed. & Trans.) *A Derrida reader: Between the blinds* (pp. 221-237). New York: Columbia University Press.

Derrida, J. (1991b). From "Living on: border lines." In P. Kamuf (Ed.), *A Derrida reader: Between the blinds* (J. Hulbert, Trans.) (pp. 254-68). New York: Columbia University Press.

Derrida, J. (1993). *Aporias* (T. Dutoit, Trans.). Stanford: Stanford University Press.

Derrida, J. (1994). *Specters of Marx* (P. Kamuf, Trans.). New York: Routledge.

Derrida, J. (2002). *Without alibi* (P. Kamuf, Trans.), Stanford: Stanford University Press.

Derek Bok Center for Teaching and Learning. (2007). Our history and mission. Retrieved May 13, 2007, from Harvard University Web site: http://isites.harvard.edu/icb/icb.do?keyword=k1985&pageid=icb.page29729

Duvall, J. N. (1998). The (super)marketplace of images: Television as unmediated mediation in DeLillo's *White Noise.* In M. Osteen (Ed.), *White noise: Text and criticism* (pp. 432-55). New York: Penguin.

Faigley, L. (1992). *Fragments of rationality.* Pittsburgh: University of Pittsburgh Press.

Foucault, M. (1972). The discourse on language. In *The archeology of knowledge and the discourse on language* (A. M. Sheridan Smith, Trans.) (pp. 215-38). New York: Pantheon.

Foucault, M. (1965). *Madness and civilization: A history of insanity in the age of reason* (R. Howard, Trans.). New York: Pantheon.

Foucault, M. (1977). *Language, counter-memory, practice: Selected essays and interviews* (D. F. Bouchard & S. Simon, Trans.). Ithaca: Cornell University Press.

Foucault, M. (1980). *The history of sexuality, Vol. 1: an introduction* (R. Hurley, Trans.). New York: Vintage.

Freud, S. (1998/1919). The uncanny (J. Strachey, Trans.). In J. Rivkin and M. Ryan (Eds.), *Literary theory: An anthology* (pp. 154-167). Malden, MA: Blackwell.

Gabriel, R. (2001). Master of fine arts in software. Retrieved May 1, 2005 from http://dreamsongs.com/MFASoftware.html

Gamble, C. (1999). *The paleolithic societies of Europe.* Cambridge: Cambridge University Press.

Gibson, W. (1984). *Neuromancer.* New York: Ace Books.

Gibson, W. (2001). Academy leader. In R. P. Packer & K. Jordan (Eds.), *Multimedia: from Wagner to virtual reality* (pp. 247-251). New York: Norton.

Gibson, W. & Sterling, B. (1991). *The difference engine.* New York: Bantam.

Gitelman, L. (1999). *Scripts, grooves, and writing machines: Representing technology in the Edison era.* Stanford: Stanford University Press.

Gitelman, L. & Pingree, P. B. (Eds.) (2003). *New media 1740–1915.* Cambridge: MIT Press.

Guattari, F. (1993). Machinic heterogenesis (J. Creech, Trans.). In V. A. Conley (Ed.), *Rethinking technologies* (pp. 13-27) Minneapolis: University of Minnesota Press.

Guattari, F. (1995). *Chaosmosis: an ethico-aesthetic paradigm* (P. Bains, Trans.). Bloomington, IN: Indiana University Press.

Hansen, M. (2000). *Embodying technesis: Technology beyond writing.* Ann Arbor: University of Michigan Press.

Hansen, M. (2004). *New philosophy for new media.* Cambridge: MIT Press.

Haraway, D. (1995). Cyborgs and symbionts: Living together in the new world order. In C. H. Gray (Ed.), *The cyborg handbook* (pp. xi-xx). New York: Routledge.

Haraway, D. (1996). *Modest witness, second-millennium: Femalemale meets oncomouse: Feminism and technoscience.* New York: Routledge.

Haraway, D. (2000). A manifesto for cyborgs: Science, technology, and socialist feminism in the 1980s. In D. Bel and B. Kennedy (Eds.), *The cybercultures reader* (pp. 291-324). New York: Routledge.

Havelock, E. A. (1963). *Preface to Plato.* Cambridge: Harvard University Press.

Hawisher, G. & Selfe, C. (Eds.) (1999). *Passions, pedagogies, and 21st century technologies.* Logan: Utah State University Press.

Hayles, N. K. (1999a). The condition of virtuality. In P. Lunenfeld (Ed.), *The digital dialectic* (pp. 68-95). Cambridge, MA: MIT Press.

Hayles, N. K. (1999b). *How we became posthuman: Virtual bodies in cybernetics, literature, and informatics.* Chicago: University of Chicago Press.

Heim, M. (1993). *The metaphysics of virtual reality.* New York: Oxford University Press.

Heim, M. (1998). *Virtual realism.* New York: Oxford University Press.

History of the internet. (2005) *Wikipedia.com* Retrieved June 16, 2005 from http://en.wikipedia.org/wiki/History_of_the_Internet

Holland, E. (1998). From schizophrenia to social control. In E. Kaufman & K. J. Heller (Eds.), *Deleuze & Guattari: New mappings in politics, philosophy, and culture* (pp. 65-73). Minneapolis: University of Minnesota Press.

Howard, R. M. (2004). Plagiarism epidemic, media epidemics. Retrieved May 22, 2005 from http://wrt-howard.syr.edu/Papers/Colby.htm

Jameson, F. (1993). *Postmodernism or, the cultural logic of late capitalism.* Durham: Duke University Press.

Johnson-Eilola, J. (2004). The database and the essay: Understanding composition as articulation. In A. F. Wysoki et al. (Eds.), *Writing new media: Theory and applications for expanding the teaching of composition* (pp.199-236). Logan, UT: Utah State University Press.

Joyce, M. (1995). *Of two minds: Hypertext pedagogy and poetics.* Ann Arbor: University of Michigan Press.

Kittler, F. A. (1996). "There is no software." In T. Druckery (Ed.), *Electronic culture: Technology and visual representation* (pp. 331-337). New York: Aperture.

Kittler, F. A. (1999). *Gramophone, film, typewriter* (G. Winthrop-Young & M. Wutz, Trans.). Stanford: Stanford University Press.

Kroker, A. (1996). Virtual capitalism. In S. Aronowitz, B. Martinsons, & M. Menser (Eds.), *Technoscience and cyberculture* (pp. 167-179). New York: Routledge.

Kroker, A. (2001). *The possessed individual.* Montréal: New World Perspective/CTHEORY Books.

Kroker, A. & Weinstein, M. (1994). *Data trash: the theory of the virtual class.* New York: St. Martin's Press.

Lacan, J. (1973). *The four fundamental concepts of psycho-analysis* (A. Sheridan, Trans.) (J-A Miller, Ed.). New York: Norton.

Landow, G. P. (1997). *Hypertext 2.0: The convergence of contemporary critical theory and technology.* Baltimore: Johns Hopkins University Press.

Leroi-Gourhan, A. (1993). *Gesture and speech* (A. Bostock Berger, Trans.). Cambridge, MA: MIT Press.

Lessig, L. (2004). *Free culture: How big media uses technology and the law to lock down culture and control creativity.* New York: Penguin.

Lucas, G. (Writer/Director). (1977). *Star wars episode IV: A new hope.* [Motion Picture]. United States: 20th Century Fox.

Lunenfeld, P. (Ed.). (2000). *The digital dialectic: New essays on new media.* Cambridge: MIT Press.

Lynds, P. (2003). Subjective perception of time and a progressive present moment: the neurobiological key to unlocking consciousness. Retrieved May 13, 2007 from http://cogprints.org/3125/

Manovich, L. (2001). *The language of new media.* Cambridge: MIT Press.

Manovich, L. (2003). New media from Borges to HTML. In N. Wardrip-Fruin & N. Montfort (Eds.), *The new media reader* (pp. 13-25). Cambridge: MIT Press.

Manovich, L. (1999). What is digital cinema? In P. Lunenfeld (Ed.), *The digital dialectic* (pp. 172-196). Cambridge, MA: MIT Press.

Massumi, B. (1992). *A user's guide to capitalism and schizophrenia.* Cambridge, MA: MIT Press.

Massumi, B. (2002). *Parables for the virtual.* Durham, NC: Duke University Press.

Miller, P. D. (2004). *Rhythm science.* Cambridge, MA: MIT Press.

Murray, J. (1998). *Hamlet on the holodeck: the future of narrative in cyberspace.* Cambridge: MIT Press.

Nancy, J-L. (1991). *The inoperative community* (P. Connor, L. Garbus, M. Holland, & S. Sawhney, Trans.). Minneapolis: University of Minnesota Press.

Nelson, T. H. (1965). A file structure for the complex, the changing, and the indeterminate. In L. Winner (Ed.), *Association for computing machinery: Proceedings of the 20th national conference* (pp. 84–100). Reprinted (2004) in N. Wardrip-Fruin & N. Montfort (Eds.), *The New Media Reader* (pp. 133-145). Cambridge: MIT Press.

Nielson, Cameron. (2003). Creating the burly brawl. *The Matrix Trilogy.* Retrieved July 15, 2003 from http://whatisthematrix.warnerbros.com

Ofek, H. (2001). *Second nature: Economic origins of human evolution.* Cambridge, UK: Cambridge University Press.

Patry, W. F. (2000). *Copyright law and practice.* Retrieved May 18, 2005 from http://digital-law-online.info/patry/patry2.html

Pfeiffer, J. E. (1982*). The creative explosion: an inquiry into the origins of art and religion.* New York: Harper and Row.

Piercy, M. (1991). *He, she, and it.* New York: Fawcett Crest.

Pink, D. (2005a) Revenge of the right brain. *Wired, 13*(2). Retrieved May 21, 2005 from http://www.wired.com/wired/archive/13.02/brain.html

Pink, D. (2005b). *A whole new mind: Moving from the information age to the conceptual age.* New York: Riverhead (Penguin).

Pinker, S. (1997). *How the mind works.* New York: Norton.

Plato. (1960). *Gorgias* (W. Hamilton, Trans.). New York: Penguin.

Plato. (1995). *Phaedrus* (A. Nehama & P. Woodruff, Trans.). Indianapolis: Hackett.

Plato. (2000a). *The Republic* (B. Jowett, Trans.). Retrieved November 5, 2004 from http://classics.mit.edu/Plato/republic.html

Plato. (2000b). *Timaeus* (B. Jowett, Trans.). Retrieved November 5, 2004 from http://classics.mit.edu/Plato/timaeus.html

Porush, D. (1996). Hacking the brainstem: Postmodern metaphysics and Stephenson's *Snow Crash*. In R. Markley (Ed.), *Virtual realities and their discontents* (pp. 107-142). Baltimore, MD: Johns Hopkins University Press.

Porush, D. (1998). Telepathy: Alphabetic consciousness and the age of cyborg illiteracy. In J. B. Dixon and E. J. Cassidy (Eds.), *Virtual Futures* (pp. 45-64). London: Routledge.

Rabinovitz, L. & Geil, A. (Eds.). (2004). *Memory bytes: History, technology and digital culture.* Durham: Duke University Press.

Rasula, J. (1996). *The American poetry wax museum: Reality effects 1940– 1990.* Urbana: NCTE.

Readings, B. (1996). *The university in ruins.* Cambridge: Harvard University Press.

Ruspoli, M. (1987). *The cave of Lascaux: the final photographs.* New York: Harry N. Abrams.

Said, E. (2000). Presidential address 1999: Humanism and heroism *PMLA, 115*(3), 285–291.

Selfe, C. (1999). *Technology and literacy in the twenty-first century: the importance of paying attention.* Carbondale: Southern Illinois University Press.

Selfe, C. (2004a). Students who teach us: a case study of a new media text designer. In A. F. Wysocki et al. (Eds.), *Writing new media: Theory and applications for expanding the teaching of composition* (pp. 43-66). Logan, UT: Utah State University Press.

Selfe, C. (2004b). Toward new media texts: Taking up the challenges of visual literacy. In A. F. Wysocki et al. (Eds.), *Writing new media: Theory and applications for expanding the teaching of composition* (pp. 67-110). Logan, UT: Utah State University Press.

Serres, M. (1982). *Hermes: Literature, science and philosophy* (J. V. Harari & D. F. Bell Eds.). Baltimore: Johns Hopkins University Press.

Shirky, C. (2005). Ontology is overrated: Categories, links, and tags. Retrieved May 21, 2005 from http://shirky.com/writings/ontology_over-rated.html

Sirc, G. (2004). Box-logic. In A. F. Wysocki et al. (Eds.), *Writing new media: Theory and applications for expanding the teaching of composition* (pp. 111-146). Logan, UT: Utah State University Press.

Slaughter, S. & Leslie, L. L. (1997). *Academic capitalism: Politics, policies, and the entrepreneurial university.* Baltimore: Johns Hopkins University Press.

Solely, L. (1995). *Leasing the ivory tower.* Boston: South End Press.

Squires, J. (2000). Fabulous feminist futures and the lure of cyberculture. In D. Bell & B. Kennedy (Eds.), *The cybercultures reader* (pp. 360-373). New York: Routledge.

Stivale, C. (1998). *The two-fold thought of Deleuze and Guattari: Intersections and animations.* New York: Guilford Press.

Thorburn, D. & Jenkins, H. (Eds.). (2004). *Rethinking media change: the aesthetics of transition.* Cambridge, MA: MIT Press.

Tofts, D., Jonson A., & Cavallaro, A. (Eds.). (2002). *Prefiguring cyberculture: an intellectual history.* Cambridge, MA: MIT Press.

Trinity Test. (2005). *Wikipedia.com.* Retrieved June 10, 2005 from http://en.wikipedia.org/wiki/Trinity_test

Udell, J. (2005). The new freshman comp. *O'Reilly Network.* Retrieved April 22, 2005 from http://www.oreillynet.com/pub/a/network/ 2005/04/22/primetime.html

Ulmer, G. L. (1983). The object of post-criticism. In H. Foster (Ed.), *The anti-aesthetic: Essays on postmodern culture* (pp. 83-110). Seattle: Bay Press.

Ulmer, G. L. (1994). *Heuretics: the logic of invention.* Baltimore: Johns Hopkins University Press.

Ulmer, G. L. (2004). Reality tables: Virtual furniture. In D. Tofts, A. Jonson, & A. Cavallaro (Eds.), *Prefiguring Cyberculture: an Intellectual History* (pp. 110-129). Cambridge: MIT Press.

Ulmer, G. L. (2003). *Internet invention.* New York: Longman.

Van Ness, E. (2005, March 6). Is a cinema studies degree the new MBA? *New York Times* (late edition-final). Retrieved May 13, 2007, from http://www.nytimes.com/2005/03/06/movies/06vann.html?ex=1267765 200&en=6294d348febb142e&ei=5088

Virilio, P. (1997). *Open sky* (J. Rose, Trans.). London: Verso.

Vitanza, V. J. (2003). Abandoned to writing: Notes toward several provocations. *Enculturation,* 5(1). Retrieved January 10, 2005 from http://enculturation.gmu.edu/5_1/vitanza.html

Wachowski, A. & Wachowski, L. (1998). *The Matrix.* Retrieved May 12, 2007 from http://www.dailyscript.com/scripts/the_matrix.pdf.

Wachowski, A. & Wachowski, L. (Writers/Directors). (1999). *The Matrix* [Motion Picture]. Warner Bros.

Wachowski, A. & Wachowski, L. (Writers/Directors). (2003). *The Matrix reloaded* [Motion Picture]. Warner Bros.

Wachowski, A. & Wachowski, L. (Writers/Directors). (2003). *The Matrix revolutions* [Motion Picture]. Warner Bros.

Wardrip-Fruin, N. & Montfort, N. (Eds.). (2003). *The new media reader.* Cambridge, MA: MIT Press.

White, G. D. (Ed.). (2000a). *Campus, Inc.* Amherst, NY: Prometheus Books.

White, G. D. (2000b). Business school: An interview with Noam Chomsky. In *Campus, Inc.* (pp. 441–456). Amherst, NY: Prometheus Books.

Wiener, N. (1988). *The human use of human beings: Cybernetics and society.* Cambridge, MA: Da Capo Press.

Wiener, N. (2001). Cybernetics in history. In R. Packer & K. Jordan (Eds.), *Multimedia: from Wagner to virtual reality* (pp. 47-54). New York: Norton.

Woods, L. (1993). *War and architecture.* Princeton, NJ: Princeton Architectural Press.

Woods, L. (1996). The question of space. In S. Aronowitz, B. Martinsons, & M. Menser (Eds.), *Technoscience and cyberculture* (pp. 279-292). New York: Routledge.

Woods, L. (1997). *Radical reconstruction.* Princeton, NJ: Princeton Architectural Press.

Wysocki, A. F. (2004). Opening new media to writing: Openings and justifications. In Wysocki et al. (Eds.), *Writing new media: Theory and applications for expanding the teaching of composition* (pp. 1-42). Logan, UT: Utah State University Press.

Wysocki, A. F. (2004). The sticky embrace of beauty: on some formal problems in teaching about the visual aspects of texts. In A. F. Wysocki et al. (Eds.), *Writing new media: Theory and applications for expanding the teaching of composition* (pp. 147-198). Logan, UT: Utah State University Press.

Wysocki, A. F. et al. (Eds.). (2004). *Writing new media: Theory and applications for expanding the teaching of composition.* Logan, UT: Utah State University Press.

Index

About the Author

Alexander Reid is an associate professor and the director of Professional Writing at the State University of New York College at Cortland. His scholarship focuses on the relationship between writing, pedagogy, and emerging technologies and has appeared journals such as *Kairos: A Journal of Rhetoric, Technology, and Pedagogy*, *Theory & Event*, and *Culture Machine*, as well as in collections such as *Culture Shock and the Practice of the Profession: Training the Next Wave in Rhetoric And Composition*, *Techknowledgies: New Cultural Imaginaries in the Humanities, Arts, & TechnoSciences*, and *Design Discourse: Composing and Revising Professional Writing Programs*, which he co-edited with David Franke and Anthony DiRenzo and is forthcoming from the WAC Clearinghouse and Parlor Press. He maintains a blog, *Digital Digs*, on the issues of new media, writing, and higher education at alexreid.typepad.com.